ITALY
100 Locals Tell You Where to Go, What to Eat, & How to Fit In

ISBN-13: 978-1499658996
ISBN-10: 1499658990

CONTENTS

ABOUT THIS BOOK

This book is for people who want to see another side of Italy.

To stroll past the main attractions, but also find the hidden-away gelato shop with the best cinnamon gelato in all of Rome. Or to discover that the best part of Genoa's Red Museum is actually its rooftop, where the panorama of the town will take your breath away. Or to know ahead of time that you shouldn't order a cappuccino after 11 a.m. or with a pizza (as one Italian says, "or we'll secretly think you should be put in jail").

In other words, this book is for people who want to get under the skin of another culture. Who want to rent apartments and live in local neighborhoods. Who want to eat in tiny restaurants without English menus. Who want to make friends with locals. Who want to deepen their experience of Italy.

Think of this as a supplement to your traditional guidebooks.
Use those for their handy place histories, lists of local hotels (if that's your style), restaurant pricing charts, and basic language lessons. And then use this to go deeper—to figure out the most colorful neighborhood in Naples, the most delicious *osteria* in Verona, the must-eat dishes of Bologna, and how to get to that hidden-away hiking path in the hills outside Positano.

Getting excited? Me too (just wait till you read some of these interviews!).

Now, a little orientation:

This book is split into two large sections: **Plan By Interest** and **Plan By Place**.

In the **Plan By Interest** section, you'll find interviews with some of Italy's top chefs, wine experts, extreme athletes, historians, and more. These interviews are designed to help you plan a trip to Italy that reflects your passion. Love food? Dig into the chef interviews to find out what dishes are a must-try and what regions they come from. Passionate about the outdoors?

3

ABOUT THIS BOOK

Check out our interviews with athletes to find the best hiking trails, cycling trips, or paragliding destinations.

In the **Plan By Place** section, you'll find interviews with people who live all over Italy. Many of them have lived in their cities for decades. Some are local Italians. Others are expats who have fallen in love with their new country. And all of them love showing travelers the best their cities have to offer. Use this section to plan your trip if you already know where your heart is set on taking you.

In every section, below each person's name, you'll see a short bio designed to help you understand his or her background. If you are traveling to Rome and interested in food, look for someone whose short bio includes "Foodie" or "Chef." If you're traveling to Sicily and want to get out in nature, look for hikers, walkers, bikers, etc.

Many of the interviewees are also tour guides, artists, Airbnb hosts, business owners, or bloggers. Watch for web addresses under their interviews if you'd like to learn more about their art, business, rental properties, or tours.

Now, then, into the book...

ON TRAVELING LIKE A LOCAL

The first time I went to Rome, I hated it.

The sun beat down mercilessly as I weaved past each cultural landmark on one of those bus tours. The earphones were broken, so I could barely make out what the guide was saying about each ruin. I was sweating so badly that I was sticking to the seat. I rushed around to some of the main monuments, but none of them spoke to me and I left each one quickly, feeling overcrowded, overly hot, and simply out of sorts.

I was supposed to stay in Rome for a week, but I left the next day.

But the second time I went to Rome—more than five years later, with a lot more travel experience under my belt, and with a brand new travel philosophy—I fell in love.

Instead of a bus tour with a big, well-advertised company, I went on a food tour with a smaller, passionate-about-what-they-do tour company (whose founder gave a Rome interview in the Rome & Lazio section of this guide!). I tasted sweet liquors in the marketplace. I had conversations with people who lived there. And I bought the best balsamic vinegar I've ever tried in my life.

I was only supposed to stay one day, but I thought, "Hmm, I could see myself spending a month here."

There were probably a number of reasons for this massively different experience. One is that it was winter (off-season) the second time I went. The streets were bustling, but not over-crowded. I was wearing a winter coat instead of sweating through my dress.

But more importantly, I think, is that fact that I was experiencing a different side of Rome.

Instead of rushing along from monument to monument with the other tourists, frantic to see everything, I was dedicating a day to the simple pleasure of discovering Italy's food—and not

ON TRAVELING LIKE A LOCAL

even through restaurants, but through small, local butchers, cheese shops, and marketplaces.

Instead of choosing a big bus tour company because it was convenient, I chose a small, passionate walking tour company that cared about connecting its tour groups with the local culture.

And this time I wasn't in a rush. I didn't have a checklist. I wasn't treating Rome like something on my bucket list.

I was, instead, trying to dig into authentic Italy, to experience what a local would experience, to meet people who really lived there, to eat what locals really ate, to shop where locals really shopped.

Which is the whole point of this book.

Yes, there are lot of amazing monuments and tourist attractions to see all over Italy. There's a reason places like the Colosseum or the Vatican attract the masses. Many of these things are worth seeing and experiencing. (And many of my interviewees will tell you so.)

BUT.

They aren't the whole story of Italy.

And, personally, I want to know more of the story, to get into the culture, to feel, even if I am only there for a few days, like I am truly living in Italy, experiencing something authentic.

In over 15 years of short-term international trips and two years of traveling full-time, mostly in Europe, I've come up with a routine that makes me feel more like a local. Before you dive into this book, I thought I'd share.

1. Travel slowly. Spend some real time in a place. Rome wasn't built in a day and it shouldn't be seen in one either.

ON TRAVELING LIKE A LOCAL

2. Rent apartments, preferably in a neighborhood full of local people. (Not sure how to find the right neighborhood? I've asked locals to tell us in the interviews you'll find in this book. Not sure how to find apartments? My personal starting point is Airbnb.com.)

3. Shop at fresh markets, small butcher shops, and neighborhood bakeries. This is where you'll find the best food (as opposed to the grocery store, though that can also be a welcome adventure).

4. Make friends with people who live there. Ask people about their lives, their thoughts, and their cultures. Expats and locals are both incredibly fascinating and every conversation will teach you a lot.

5. Try to fit in. In Italy, this means dress nicely, don't wear flip-flops if you aren't at the beach, order cappuccino at the right time of day, and offer a hearty *buongiorno!* to the proprietor when you come into a restaurant or café.

It is these principles and this type of travel that I've molded the questions in this book around. So if you, too, want to slow down and experience Italy in a different way, these interviews should provide a very solid foundation indeed.

PLAN BY INTEREST

Plan your trip based on what you love to do.

ITALY FOR WINE LOVERS

Alfonso Cevola
The Italian Wine Guy.

First, tell us about you.

I was born in a vineyard. (*Literally*. The hospital I was born in was surrounded by vines.) My grandfather had vineyards in Cucamonga. When I went to Santa Clara University, the president was a Jesuit and a winemaker. And many of my college pals were from winemaking families in Napa, Sonoma, and Santa Clara Valley.

My heritage is Italian and I naturally gravitated to Italy. I was very fortunate to have that random luck.

What I love about wine is *the connection people have to their little corner of earth*. I love the stories, the passions, the arguments, and the dreams.

If someone is visiting Italy for the first time, what are the top 10 wines you recommend they try and why?

10 wines is a lot. And it all depends where you land. Let's say you land in Rome. Start with a carafe of the house red or white. (Really. Get an idea for the baseline. I still do it to this day.) Then, find a cool wine bar and settle in. If you're looking for a great place, consult The Rome Digest (.com), and Katie Parla's app.

So, my 10 wines for beginners? *Frascati, Pinot Grigio, Orvieto, Verdicchio, Chianti, Montepulciano d'Abruzzo, Nero d'Avola, Barbera d'Asti*, and *Prosecco*. These are gateway wines, easing you into the Italian landscape softly, gently.

For more experienced wine lovers, what are some of the hidden gems you'd recommend?

I'd say wines from the Langhe: *Nebbiolo, Barbaresco*, and *Barolo*. From Tuscany: *Brunello, Vino Nobile*, and *Chianti Classico Riserva* (or *Rufina*). *Etna Rosso* from Sicily, *Aglianico*

ITALY FOR WINE LOVERS

from Basilicata, *Inferno* from Valtellina, and *Lambrusco di Sorbara*.

If someone is planning a wine tour around Italy, what regions and towns do you recommend they visit?

I am not a city person when it comes to Italy. If you think you need to see Rome, Florence, Milan, and Venice because they are on your bucket list, by all means, have at it. When you get them checked off, head out to the country. Tuscany, Piedmont, Abruzzo, Marche, Sicily, Trentino-Alto Adige, and Veneto…all these places are, at most, a few hours by car from those four cities.

Hint: don't try to do Italy in one fell swoop. Go to one place for a week or 10 days and get to know the locals. I once took a friend who had never been to Italy to an island off the coast of Sicily. Now, *that* was true immersion.

Italy is very easy and very forgiving once you get out of the larger urban areas. Save those places for when you start to get a feel for the real Italy. Then a place like Rome will make more sense.

Where, in your opinion, are the best vineyard tours?

Well, it seems Tuscany is the best-organized place. But you can also find tours in Puglia, Sicily, Piedmont, Liguria…almost anywhere there is a vineyard, there is a tour. Italy, after all, is one giant vineyard. *25% of the wine produced in the world comes from Italy.*

For a general experience, though, I'd start with Tuscany.

Can you tell us a little about the regional differences in Italian wines?

One should drink the wines from the region they are in unless they are in a large urban area (such as Rome) and they are at a restaurant that specializes in the food of, say, Abruzzo. (In which case, order a *Montepulciano d'Abruzzo*.) Or if you are in Milan and in a restaurant where everyone is from Sicily, then by

10

all means order a Sicilian wine. "If it grows with it, it goes with it," as Danny Meyer likes to say.

Generally, the wines of Italy are very diverse, but they have evolved with the food from the regions from which they come. Crisp whites from the Adriatic Coast, Marche, or Abruzzo (like *Verdicchio* or *Trebbiano*) go very well with the fresh seafood from the Adriatic, for instance.

If you are in Piedmont during truffle season, then a *Barolo* or *Barbaresco* is a terrific match.

If you are in Tuscany and they are firing up thick, hearty steaks, nothing is better than a *Chianti Classico*, *Vino Nobile*, *Brunello*, or *SuperTuscan*. They complement each other. And with wine it's all about the harmony.

How can a traveler experience Italy's wine like a local?

Try and speak a few words in the language. Smile. Envision humility; many people in Italy never really travel any further than their regional capital. Be patient. And kind. Go to local little places and order the house wine. Don't order a *Barolo* in Tuscany or a *Brunello* in Piedmont (for now). Slow down. Breathe. Keep your heart open. I know this sounds a little corny, but it will work.

What's your best piece of advice for travelers who want to have an amazing Italian wine experience?

If you can stand it, I'd say to go to one place, a vineyard, maybe one that has a nice B&B or an apartment for rent. Stay there and explore the region from that home base. Get to know the locals, the baker, the cheese-maker, and the local tavern folk. I cannot tell you how rewarding something as simple as that can be.

Anything else we should know about wine in Italy?

Don't try and understand all of Italy or all of Italian wine in one trip. Enjoy the moment and the experience. When in Rome, enjoy life as the Romans do: leisurely, unrushed, and with a sense of joy and celebration of life and being alive.

ITALY FOR WINE LOVERS

Find Alfonso at: www.acevola.blogspot.ch.

Cindy-Marie Harvey
Wine Expert. Senior Programme Manager with Arblaster & Clark Wine Tours.

If someone is visiting Italy for the first time, what are the top 10 wines you recommend they try and why?

Sparkling wine from Franciacorta: to showcase how world-class Italian sparkling wines can be.

Greco di Tufo from Campania: to demonstrate native white variety from the south.

Frappato from Sicily: to show that the region can do elegant reds, as well as blockbusters.

Chianti Classico: the perfect introduction to Sangiovese.

Salice Salentino: a big, gutsy red from Puglia.

Lambrusco Cru de Sorbara: to discover what this much maligned wine tastes like when properly made (paired with local salami!).

Barolo: king of all red wines in Italy. Need I say more?

Aglianico: to prove the power and complexity of reds from the south, especially Basilicata.

Passito de Pantelleria: sheer nectar in a glass from the volcanic island close to the African coast.

Moscato D'Asti: at 5.5% ABV, it's the perfect end to a meal or even as a mid-morning welcome drink.

For more experienced wine lovers, what are some of the hidden gems you'd recommend?

Barbaresco: ethereal, complex, elegant...this has a small production zone and some outstanding wines.

Alto Adige: quality levels across the board in this region are stunning. Try their *Pinot Biancos* and *Sauvignon Blancs* as well as *Pinot Noir*.

Pecorino: no, not the cheese, but a variety of re-emerging wines in Le Marche.

Nerello Mascalese from Etna: proving what an exciting sub-region of Sicily this famous volcano is at the moment.

If someone is planning a wine tour around Italy, what regions and towns do you recommend they visit?
I recommend Piemonte during white truffle season, with its beautiful colors in the vineyards and gorgeous market towns like Alba, or Sicily, with its wide range of wine styles and historical places to visit, such as temples in Agrigento and Siracusa.

Can you tell us a little about the regional differences in Italian wines? Why should someone choose one region over another?
Regionality is the key in Italy (thankfully they still keep to it!). When choosing a region, ask yourself if you like white, red, a mixture of both, or (indeed!) sparkling. That is a good starting point, as some regions concentrate on one style of wine, while others make across the board.

How can a traveler experience Italy's wine like a local?
Travel on a good tour (like ours) and you'll get to speak to the people who make the wine—the owners of the estate—so you get to know the real, current story rather than just reading what's in wine books.

What's your best piece of advice for travelers who want to have an amazing Italian wine experience?

ITALY FOR WINE LOVERS

Be open-minded. Try grape varieties that you have never heard of (there are hundreds in Italy) and experiment!

Anything else we should know about wine in Italy?

Good wine should be enjoyed with good food. One cannot exist without the other. Italian wines are designed to balance out the flavors and components of the local food—not to be entered into wine competitions to impress judges. So try them with the local food (try anything that is recommended by the Slow Food Association, as it will be typical of the region)!

Find Cindy-Marie at: www.winetours.co.uk.

ITALY FOR FOODIES

First, tell us about you and your restaurant.

My kitchen can be defined as "tradition seen from 10 miles away." I revisit traditional recipes and ideas and make them contemporary. This is my specialty.

I try very hard to respect tradition, but also to respect ingredients and heroic farmers, butchers, and fishermen. Sometimes I have to ask if our traditions respect the ingredients and, if they don't, then it is time to rework them. I call this "tradition in evolution."

As a kid, I was always under the kitchen table. It was my refuge from three older brothers' torments and threats. I found peace at my grandmother's feet as she rolled out the dough for tortellini, among the smells of broth and roast meats and the constant chatting of my grandmother, mother, and aunt, who prepared meals for the 10 of us every lunch and dinner.

Those memories are probably why I became a chef.

When my brother told me about a *trattoria* on the outskirts of Modena for sale in the early 1986, I just knew that was the right thing to do. So I quit law school, bought that trattoria, and opened it a week later. I didn't really know what I was doing, but with lots of help from my mother and a cook named Lidia Cristoni, who happened to live around the corner, I began my career.

Osteria Francescana is in the heart of Modena. It is a hundred-year-old *osteria* transformed into an intimate fine dining restaurant where contemporary art and contemporary Italian cuisine share the same table. In addition to the *a la carte* menu, we offer three tasting menus to explore our kitchen: Tradition in Evolution, Classics, and Sensations. Each has its own personality; each focuses on a different aspect of our kitchen. This makes each dining experience unique. One table can be

15

ITALY FOR FOODIES

eating *tagliatelle al ragu* in the Emilian traditions menu and the next a Livornese red mullet from the new "Come to Italy with Me" sensations menu. Or a revisited classic Osteria Francescana plate, "All The Tongues of the World," which was recently featured in an art exhibition at the Beaux Arts in Paris.

What is most important to us is sharing time with our guests. Perhaps we are old fashioned in this sense, but hospitality is very important. And everyone should feel at the end of a meal that the journey was worth the trip. I often say that our biggest compliment is not the awards or the stars, but the people who travel halfway around the world to Modena, to Osteria Francescana, to have a meal with us. Nothing could make me more proud than to share my kitchen, my stories, and the unique culinary gastronomy of Italy.

When visiting Italy for the first time, what should we try?
In the north, Piedmont and Lombardy, rice and *polenta* are native. In Piedmont, try the *risotto* with *castelmagno* cheese (or white truffles in season). In Lombardy, *polenta concia* (with cheese).

In the region of Emilia-Romagna, the handmade egg pastas are divine. In Modena, try *Modenese tortellini* in broth or *tortelli* with pumpkin. In Bologna, *tagliatelle* with *ragu*. And, near the Adriatic sea in Romagna, homemade *passatelli* in broth, naturally with a glass of *Sangiovese* wine.

Crossing the Apennines toward Tuscany, the famous *ribollita* vegetable soup is a must.

In Rome, seek out the best *pasta carbonara* and *cacio pepe* (Roscioli in *Campo dei Fiori* is our favorite restaurant for this).

East, over the Po River into Veneto, there is the tradition of *baccalà mantecato* (salt cod mixed with olive oil in a flavorful puree).

ITALY FOR FOODIES

In Naples, there are incredible products like capers and Vesuvian tomatoes and mozzarella, so I would say *pizza*, but only in Naples, not the rest of Italy.

Toward the Adriatic, the seafood is so abundant, especially bluefish and baby squid which are perfect for *fritto misto di pesce* (mixed fried fish).

And, of course, in Sicily, pastries of any kind, especially from Caffe Sicilia, located at *125 Corso Vittorio Emanuele* in Noto.

If someone is planning a food tour in Italy, what cities should they make sure to visit?

I am very spoiled living in Italy where we have so many amazing products—from capers from Panterlleria to traditional balsamic vinegar from Modena, tomatoes from Naples, fish from the Adriatic, prosciutto from Parma, and beef from Piemonte.

If I were travelling through Italy, I would go to the cities with the best restaurants, whether they were big cities or small cities. If a chef has decided to set up shop and done so with success, that means that this town or area of Italy offers something very special: unique landscape, geography, culture, and, naturally, gastronomic products and traditions that are worth discovering.

There are a group of Italian chefs who represent the future of Italian cuisine: Massimo Alajmo, Davide Scabin, Ciccio Sultano, Norbert Neiderkofler, Mauro Ulliassi, Moreno Cedroni, Carlo Cracco, Chicco Cerea, Antonino Canavacciuolo, Andrea Berton, Giancarlo Perbelini, Gennaro Esposito, Nico Romito, Heinz Beck, and Giovanni Santini.

Stop at any of their restaurants, sprinkled all over Italy, and you will have an incredible experience.

In other cities, ask for advice from the fine dining establishments. The chefs in these restaurants are part of a larger community of excellence that, at times, can only be

17

discovered by word of mouth. We do our best at Osteria Francescana to guide our guests through Modena and the area of Emilia-Romagna because there is so much to discover just steps beyond our own threshold.

In addition to your own restaurant, what other restaurants do you recommend in your area or other parts of Italy?
The talented chefs I mentioned above would be my starting point. From there, I would seek out *trattorias*, markets, and *enotecas* offering a tasting of local fare.

A few more of my favorites: in Modena, there is the Franceschetta58. The atmosphere is ultra casual and the selection of Italian traditions is vast. The food is welcoming and comforting with very well-sourced ingredients. Address: *Via Vignolese 58*.

Trattoria Bianca, located at *Via Giovanni Battista Spaccini 24*, is another a local favorite, serving *gnocco fritto* with Emilian *prosciutto, mortadella,* and *salami*, as well as handmade pastas.

On the way to Bologna, in nearby San Giovanni in Persiceto, there is the rustic Osteria Mirasole. Franco grills excellent cuts of Italian *Piemontese* beef on a grill in the restaurant. His selection of reds pairs perfectly with the food. Address: *Via Giacomo Matteotti 17*.

In Imola, just past Bologna on the way to the Adriatic, there is a beautiful restaurant called San Domenico with wonderful Italian traditional plates. Address: *Via Gaspare Sacchi nr.1*.

On the Tuscan seaside, in the medieval city of Pietrasanta, I love Enoteca Marcucci where fine wine accompanies a simple meal in a unique setting. Address: *Via Garibaldi 40*.

In Rome, I can be found at Roscioli in *Campo dei Fiori* (at *Via dei Giubbonari 21*) for a quick snack or a plate of *carbonara*, or at EATaly (*www.eataly.com*) for my grocery shopping.

ITALY FOR FOODIES

In Noto, Sicily, I am always at Caffe Sicilia (at *Corso Vittorio Emanuele III 125*) for the pastries and granita created by Corrado Assenza.

In Venice, you'll find me at Caffe Quadri (at *Via Liguria 1*) run by the Alajmo brothers (who also run Le Calandre in Padova).

Find Chef Massimo at: www.osteriafrancescana.it.

CHEF MASSIMO'S CHEAT SHEET

For Eating Your Way Across Italy

Emilia-Romagna: handmade egg pastas like *tortellini, tortelloni di zucca* (pumpkin ravioli), *tagiatelle al ragu,* and *passatelli in brodo.*

Tuscany: *ribollita* (a black cabbage vegetable soup) and *fagioli all'uccelletto* (white beans with sage and olive oil).

Lombardy: *polenta concia* (polenta with cheese) or *risotto alla zafferano* (risotto with saffron and bone marrow).

Veneto: *baccalà mantecato* (creamed cod).

Rome: *pasta cacio e pepe* and *carbonara.*

Naples: *pizza.*

Sicily: *cannoli alla Siciliana* with ricotta cream filling.

Marche to Puglia (Adriatic Coast): *fritto misto di pesce* (mixed fried fish).

ITALY FOR FOODIES

Chef Massimiliano Alajmo
Chef Patron, Le Calandre—a Worldwide Top-50 Restaurant.

First, tell us about you and your restaurant.

Le Calandre is a fine-dining Italian restaurant located in Sarmeola di Rubano, a small town just outside the city of Padua in Italy's Veneto region.

We believe in dishes that capture all of our senses, beginning with the most evocative of the five, our sense of smell. Aromas have a special ability to create lasting memories, particularly in relation to food.

We also believe that every element in a recipe must make its own contribution to create harmonic balance, carrying with it the memory of where it has been.

The result is combination of intense sensations—an original presentation of ancient flavors using a fresh and reassuring approach.

Of course, dining is about more than food. Which is why Raffaele (Chef Massimiliano's brother) gives special attention to the restaurant's wine list, the knowledge of his staff, and the warm, loosen-your-tie-and-get-comfortable atmosphere of the dining room.

In your mind, what sets Italian food apart from other cuisines around the world?

All cuisines are based on the search for pleasure. Italians certainly know how to enjoy the pleasures of the table, including good company.

If someone is visiting Italy for the first time, what are the must-try dishes?

I would begin with, in no particular order, *spaghetti aglio* (spaghetti with a garlic sauce), *olio e pepperoncino* (spaghetti with garlic, olive oil, and chili pepper), *baccala mantecato*

21

(Venetian-style whipped salt cod), *tortellini in brodo* (tortellini in broth), *fave e cicorie* (fava beans and chicories), *granite di gelsi neri e mandorle* (black mulberry and almond granita—a Sicilian sorbet-type dessert), *panettone* (sweet leavened bread typically served at Christmas), *brasato al Barolo* (beef braised in Barolo wine), *mailalino sardo* (Sardinian roast suckling pig), *caprese* (the original tomato and mozzarella salad), and *risotto alla Milanese* (saffron risotto).

If someone is planning a food tour in Italy, what cities and regions should they make sure to visit?
Any and all. The Italian foodscape is so rich and varied that no matter where you go, you are certain to discover something wonderful to eat.

In addition to your own restaurant, what other restaurants do you recommend in your area or other parts of Italy?
Aimo & Nadia at *Via Privata Raimondo Montecuccoli 6* in Milan; Ristorante Duomo at *Via Captain Bocchieri 31* in Ragusa (Sicily); and Spinechile at *Contra Pacche 1* in Schio (outside Vicenza).

Is there anything tourists do that would be considered strange or rude in Italy?
Avoid drinking a cappuccino with lunch or dinner.

What's your best piece of advice for travelers who want to have an amazing Italian cuisine experience?
Travel in good company. And be sure to visit a cultural heritage site or museum before sitting down to lunch or dinner.

Find Chef Massimiliano at: www.alajmo.it.

ITALY FOR THE OUTDOORSY

Maurizio di Palma
BASE Jumper. Skydiver. Paraglider. Professional Badass.

First, tell us about you.
My name is Maurizio di Palma. I'm 34 years old and was born in a little country town close to Milan. Five years ago, I moved to a town in the Trentino Alto Adige region close to Lake Garda.

I moved to Trentino because it's the home of one of the most famous and beautiful cliffs for BASE jumping, a sport I've been in for 12 years (after five years of skydiving).

I've done over 3,000 jumps from cliffs, antennas, buildings, and anything else that's jumpable. I love BASE because it's like nothing else on earth. The feeling you get from jumping is totally unique (and very hard to describe to those who don't jump). The second reason is because BASE allows me to travel a lot and see so much. I can jump some beautiful cliffs in Dolomites or a big building in center of New York, a big antenna in the desert or a natural cave in China.

Where are the best places in Italy for a beginner BASE jumper or paraglider?
In Italy, for sure, the best place for a beginner BASE jumper is Monte Brento, a cliff over 1,000 meters high close to Arco (in Trentino-Alto Adige). It's a big cliff with a perfect shape for BASE and throughout the year there are many jumpers from all over the world who travel here to jump.

About 20 kilometers south of Brento, there is a very famous place for paragliding. It's called Monte Baldo and is a big mountain just over the village of Malcesine. This is a perfect place for paragliding at any level—from beginner to expert pilot. Plus, with 1,600 meters of elevation on Lake Garda, paragliders enjoy a beautiful view.

To get to Monte Baldo for paragliding, take the convenient cable car only 15 minutes from Malcesine. Tandems are also available here (*tandemparagliding.eu*).

23

ITALY FOR THE OUTDOORSY

Where are the best places in Italy for an advanced BASE jumper or paraglider?

One of the most beautiful places in Italy for advanced jumpers and paragliders is the Dolomites. Every flight is breathtaking. One of the most famous places is Col Rodella (2,450 meters above sea level) in Val di Fassa.

Keep in mind that the weather condition in the Dolomites changes very quickly, especially in summer (which is why it's a good place to gain experience).

For BASE jumping, the most famous spot is Sass Pordoi, which is also in Val di Fassa. It's a big mountain (2,950 meters above sea level) from which, with use of a wing-suit, the jumpers are able to do a nice jump with close to one minute of free-fall.

A convenient cable car brings the jumpers to Sass Pordoi in less than 10 minutes and the exit point is only a five-minute walk down. It's a technical spot, *not* recommended for beginners or for jumpers without solid wing-suit BASE experience.

What is your favorite place to BASE jump and paraglide?

My favorite places for BASE in general are the Dolomites and Monte Brento (when I'm not around for jumping from other objects like antennas or buildings). I live very close to Monte Baldo and, when there is an opportunity, I fly there.

There are other interesting take off areas for paragliding in Sarche Valley (where I live). One of my favorites is Monte Gazza, where my friend and coach, Roberto Cappelletti, also flies.

What should we do if we visit your favorite place?

Each BASE jumper that comes to Monte Brento goes directly to the unofficial BASE headquarters: Bar Parete Zebrata (at *Localita Gaggiolo* 4). It's the best place to meet other jumpers and organize a jump. Inside the bar, there is a meteo station for checking the wind before a jump and any jumpers can find some important info for a safe jump.

ITALY FOR THE OUTDOORSY

In the evenings, usually all the jumpers go for dinner at Pizzeria Alfio at *Strada Gardesana Occidentale 7/B* in Dro.

This pizzeria is only three kilometers from the Bar Parete Zebrata and the landing zone of Monte Brento. Ask the owner, Matteo (a cool guy who is very friendly with the jumpers [and whose interview you can find in the Trentino-Alto Adige section of this book]), to recommend some very local dishes (or enjoy a lovely Italian pizza).

The area of Lake Garda and the Sarche Valley offers many opportunities for outdoor activity: canyoning, mountain biking, climbing, etc. During days off or when the wind from Lake Garda is too strong for jumping or flying, you can enjoy the *via ferrata* (literally "iron roads," *via ferratas* are protected climbing routes). The best and easiest is the *via ferrata* of Monte Colodri in Arco. For experts, try the Rino Pisetta on Monte Dain in Sarche village.

For hiking, there are many trails, including the nice trail from Monte Bondone to Monte Cornetto, which takes you to 2,126 meters above sea level and offers a view of entire Sarca Valley.

Is there anything visitors should know about doing BASE or paragliding in Italy?

In Italy, BASE jumping is only allowed from cliffs. Jumps from other objects, like buildings, antennas, etc., are forbidden (as in many other parts of the world).

In Trentino-Alto Adige, there aren't any problems with jumping because it's well-known and tolerated. That said, it's really important for all the jumpers who decide to come in Monte Brento to know and respect the rules of this cliff, which are showcased just before you arrive at the exit point.

For jumpers who come to Italy to jump, the best way to connect with the BASE community is the association: *basejumper.it*.

ITALY FOR THE OUTDOORSY

Find Maurizio at: www.mauriziodipalma.com.

Anna & Isabelle
Owners, Dolomite Treks.

First, tell us about you and your business.
We both spent years working for an English walking tour company before deciding to set up our own. One of us (Anna) has a background in tourism, studied languages, and is Dolomite born and bred and the other (Isabelle) works in tourism, teaching, and translation and is a UK-born history graduate.

We specialize in Dolomite walking (hence the name of our company, Dolomite Treks), but we have run walking tours all over Italy and sometimes further afield. We run small group walking tours and often take private groups and we also organize tailor-made, self-guided holidays for individuals and groups in the Dolomites where we both live.

The best thing about walking in Italy is the immense range of walking available—there is everything from vineyard walking to rolling hills and the most dramatic mountains in Europe.

Where are the best places in Italy for a beginner hiker?
There are good marked trails that can be easily combined with good food and wine in Piedmont, particularly around Alba, and also in central Italy in Tuscany, Umbria, and the Marche.

The Italian lakes are also a great place for walking of every sort with every kind of view imaginable. Beginners should not be put off mountain walking either, as the great thing about Alpine walking is the ski lifts, which can take you to the peaks in summer for a relatively gentle or mainly downhill walk. The Dolomites are obviously great for this, but so is the Valle d'Aosta and, in fact, the whole of the Alpine chain.

ITALY FOR THE OUTDOORSY

Where are the best places in Italy for an advanced hiker?

If lots of ups and downs is what you're looking for, I would suggest, once again (obviously we are biased!) the Alps, where you can try your hand at the long distance mountain routes called *Alte Vie*, with altitude gain and loss every day of around 1,000 meters or more. In the Dolomites, one of the best and most accessible is *Alta Via number one*, which starts in Braies and ends in Belluno and usually takes 10 – 15 days. I would also recommend Liguria and the Amalfi Coast for demanding coastal walking with spectacular views and pretty towns in the middle. The Cinque Terre is the most famous area in Liguria for international travellers, but there is dramatic walking to be had all over the region.

What are some of the best long treks you can take in Italy?

Well, the most famous long hike is the *Via Francigena*, which is Italy's equivalent of the *Camino de Santiago*, a pilgrim trail that takes you along the whole length of Italy through an enormous range of scenery. The most famous and best-marked sections are in central Italy in Tuscany—from Siena to Florence, for example—and Umbria, but the whole route would take several months. In the mountains, the best long routes are the *Alta Vie*, which are normally 10 to 14 days long.

What are some of the best short hikes?

There are short hikes everywhere in Italy and all the places we have mentioned so far have beautiful short hikes including the mountains where, as we said earlier, the ski lifts are a big help.

Into long hikes? Check out the Via Francigena—Italy's version of the Camino de Santiago.

ITALY FOR THE OUTDOORSY

What are your personal favorite places to hike?

Well, we are biased and think that the Dolomite landscape is truly unique! Its spiky profiles and unusual pink colors at sunset and dawn contrasting with the soft contours of its verdant pastures and forests gives it a very different feel from other Alpine areas. We are also huge fans of walking in Liguria, the Italian Lakes (particularly Lake Garda), Tuscany, Umbria, the Amalfi coast, Sardinia for wild walking, and Sicily for food, wine, and history.

Is there anything visitors should know about hiking or trekking in Italy?

Walking in Italy is totally straightforward in this respect, as long as you do not touch any crops at all or damage fences or gates. Of course, if you come across a locked gate or high fence, it is clear that the owner does not want you to enter his or her land and you should respect this.

Find Anna and Isabelle at: www.dolomitetreks.com.

Gabriel Del Rossi
Professional Bicycle Tour Guide for Trek Travel.

First, tell us about you.

My name is Gabriel Del Rossi and my work and fun is wrapped up in the same activity: I am a professional bicycle tour guide for Trek Travel. I have been leading trips all over Europe for 20 years, showing my guests the quiet roads of the countryside and the unique subtleties of the regional European cuisine.

I also expose them to the depth of culture and history that is here in Europe. I'm from the Boston area originally, but now spend my time between Sicily (my home in the cycling months) and Vail, Colorado (where I am a ski instructor in the winter).

Where are the best places in Italy for a beginner biker?

ITALY FOR THE OUTDOORSY

For beginner bicycle riders, the best places to ride are flat. The *Val Padana* (otherwise known as the Po River Valley) is a fantastic area for new cyclists.

Any new rider could spend a few days in the marvelous city of Venice, then ride along the *Lido di Venezia* heading south. This area of Italy is speckled with beautiful villages that are both historic and quaint. Ferrara is the old town that belonged to the powerful Este family back in the medieval ages and is now a UNESCO World Heritage Site. A university city, it is young and vibrant with a popular jazz festival every year. Ravenna is another city along the itinerary, with its beautiful Byzantine baptisteries and breathtaking mosaics. A week could be spent in the Val Padana, connecting Venice all the way to just outside Bologna, and the riding is never too challenging. The food is delicious, the people are fun, and the history is endless.

Where are the best places in Italy for an advanced biker?

For advanced cyclists, the Dolomites and the Alps are the most popular destinations. The *Sella Ronda* in the Dolomites has a number of astonishing mountain passes made famous by Fausto Coppi and the Giro d'Italia. Gavia, Sella, Pordoi, Pellegrino, and Falzarego are just a few of the mammoth passes that attract thousands of cyclists to this part of the world every year. The Dolomites also have a unique WWI history and many historians make their way to these passes to test their legs and their knowledge throughout the season.

The Alps are also a popular destination with great ascents, like the Grand and Petit San Bernard in the Valle d'Aosta in northwestern Italy. Other climbs include Stelvio, Mortirollo, Monte Grappa, Zoncolan, and Ghisallo in Lombardy and Trentino (ranging from challenging to extremely difficult). Possibly the hardest climb I have ever ridden is the Scanuppia near a town called Trento in northeastern Italy—absolutely brutal at an average 17.5% grade for 7.5 kilometers. Make sure if you're doing these climbs you have the right gearing or else you won't be happy. Oh yes...and having a good training program helps too!

ITALY FOR THE OUTDOORSY

There're other areas in Italy, such as the Gran Sasso, the Alpi Apuane near the Cinque Terre, and the islands of Sicily and Sardegna, that have very challenging riding for intermediate riders. These are areas that aren't easy, yet aren't overly difficult either. What makes these destinations great is the food and wine you can get along the way and the views are worth the trip alone!

What are some of the best long bike rides in Italy?

For me, long bike rides last for days, if not weeks. Some good rides are on the islands of Sicily and Sardegna, where you can tackle a large distance and see a number of small, quaint towns (Calvi and Ragusa, for example) and get back to the hotel feeling like you've had an amazing day on the bike. I also find some of the best long rides are in Tuscany where you can connect hilltop town to hilltop town and then circle back to your hotel. San Querico, Pienza, Sinalunga, and Chianciano are a few of the towns in central Tuscany near Siena. Also, the area around Cortona in southern Tuscany is fantastic for rides to Montepulciano, Montalcino, and the beautiful Lago Trasimeno. These are challenging rides, but the days are incredibly rewarding.

What are some of the best short rides?

Most of the best short rides are along the coast. In the region of Le Marche, for example, you can ride north or south along the coast, have great food, and shop local products during the day. Or just hang out at the beach all day.

Puglia is very similar: amazing seafood and beautiful, simple bike rides up and down the Salento area (departing out of Otranto, there are few roads to take to some great beach spots along the peninsula). There are a number of towns along the coast that boast local ceramics and art, delicious *primitivo* and *negramaro* wines, and the roads are not too busy in the off season (any month except June, July, and August).

What are your personal favorite places to bike?

Piedmont and Sicily. These regions offer challenging rides, yet nothing too difficult. The cuisine is fantastic and the wines are delicious (after all, a bike ride is only as good as the wine you drink at the end!). There are also plenty of options for cyclists looking for easier rides.

There is also a depth of culture that allows for time off the bike and to appreciate the area a bit further. In Serravalle (Piedmont), there is a cycling museum dedicated to Fauto Coppi and there are many *grandfondo* (amateur cycling competitions) that give you the opportunity to ride long distances that are supported and to meet locals at the same time.

There is something about riding along the coast of Sicily that has a unique flair to it, especially when you can look out into the Mediterranean and feel the sea spray on your face. It is a great feeling of freedom.

Is there anything visitors should know about biking Italy?

Cars in Italy are very respectful of cyclists, but that means that the cyclist must act like a car (obeying stoplights and one-way signs, stopping at stop signs, etc.). People say Italians are crazy drivers. I think Italians understand the power and the size of their automobiles a lot better than most North Americans do. As a result, they can travel on smaller roads and don't need as much space to pass. That may seem narrow for most Americans, but after a few days you get used to the drivers and understand their respect for cyclists.

There are no helmet rules, but you'd be better off always riding with a helmet for your own safety. Italian law requires that bikes have lights on them when the day is dark or cloudy, so make sure you have lights on the front and back of your bike.

Anything else you want us to know?

I love the respect cyclists receive in Italy. The Italian cycling culture is vastly different than the states and, as a result, people are surprised how respectful the cars are when passing.

ITALY FOR THE OUTDOORSY

I also love how the bicycle is a means of conversation and not only transportation. The bicycle opens doors, gets people talking, creates friendships, and is the foundation to many great memories. There are a number of shop owners and restaurateurs who connect on a higher level with cyclists since those who ride bikes are not their typical customer.

As I write this, I think of all the amazing rides I've been on in Tuscany, Piedmont, Sicily, and Puglia. Each one was a great adventure and I've met some unbelievable people along the way.

Find Gabriel at: www.trektravel.com.

ITALY FOR HISTORY BUFFS

Christopher Duggan
Professor of Modern Italian History. Author.

First, tell us about you.

I've worked on the modern history of Italy ever since graduating from Oxford back in the late 1970s. I guess I've always been fascinated by Italy. I spent many summer holidays there and my first love was for the Renaissance period. Venice, Florence, and Siena were the places that I was really smitten by and it was the extraordinary art and architecture—so far in advance of anything that you could find in England in the same period—that I found really exciting.

I guess I belong to that tradition of English Italophilia, which goes back to the time of the Grand Tour in the 18th century and, to some extent, beyond. I started work on a doctorate in 1980 and decided to concentrate on a topic in the modern period, as one of the things that I had become interested in was how a country with such a remarkably strong tradition of cities and regions with independent identities and histories could have successfully been unified into a single state in 1860.

I studied the campaign conducted by the fascist government against the Sicilian mafia in the 1920s and was intrigued to see just how deeply embedded in the fabric of Sicilian society the tradition of private violence was—and just how difficult, as a result, it was even for an authoritarian police state like fascism to tackle organized crime.

If someone is visiting Italy for the first time and is interested in modern history, where would you recommend that they travel and what should they see?

For modern history, that is since Italy was unified in 1860, you might want to start in Turin. This was the capital of the dynasty, the House of Savoy that spearheaded the unification process in the 1850s. There are many monuments and palaces connected to the Savoys in and around the city.

ITALY FOR HISTORY BUFFS

The Savoys were a highly ambitious dynasty, with territories on both sides of the Alps, and they were always looking to take advantage of the international situation—especially during wars—to improve their standing. They were extremely conscious of their status and this is reflected in the magnificence of their royal buildings—such as the royal palace in the center of Turin or Palazzo Racconigi, a few miles to the south.

Turin was the capital of Italy for a few years after unification; Palzzo Carignano, a splendid baroque palace, was home to united Italy's first parliament. The capital moved to Florence in 1865—where the *Palazzo della Signoria* became the parliament building—and then to Rome.

If you want to get a sense of modern Italian history in Rome, you need to look out for all the signs of how the new Kingdom of Italy looked to imprint itself on a city which was home to the papacy—and the papacy, it is important to recall, refused to recognize the Italian state until the so-called "conciliation" of 1929. Until then, the pope and the Italian king were rivals in Rome. The popes had, for centuries, ruled over a large swathe of territory in central Italy until these lands were invaded by Piedmontese troops in 1860 as part of the unification process—this was the main reason for the refusal of the pope to recognize the Italian state.

Huge monuments—above all, the massive white memorial to King Victor Emmanuel II, the first king of united Italy, in *Piazza Venezia*, known as the Vittoriano—along with statues and public buildings were constructed in an attempt to show that Rome now belonged to Italy and not just to the papacy. A key figure celebrated in statues was Giuseppe Garibaldi, the flamboyant soldier who played a vital part in the unification process in 1860. In Rome, he is commemorated in a fine equestrian statue on the Janiculum Hill, gazing out significantly over the Vatican. His statue can be found everywhere around Italy.

ITALY FOR HISTORY BUFFS

For more seasoned history lovers, are there any lesser-known sites you would recommend visiting?

For those interested in the fascist period, a visit to Predappio, the small town in the Romagna in northeastern Italy where Benito Mussolini was born, and is now buried, is fascinating. The town was turned into a site of mass "pilgrimages" during the 1920 and 1930s, with thousands visiting it on a daily basis to see the small house where the Duce was born and pay their respects at the tombs of Mussolini's parents in the cemetery of Cassiano.

The town has good examples of fascist modernist architecture, especially the Casa del Fascio, once the headquarters of the local fascist party.

There are also very disturbing elements to visiting Predappio—or the Villa Carpena, a few miles outside the town, which was the Mussolini family's summer retreat and now a museum. Italy has still not exorcised its fascist past and many people come to Predappio out of a sense of nostalgia; the often highly celebratory comments left in the register in front of Mussolini's tomb in San Cassiano seem extraordinary given the extent to which almost everywhere else fascism has come to seem an unconditionally evil regime.

What are three historic sites or cities in Italy that you find personally fascinating and why?

Palermo, the capital of Sicily, gives you a remarkable sense of the different cultural layers of Italian history. The Arabs turned the city into a glittering capital between the 9th and 11th centuries, before the Normans and later the Aragonese and Spanish took it over. Traces of all these different civilizations abound in and around the city. I spent a lot of time in this city back in the 1980s when I was researching my first book on the fascist campaign to eliminate the Sicilian mafia and it gave me a sense of just how distinctive—culturally and historically—the various cities of Italy are.

Another city that, of course, gives you this sense is Venice. Its wealth was built on its maritime dominance of the

ITALY FOR HISTORY BUFFS

Mediterranean, the eastern Mediterranean especially, and its art and architecture were heavily imbued with influences from the Byzantine world. Venice was not only stunningly wealthy in the medieval and Renaissance period—it also had an extraordinary sense of civic identity and a highly complex system of governance, at the heart of which was the figure of the doge.

A place that I recently enjoyed visiting was San Martino della Battaglia on the south edge of Lake Garda. This was the site in June 1859 of one of the key battles of unification movement and is commemorated with an enormous tower, more than 70 meters high, with splendid views from the top. Inside are frescoes celebrating King Victor Emmanuel II (who led the troops against the Austrians at the Battle of San Martino in a very inconclusive engagement) and the unification movement.

The Battle of San Martino was the Piedmontese contribution to a much larger battle being fought in a long line running south from Lake Garda on 24 June, 1859 between French and Austrian troops. This battle, the Battle of Solferino, was one of the bloodiest engagements of the 19th century. A Swiss businessman, Henry Dunant, happened to be passing in the vicinity when the battle was being fought and was so horrified by the lack of proper care for the wounded that he was inspired subsequently to set up the Red Cross. At San Martino there is a good museum with information about the Battle of Solferino, as well as a rather gruesome ossuary of bones collected from the battlefield.

Find Christopher's books on Amazon.com (search Christopher Duggan).

PLAN BY PLACE

Plan your trip based on where you want to go.

VENICE & THE VENETO

Canals, glassblowing, and a giant masquerade ball are just the beginning in this vibrant region.

In this section: Venice / Verona / Padova / Vicenza / Treviso

Venice (Venezia)

A sinking city full of Carnival masks, singing boatmen, and delicate glasswork.

Jennifer Dombrowski
Blogger. Dog-Lover. American Expat.

First, tell us about you.

I was born and raised in Pennsylvania, moved to Las Vegas for college, and then lived in Arizona and Italy with my husband. We've been living in Italy for five years now and what an experience it has been! In my free time, I like to go to Italian markets and read. Now that it's nearly summer, I can be found playing at the beach with my dog, Emma.

If someone is visiting Venice for the first time, what do you recommend they see or do?

The best thing to do for first time visitors to Venice is to just walk around and get lost. (Don't worry; you can't get too lost. You are on an island, after all.) Some not-to-be-missed highlights are the Rialto Bridge, St. Mark's Cathedral, and Doge's Palace. Take a *vaporetto* (water bus) over to the island of Murano and forget the over-priced Disneyland-like gondola ride—take gondola rowing lessons instead.

What neighborhoods or parts of town are best to stay in?

VENICE & THE VENETO

Venice is pretty small, so everything is close to the center. I personally like Cannaregio, the northernmost of the six historic *sestieri* (districts) of Venice. It's the off-the-beaten-path area of Venice packed with delicious *bàcari* (wine bars) and locals.

Let's talk about day trips...what nearby places should everyone make sure to visit?

Venice is just one of hundreds of islands in the Venetian Lagoon and you can easily use the *vaporetto* to visit Murano, which is famous for its glass making factories, or Burano, which is famous for its lace making. Hop on the train and visit Verona, the inspirational setting of *Letters to Juliet*. You can also rent a car for the day and travel Italy's wine roads, sipping bubbly *Prosecco* or velvety *Amarone*.

Tell us about the local dishes. What should people try?

When people think of Italian food, the food they know is an Americanized version of southern Italian dishes. Venetian dishes are much different. The best way to experience Venetian food is to take a *cicchetti* tour. *Cicchetti* (pronounced chi-KET-tee) are like Spanish tapas—small snacks or side dishes that are prepared fresh daily. The Venetian thing to do is eat a couple at each *bàcari*. A couple of my personal favorites are all located just steps away from the Rialto Bridge and frequented by locals.

What are your top three favorite bars and restaurants?

For *cicchetti*, try: Cantina Do Mori at *Sestiere San Polo 429* or All'Arco at *San Polo 436*. For a sit down, you can't go wrong by booking a table at L'Alcova (at *Campo Santa Sofia*). Executive Chef, Josef Klostermaier, likes to put his own unique spin on traditional Venetian cuisine and he even takes the traghetto gondola across the Grand Canal to personally hand-select fresh fish and vegetables from the Rialto Market daily.

Is there anything tourists do that locals find rude or strange? What can we do to better fit in with the culture?

Venetians are definitely no strangers to tourists. But something tourists can do is remember that the *calle* (streets) are very narrow. Don't walk with your group side by side, especially when there is pedestrian traffic on the *calle*.

What is the best way to meet locals and make friends?
Visit the *bàcari*! The best friendships are made over a carafe of the house wine.

When in Venice, forget the overpriced gondola ride...take gondola rowing lessons instead!

Why should people make sure to visit Venice?
Venice is one of the most unique and beautiful cities in the world. Sadly, it is sinking and experiences more and more *Acqua Alta* (flooding) each year. It may not be around forever and you wouldn't want to miss out on this Italian gem.

Where can we go to take beautiful photos?
Venice is very picturesque. Of course, everyone knows photos of the Rialto Bridge and *Piazza San Marco*. But wander around and you'll find colorful laundry precariously hanging above canals and bursts of bright pink azaleas climbing the old brick walls.

Anything else you want us to know?
If you're coming to Italy, surely you'll be eating a lot of *gelato*. Here's a tip for being able to tell the fake stuff from artisanal *gelato*: always check the banana, mint, or pistachio for their coloring. Artisanal *gelato* uses only fresh, natural ingredients so banana will be slightly gray, mint will be white, and pistachio will be a muted gray-green.

Find Jennifer at jdombstravels.com.

VENICE & THE VENETO

Andrea Villani
Reader. Wanderer. Traveler.

First, tell us about you.
I come from Piemonte, which is a region in the northwest of Italy. I've lived in Venice for three years now and when I have free time I like to go rowing, jogging, wandering around, and sometimes visiting museums. I love reading, of course, and travelling!

If someone is visiting Venice for the first time, what do you recommend they see or do?
The first time in Venice is always a bit dreamlike. I advise you to visit as many churches as possible (not only Saint Mark's!) and to try and lose yourself in the narrow streets. The beauty of Venice is for all to see; you don't have to make much effort to appreciate it.

What neighborhoods or parts of town are best to stay in?
If you are here for a short time, *Santa Croce* and *Dorsoduro* would suit you best; they are full of hotels, B&Bs, and restaurants and are the nearest *sestiere* (neighborhoods) to train, bus, and water-bus stations.

Let's talk about day trips...what nearby places should everyone make sure to visit?
If you have time to make a day trip, go straight to Padua, Verona, and Trieste. The countryside of the Euganeean Hills is peaceful and nice to visit and the tour of the Venetian villas is wonderful!

Tell us about the local dishes. What should people try?
Polenta, baccalà (salted cod), and *sarde in saor* (sweet and sour sardines) are the best dishes to try!

What are your top three favorite bars and restaurants?
Bars? El Chioschetto on the Zattere promenade (*Dorsoduro 1406*), Bacareto de Lele near Tolentini's church (*Campo dei*

Tolentini, Santa Croce 183), and Al Bocon DiVino in Santa Margherita Square.

Restaurants: Frary's in the *Frari Square*.

Is there anything tourists do that locals find rude or strange? What can we do to better fit in with the culture?

A very wise question! First of all, don't walk too slowly or, worse, stop in the center of the street or at the crossroads. Space is more valuable than gold in Venice; if you are not sure where to go, step aside in a corner while you figure it out.

For lovebirds, newlyweds, and similar: please, do not walk continuously holding hands; it's not practical in our narrow streets, since two people are difficult to pass when we're on our way to work, school, etc.

During the night, don't sing too loud; every noise is heard in the houses as if windows don't exist and the narrowness of the *calli* (streets) enhances the sound.

What is the best way to meet locals and make friends?

Have a *spritz* (drink) and start talking with the friendliest students you can find; an entire world will be open to you!

Why should people make sure to visit Venice?

Venice is like magic become stone. There's an unforgettable light between her streets, reflected in thousand of windows and canals, and history taps you on the shoulder at every corner. You will fall in love in an hour or even less, and you'll forget about everything you could complain about: transportation, crowds, expensive food, Venetians who don't speak a single word of a foreign language...

Where can we go to take beautiful photos?

Saint Markus' Square is breathtaking, especially during the high tides or when the sun shines brightly and dances on the white façades. From Giudecca Island, you can take shots of the skyline of the southern part of Venice, while travelling on the *vaporettos* (small boats) allows you to capture the corners and entryways of buildings. I think every little *campo* could be a Hollywood set, if anyone has eyes to see their richness.

Anything else you want us to know?
Try to listen to Venetian dialect; it's hilarious and might remind you a slurred Spanish. Don't forget natural reserves and the mountains if you got a chance to visit them. If you are a water person, look for trips on the many rivers of Veneto. That can be quite amusing and original.

Giulia Gabrielli
Student. Production Art Assistant. Traveler.

First, tell us about you.
I came from Verona and moved to Venice to study about 14 years ago. I am a production art assistant and dogsitter. In my free time, I like to travel with friends.

If someone is visiting Venice for the first time, what do you recommend they see or do?
Go visit the Doge's Palace and other *palazzi* in town. Most of the beauty is inside the buildings.

What neighborhoods or parts of town are best to stay in?
In Venice, I suggest *Dorsoduro* or *Cannaregio* because they are both very nice and typical.

Let's talk about day trips...what nearby places should everyone make sure to visit?
Treviso, Asolo, and Verona are good for food and wine and things to do and see.

Tell us about the local dishes. What should people try?
Sarde in saòr (sardines in onion sauce), *spaghetti alla busara* (prawns in tomato sauce), and *bigoli in salsa* (pasta in

anchovy sauce) are the most famous dishes and in the *bacaro* (Venetian bars) there is a variety of *cicheti* (like tapas).

What are your top three favorite bars and restaurants?
Anice Stellato, on *Sestiere Cannaregio* in the *Cannaregio* neighborhood, Zucca, at *Santa Croce 1762* in *Santa Croce*, and Osteria da Carla at *Corte Contarina N 1535* in San Marco.

Is there anything tourists do that locals find rude or strange? What can we do to better fit in with the culture?
Do not scream when you talk, especially if you walk at night. And don't put your feet in the canals (this is not healthy).

Sometimes you could run into streets that are really tiny; remember to walk on the right side (as you drive your car...there's traffic even though we don't have cars).

What is the best way to meet locals and make friends?
Have a *spritz* in a bar.

Where can we go to take beautiful photos?
San Marco Square, Zattere, and Academia's Bridge.

Anything else you want us to know?
All the cheap things are fake for sure—it is impossible to find Murano glass and Venetian handmade masks for one euro. If you want the real thing, you'll need to do a little digging and pay a little more.

Verona

Home of the world's most well preserved functioning coliseum, Romeo & Juliet, and a population known for being a little nuts.

VENICE & THE VENETO

Anna Colage
Web Writer. Foreign Language Enthusiast. In Love With Verona.

First, tell us about you.

I was born in Verona and I moved to another town when I was a little girl. Then I came back here for college and decided it was the best place to stay for me. So it is about 20 years now that I am living here and I have seen the city change over time. I am a web content writer and in my spare time I like to go out to eat with my fiancé and friends, go to the cinema, play tennis, and learn foreign languages (I am actually learning Portuguese).

If someone is visiting Verona for the first time, what do you recommend they see or do?

Verona is well known in the world as the city of Opera because of its ancient Arena, and also for the sad love story between Romeo and Juliet (the famous balcony was re-built here), but I would say there are so many other things to see: the ancient Roman Theater during the summer theatric season is worth well a visit and, of course, *Piazza delle Erbe* (the most beautiful square in the world, as it was voted by tourists in a recent survey), with its beautiful frescos all around. And do not forget to come for Carnival: we have the most ancient Carnival of Europe – it is 600 years old!

What neighborhoods or parts of town are best to stay in?

Well, of course, the center is the best place to stay to catch all the beautiful glimpses as a tourist. But as a citizen, the most desired is *Valdonega*, which is a quiet, green place on the hill.

Let's talk about day trips...what nearby places should everyone make sure to visit?

Verona has a lucky position. Near Lake Garda with cute villages like Bardolino, Garda, Torri del Benaco, and Malcesine (you can cross it by boat or make a tour and go on the other side to visit other villages). On the north side, there are hills (with vineyards and many famous wine cellars and wines like *Soave*, *Valpolicella*, and *Recioto*, just to name a

45

few) and mountains where you can go walking and skiing. At the southwest, about 35 kilometers away, there is a very nice village called Borghetto with a typical watermill (people go there to take pictures on their wedding day). And, also, Verona is just 1.5 hours away from the sea by car. So there are really a lot of things to do in every season.

Tell us about the local dishes. What should people try?

My advice is to eat local and, in the case of Verona, that means: *risotto al tastasal* (risotto with sausage dressing) or *risotto with radicchio* (risotto with a typical salad of Treviso often eaten here as well), *pastisada de caval* (horse meat pasta), *polenta* (thick porridge made with maize flour) with cheese or mushrooms on top, and different lake fish.

As sweets we have: *baci di Giulietta* (Juliet's kisses), *pandoro of Verona* (a type of sponge cake eaten at Christmas), *zaletti* (biscuits), and *castagnaccio* (made of chestnut flour). All this food connects to the country origin of the town.

What are your top three favorite bars and restaurants?

My favorite restaurants where I often go are: a pizzeria called Corte Farina (at *Via Corte Farina 4*) that cooks excellent pizza. The sfilatino (rolled pizza) with cheese and zucchini inside is the best, in my opinion. They also prepare excellent salads and some food of the tradition up-to-date with modern taste.

The best bar to have an *aperitivo* (aperitif) is Aquila Nera (Black Eagle) in the center (at *Galleria Pellicciai 2*). You can have a *spritz* (a glass of white wine or *Campari* with seltzer and a slice of lemon) and an appetizer. You can also have lunch here or a cup of tea with cookies in the afternoon.

Last, but not least, is a trattoria called le Vecette (the two old ladies) that cooks the traditional food I mentioned in my previous answer with a good cantina of wines. Address: *Via Pellicciai 32/A*.

Is there anything tourists do that locals find rude or strange? What can we do to better fit in with the culture?

Well, Verona is a very touristic town, so thousand of people come and walk and eat in its streets and...in the past just sat in front of monuments. That is now forbidden and I noticed that tourists pay more respect to our sometimes very ancient monuments. But still there is one thing that I don't really understand: why do they write love phrases and put chewing gum to hold the love cards on the walls in the gallery to go to Juliet's balcony? This is very rude; they can write directly to Juliet and a committee replies to every single letter coming from all over the world. They should also know that it costs a lot of money to clean all up every year!

What is the best way to meet locals and make friends?

Definitely go to *Piazza delle Erbe* at about 6 p.m. every day and have an *aperitivo* in one of the several bars there, especially near the column with Venetian lion at the end of the square. Young people meet here to have a chat, drink together, or just gather.

Where can we go to take beautiful photos?

The best place to take pictures in Verona is *Castel San Pietro*, which is up on the hill. There is a magnificent view of the river Adige and its bridges, including *Ponte Pietra*, the ancient one. You can see all the rooftops of the historical center.

Why should people make sure to visit Verona?

Because it is a jewel rich in history and culture from ancient Roman times to nowadays. There are lots of things to do, from opera to modern ballet to photography. You should spend at least one week in order to see everything calmly and enjoy our lifestyle.

Anything else you want us to know?

We are known as mad people who like having fun. There is a nursery rhyme about the region Veneto where all these towns belong: "*Veneziani gran siori, Padovani gran dottori, Vicentini magna gati, Veronesi tuti mati.*" It means: people from Venice are well-known as famous lords, people from Padova as doctors, people from Vicenza as cat eaters (yes, in the poverty times!), and people from Verona as all mad.

We are always available for a chat even if we do not know each other well. But pay attention: we often speak dialect, which is part of our culture and applies to everyone - from the young to the elderly. English is spoken by many, but German also plays an important role here, as most tourists come from Germany.

Ilaria Roveran
World-Traveler. Entrepreneur + Landlord. Local.

First, tell us about you.
I have lived in Verona since I was born. I love my city because it isn't a metropolis and you can move around by bicycle. In my free time, I go out with my friends; in my city there are many pubs and restaurants.

Verona is very convenient. I can get to Lake Garda in just 30 minutes or be skiing in the Dolomites in an hour.

In the city itself, just a short walk from the city center, there are beautiful, green nature walks called *torricelle* (I have a dog and this is perfect for us!).

If someone is visiting Verona for the first time, what do you recommend they see or do?
Verona is the city of Romeo & Juliet, but it also has a lot more to offer. If you visit Verona for the first time, you have to see the *Ponte Pietra, Castel San Pietro* (you'll see the city from the hill), *Palazzo Giardino Giusti, Piazza Bra* (home of the Arena), *Piazza Erbe*, and *Piazza Dante*.

What neighborhoods or parts of town are best to stay in?

I live between the Roman theater and *Ponte Pietra*...and I *love* this neighborhood. It is very quiet and we all know each other. Plus, I can be in *Piazza Erbe* or at the *torricelli* paths in just two minutes.

The other neighborhood I would recommend—quiet, safe, and very central—is close to the Arena (where my holiday rental, Come Casa Tua, is located).

Let's talk about day trips...what nearby places should everyone make sure to visit?

Lake Garda: Bardolino, Lazise, or Sirmione. I would recommend those towns for both summer and winter (though they are, of course, very different in each season).

Venice: we are only an hour away from the lovely sinking city by train.

Tell us about the local dishes. What should people try?

Stroll between Verona's collection of small and laid-back *osterie* (wine + small plates bars) and stop in one or two for a glass of local wine (*Valpolicella*) and an entrée. This is one of the city's culinary pleasures.

Typical dishes include *monte Veronese* (local cheese) and *bigoli* pasta with donkey *ragu* (yes...donkey).

What are your top three favorite bars and restaurants?

El Bacarin/Montebaldo, located on *Via Rosa 12*, has plates of local cheese and cut meats, as well as hearty *polenta*. Osteria del Bugiardo, located on *Corso Porta Borsari*, is another favorite. Osteria Torre del Gardello, located on *Corso Sant'Anastasia*, is a new, typical *osteria* and you can taste wine with good dishes. Terrazza Bar al Ponte is one of my favorite places, too, because of the awesome view from their balcony (at *Via Ponte Pietra 26*).

Is there anything tourists do that locals find rude or strange? What can we do to better fit in with the culture?

49

Personally, I love when my city is full of different nationalities and cultures. The only thing is when they put chewing gum on the wall of Juliet's house. This is incredibly rude.

What is the best way to meet locals and make friends?
Go to *Piazza Erbe* (Mazzanti Cafe) on the weekend. It is full of people until 2 a.m.!

Why should people make sure to visit Verona?
Smaller than Rome, Verona is magic...every time you raise your head, there are new things to discover.

Where can we go to take beautiful photos?
I think *Ponte Pietra* is the best place to take a photo...or from *Ponte Pietra* to *Castel San Pietro* (you have to climb the stairs but the effort is well worth it).

Anything else you want us to know?
There is a typical proverb that says: *"Veronesi tuti mati"* (people from Verona are all mad). Come here and find out!

Find Illaria at: www.comecasatua.com.

Padua (Padova)

The setting of Shakespeare's Taming of the Shrew and home of the largest square in Europe.

Leonardo Maglio
Police Officer. Native Italian.

First, tell us about you.
I have lived in Padova for about eight years (before that, I lived in Venice and I'm originally from the beautiful southeast of Italy—a micro-region called Salento in Puglia). I'm a

policeman. In my free time, I go out with my friends to a good restaurant, to drink good wine, or to dance.

If someone is visiting Padova for the first time, what do you recommend they see or do?

Padova is a beautiful, ancient city and (fortunately!) not as touristy as Venice. It is a very important university city (we've got the second most ancient university in the world). And the historic center is interesting to see, including *Prato della Valle Square* (the largest square in Italy), *Basilica di Saint Antonio*, the biggest botanic garden in Europe, *Dei Signori Square*, *Della Frutta* and *Delle Erbe* squares, *Palazzo degli Zabarella*, *Palazzo Moroni*, *Cappella degli Scrovegni*, *Museo degli Eremitani*, the ancient Café Pedrocchi (at *Via VIII Febbraio 15*), *Palazzo della Ragione*, Bó University (where Galileo Galulei used to teach), and *Ghetto Ebraico*.

What neighborhoods or parts of town are best to stay in?

The historic center and the *Arcella* quarter.

Let's talk about day trips...what nearby places should everyone make sure to visit?

Nearby, you'll find *Abano Terme*, which has many natural thermal pools. If you like nature and woods, go in *Euganei Hills Park*. I also love the ancient towns of Cittadella, Este, Piazzola sul Brenta, and Monselice.

Tell us about the local dishes. What should people try?

The typical food is *baccalà alla Vicentina* (Vicenza-style cod), *bigoli* pasta with boar meat or *ragú*, *gelato*, and any kind of cake.

While you're here, you must drink a *spritz* (*Prosecco di Valdobbiadene*, Aperol, a piece of orange, one olive, and little water).

What are your top three favorite bars and restaurants?

Bars: Kofler (at *Via Pilade Bronzes 34*), Enoteca dei Tadi (at *Via de Tadi 16*), and Café Baessato (at *Largo Europa 14*).

VENICE & THE VENETO

Restaurants: Pizzeria agli Eremitani (located at *Via Porciglia 29*), Granchio Blu (located at *via Postunia 2 a Selvazzano Dentro* and serving very good pizza and fish plates), and Pizzeria Puri e Folli (located at *Via Giuseppe Perin 21*).

That said, in Padova there are many good restaurants, pubs, clubs, and bars, especially in the center!

Is there anything tourists do that locals find rude or strange? What can we do to better fit in with the culture?

In Italy, the culture varies greatly in the north, center, or south. In general, northern Italians do not like people littering in the streets. Never refuse if something is offered to you. Do not be pushy. Every time, eat everything you're served and drink good wine together.

In general, Italian people like to be ironic and like so much to woo women (especially with many compliments, offering a good dinner with good wine).

What is the best way to meet locals and make friends?

Throughout Padova's historic center are many bars, pubs, clubs, and restaurants where you can meet people.

Why should people make sure to visit Padova?

If you like art, you have to come to Padova. Also, it's a romantic and quiet city and, in the evenings, a university city with many clubs. Finally, if you come just to the amazing S. Antony Basilica, you won't be disappointed.

Also, Padova is located in the perfect center of the region, so it's a great home base for exploring everything nearby. We've got great bus connections, so it's easy to get to Venezia, Verona, Vicenza, Treviso, Lake Garda, Sirmione, the Dolomites, and the sea in Chioggia Sottomarina. If you stay for a week, it's possible to see much of the region without spending much money.

Where can we go to take beautiful photos?

Prato della Valle, *Piazza dei Signory*, and the historic center.

Anything else you want us to know?
If you need free Wi-Fi, try the airports, train stations, or by requesting it in bars, pubs, and hotels.

Vicenza

A UNESCO World Heritage Site, architecturally significant, and one of Italy's wealthiest cities.

Noemi Meneguzzo
Teacher. Philosopher. Dancer. Traveler. Artist & Cancer Survivor.

First, tell us about you.
I was born in Vicenza and lived there until 2005. Then I migrated to San Diego, California for three years and now I'm back in Italy. In my spare time, I love studying modern and contemporary dance, reading, going out with friends, or just walking in the countryside.

If someone is visiting Vicenza for the first time, what do you recommend they see or do?
Downtown Vicenza is beautiful and charming. I love walking in *Corso Palladio* early in the morning or during the night. The buildings are wonderful, elegant really, and nobody is there during those times of day.

In my personal opinion, the places you have to see are *Basilica Palladiana* and *Piazza dei Signori*, *Teatro Olimpico*, *Chiesa di San Lorenzo*, *Museo di Palazzo Chiericati*, *Museo Dicocesano*, *Chiesa di Santa Corona*, The *Rotonda*, *Monte Berico* (for the city view), and *Villa Valmarana ai Nani*.

Also, the countryside is beautiful: Bassano del Grappa and Marostica are very nice and are livelier than Vicenza.

53

VENICE & THE VENETO

What neighborhoods or parts of town are best to stay in?
Vicenza is very quiet and generally safe, but the neighborhood around the train station is not very safe at night. If you are in Vicenza as a tourist, the hostel is right downtown. The city is well served by public transportation compared to the American cities in California where I lived.

Let's talk about day trips...what nearby places should everyone make sure to visit?
Bassano has a cute center with a famous bridge. It's also famous for the ceramic art pieces and for the *Grappa Nardini* wine. In Bassano, nights are very lively. People are all around and you feel safe. There are many cultural events all year around.

Marostica is known for the *Partita a Scacchi*, a living chess game (real people play the roles of the chess pieces) performed every two years in the beautiful *Piazza degli Scacchi*.

The Altopiano di Asiago is a touristic and popular place in the mountains. If you would rather get off the beaten path, you can visit Campogrosso instead—or Monte Pasubio, with its trail of 52 galleries. The mountains that surround Vicenza were involved in WWI and you can see interesting foxholes, trenches, and forts there.

Close to Vicenza, there is a small lake called *Lago di Fimon*, where you can go for a walk and a picnic. There are also places where you can go rafting, like Valstagna.

Tell us about the local dishes. What should people try?
Vicenza is well known for the *polenta* (cornmeal porridge) and *baccala' alla Vicentina* (Vicenza-style cod), but each village has its own specialties. For instance, Creazzo is very popular for the *broccolo fiolaro* (Venetian broccoli), Bassano for the asparagus, Grumolo della Abbadesse for the rice, and Asiago for the cheese.

VENICE & THE VENETO

There are many *gelaterie* downtown. The most elegant is Caffe' Garibaldi, but I highly recommend OLLY, a bio-ice cream shop in *Corso Fogazzaro*. The *gelato* is very good...better than Grom (the popular gelato)!

The most popular cake is the *puttana* or *pinza*, which was the cake of poor people, made with leftovers, like polenta, bread, pinoli, and raisin.

In Vicenza, you eat very well, even though the restaurants are not very cheap. I won't recommend any international restaurants because they are expensive and the quality of food is not so high.

In Vicenza, you also can enjoy wine. I like the *Prosecco* from Gambellara, but also the red wine made from local wineries. You should visit some *cantine* (Italian bistros) in Gambellara or Breganze!

There is a popular saying *"Vicentini magnagati,"* meaning that the people here (Vicentini) are cat (yes...cat!) eaters. Is it true? Well...every Vicentino seems to know someone who says he/she has eaten a cat.

What are your top three favorite bars and restaurants?
I like Righetti, at *Piazza Duomo 3*, which is a self-service restaurant with popular meals. Food is fresh and homemade. You find the real *Vicentini* (locals) eating here during their lunchtime.

Cafe' Borsa (at *Piazza dei Signori 26*), The Grottino (at *Piazza delle Erbe 2*), and L'Antica Casa della Malvasia (at *Contrà delle Morette 5*) are nice bars where you can find a good selection of wines and good music.

My favorite place is Osteria al Centro on *Via Valle dei Mulini* in Fimon, which is about 15 kilometers outside Vicenza. The owner is Carletto, a real character. He is a musician and a painter; he loves to talk and complain about politics; and he serves good wines, beers, and *bruschette* (sandwiches). He used to serve the *fragolino*, a sweet red wine, but now the production of this kind of wine is prohibited. The place is very social; you sit with other people, and there is a good selection of table games.

Is there anything tourists do that locals find rude or strange? What can we do to better fit in with the culture?

After the invasion of Iraq and the construction of a new base, some of the locals don't like American soldiers...especially when they are drunk and walk downtown.

What is the best way to meet locals and make friends?

Go out at 6 p.m. and have an aperitif (I recommend a *spritz*, a sparkling, wine-based cocktail) with local people if you are downtown. Other places to go are the Wenge Café (at *Viale della Scienza 9/11*) and Feel (a restaurant, pizzeria, wine cellar, show club, and dance club at *Via Vecchia Ferriera 22*). You can also meet interesting people in local activity clubs, like Teatro Kitchen (at *www.spaziokitchen.it*, for theater buffs) or Cai (at *www.caivicenza.it*, for hikers).

Why should people make sure to visit Vicenza?

Vicenza offers many ways to enjoy life. First of all, the city is a Palladio jewel. The countryside is beautiful too. Just take a look from the *Piazzale della Vittoria*, a square on the top of a hill behind the train station, for a stunning view of the surrounding beautiful hills and mountains.

Where can we go to take beautiful photos?

Downtown. *Ponte San Michele* and *Ponte Furo* offer you a beautiful view of the city, buildings with terraces and flowers, and the roof of *Basilica Palladiana*.

Anything else you want us to know?

Vicenza has a good location. You can stay here and visit the other Venetian towns easily. Verona and Padua are just 30 minutes away and Venice is less than one hour.

Vicenza is beautiful all year around, but in the summer it is very hot, so I suggest you come here in spring or fall.

Find Noemi at: www.tucancroiodonna.it.

Treviso

The original home of Tiramisu is also a charming and central home base for exploring the region.

Federico di Appiani
Designer. Journalist. B&B Owner.

First, tell us about you.
I am French and Italian. I spent some years living in London, Rome, and Milan. Now, I am in Treviso (for the past 10 years). I run a B&B and work as a freelance web designer, journalist, and writer.

If someone is visiting Treviso for the first time, what do you recommend they see or do?
My top picks: the ancient wall and stone gates (*Porta S. Tomaso* and *Porta S. Quaranta*), the *Restera* walk alongside the Sile River, and a wine and finger-food tour in the *osterias* of Treviso. I also love the frescoes by Tomaso da Modena in the ancient Seminary of *San Nicolò*, the canals of *Buranelli*, and the *Isolotto della Pescheria* (fish market Island).

What neighborhoods or parts of town are best to stay in?
The hills are very nice. Particularly, the small towns of Conegliano, Asolo, Valdobbiadene, and Cison di Valmarino.

Let's talk about day trips...what nearby places should everyone make sure to visit?
Gipsoteca di Antonio Canova (the "graces" by Antonio Canova—an art exhibit in Possagno) is worth seeing. *Castello di San Salvatore*'s book fair (held in October) in Susegana

(where you can also visit the *Castello di Collalto* market) is another favorite, as is a walk and dining experience in the restaurants around *Cison di Valmarino Castello*. Also, check out the Gambrinus Restaurant at *Via Capitello 18* in San Polo di Piave and try *il piatto del giorno* (the dish of the day) in the *osteria*.

Finally, I recommend a visit in the cantine of Valdobbiadene to buy *Prosecco*.

Tell us about the local dishes. What should people try?

Tiramisu is originally from Treviso (so definitely try some here). Also: *casatella* (a fresh cheese), *radicchio rosso di Treviso* (red radish), asparagus, *spritz* (a drink), *Prosecco*, *Raboso del Piave* (a local red wine), and *risotto*.

What are your top three favorite bars and restaurants?

Osteria al Radicchio Rosso (at *Via Tolpada 25/27*) for amazing fish, Ke Vin bar at *Via Sant'Antonino 4* (which means "what a wine") for local flavor without the flashy, up-to-date interior, and Pizzeria la Finestra (on *Via Diaz TV*) for very good pizza.

Is there anything tourists do that locals find rude or strange? What can we do to better fit in with the culture?

Treviso is not Venezia, so it is not touristy. This makes it a very genuine place to visit, but also means most people don't speak other languages, so you should try to learn a little Italian.

Why should people make sure to visit Treviso?

It's a great home base for exploring the area. We are 30 kilometers from Venezia with a direct train and it's very easy to go to Padova and Vicenza. Plus, there is an airport served by Ryanair less than a kilometer from the historic center of Treviso.

Where can we go to take beautiful photos?

Penisola del Paradiso around the ancient wall.

Find Federico at: www.appiani36.it.

TRENTINO-ALTO ADIGE

Welcome to the Italian Alps with their limestone cliffs, snowy forests, and ancient mountain towns.

In this section: Trento / Bolzano / Dro (Lake Garda)

Trento

An ancient mountain town and gateway to the Dolomites— the mountain range of UNESCO fame.

Edy
Theater Buff. Sports Enthusiast. Trento Native.

First, tell us about you.
I've been living in Trento my whole life (41 years). In the last 10 years, I've had to go elsewhere for work, but during weekends I tend to come back to Trento.

In my free time, I love alpine hiking, skiing (both mountain and distance), biking (both mountain and road), and playing indoor soccer. I'm also interested in culture, museums, cinema, and theater.

If someone is visiting Trento for the first time, what do you recommend they see or do?
Trento is a very old town and a mountain town, so the first things to see are its historical landmarks and mountain environment.

Specifically: the old center of Trento is wonderful (particularly the dome square with the cathedral), as are *Buonconsiglio* Castle (and its museum), and the Muse Museum (designed by

59

architect Renzo Piano). You can easily stroll around the center and see everything because it is a car-free area.

What neighborhoods or parts of town are best to stay in?

I suggest staying in the center of Trento. And if you're staying for a while, consider spending some of your days in the mountains or at Riva del Garda. (And if you do go to Riva, make sure to visit Arco Castle and the beautiful medieval village of Canale.)

Let's talk about day trips...what nearby places should everyone make sure to visit?

Very close to the city, you can visit some of the most beautiful mountains and lakes, including Gruppo di Brenta, Val di Fassa, Val di Fiemme, and Lake Garda, Caldonazzo (where there are tons of lake sports to participate in), Levico, Tenno, and Molveno.

Roverto and its Museum of Modern and Contemporary Art are also worth a visit.

Tell us about the local dishes. What should people try?

The traditional food in Trento is the poor man's food. In the winter season, try *tortel di patate* (fried potatoes), *carne salada* (meat), *speck* (bacon), *canederli in brood* (dumplings in broth), potato *gnocchi*, *strangolapreti* (literally, "priest stranglers" because, according to legend, the clergy liked them so much that they would eat until they choked), *crauti* (sauerkraut), and *polenta* (cornmeal). Also trout is quite common.

What are your top three favorite bars and restaurants?

Bars: Plan (at *Largo Giosue Carducci 38*), Cantinota (at *Via S. Marco 22/24*), Pasi (located at *Piazza Mario Pasi 1*), Feeling (at *Via Androna 1*), Accademia (at *Vicolo Colico 4/6*), Willy (at *Via Pranzelores 46*), and Simposio (at *Via Rosmini 19*).

Restaurants: Loto (at *Via Gocciadoro 62*), Forst (at *Via Paolo Oss Mazzurana 38*), and Pedavena (at *Piazza Fiera 13*).

Pizzerias: Oro Stube (located at *Via Sommarive 10*) and Grotta (at *Vicolo San Marco*). Grotta is famous for its huge portions.

For students and young people, Picaro (located at *Vicolo San Giovanni 36*) is also a popular restaurant.

What is the best way to meet locals and make friends?
Visit the bars I suggested above or go to university, which has events designed for meeting new people. People from Trento are not so open in the beginning. Remember: We are Nordic mountain people, not at all similar to people from Rome or southern Italy.

Why should people make sure to visit Trento?
Architects say that Dome Square is the most beautiful square in Italy.

Where can we go to take beautiful photos?
Dome Square, *Giro al Sass* (a road-running competition in mid-October), the Muse Museum, and Monte Bondone (a nearby mountain with wonderful views of the city).

Also, Martignano and Sardagna, two hilltop villages, offer great views of the city.

Anything else you want us to know?
The university is very important and they are trying to develop something similar to a Silicon Valley in Trento by supporting a lot of research and start-ups.

Serena Fusaro
Hiker. Climber. Theater Buff. Trento Native.

First, tell us about you.
I have always lived in Trento, with the exception of about a year when I lived in France and Germany. In my free time, I love to go to the mountains. And I often go to the cinema and theater.

TRENTINO-ALTO ADIGE

If someone is visiting Trento for the first time, what do you recommend they see or do?
Visit the town center and do the *Giro al Sass*—a traditional walk through the historic city center. The museums of Trent are also very interesting, including the newly opened Muse. Finally, the Buonconsiglio Castle is always interesting.

What neighborhoods or parts of town are best to stay in?
It's best to stay in the historic center, near the train station and Cathedral Square. Next to the train station, there is a hostel.

Let's talk about day trips...what nearby places should everyone make sure to visit?
Take a short hike in the mountains to enjoy the view of the Valley dell'Adige (Sardagna, Bondone, and Marzola). And spend a day at Lake Garda to lay in the sun or do some water sports.

Tell us about the local dishes. What should people try?
Our dishes are a bit similar to German food here in the north. *Polenta* (cornmeal porridge) is a must! You can get it with meat or cheese and herbs. Alternately, try the *tortel di patate* (potato omelet) or *strozzapreti* (pasta).

What are your top three favorite bars and restaurants?
Caffe della Paix (a traditional café at *Passaggio Teatro Osele 6/8*), Osteria San Martino (a very typical local restaurant at *Via San Martino 42*), and Pizzeria Da Albert (at *Via Bomporto 2*).

What is the best way to meet locals and make friends?
Join a local association, play sports, or attend the university. Couchsurfing.org can also help people socialize.

Why should people make sure to visit Trento?
Trento is very welcoming. It's also the city that won the first place prize for quality of living in Italy in 2013. Plus, it is surrounded by breathtaking mountains.

There isn't a lot of nightlife, but for sports lovers, the possibilities are infinite, whether in winter or summer. The Dolomites (a UNESCO World Heritage Site) are always open.

Where can we go to take beautiful photos?
Da Sardagna (take the cable car from the Trento city center) or on the city center walk I mentioned above.

Anything else you want us to know?
Absolutely do not miss *La Festa Medievale del Patrono* in June.

Anna Bortoli
Social Worker. Dancer. Lover of Life.

First, tell us about you.
I have lived in Trento since I was born (so, for 26 years). Now, I live in a nearby village, 20 minutes from Trento. In my free time, I love listening to the radio/music, reading with my cat on my lap, going to the gym, and dancing (I'm taking a lindy hop class right now).

If someone is visiting Trento for the first time, what do you recommend they see or do?
Trento can easily be seen in one day. I would recommend the town center (cathedral, squares, and old streets), the Buonconsiglio castle and, if there is no queue, the new modern museum: MUSE.

What neighborhoods or parts of town are best to stay in?
Trento is very small and you can go from south to north easily by bike. From west to east is a bit more complicated because the land is not flat, but a little hilly.

I would recommend the center/south of the town (*Trento, Piedicastello, San Giuseppe, Clarina, San Bartolameo*).

Let's talk about day trips...what nearby places should everyone make sure to visit?

63

TRENTINO-ALTO ADIGE

Surely *Lago di Garda* and Arte Sella in Val di Sella (near Borgo Valsugana), which are both nice places to visit and to have walk.

Tell us about the local dishes. What should people try?

Trento is not famous for cooking, I'm afraid. But it is quite typical to try *polenta* and melted cheese with sausages and mushrooms.

What are your top three favorite bars and restaurants?

Bars: Accademia (located at *Vicolo Colico* 4) and pub Posta (at *Via Roccabruna 2*).

Restaurants: Patelli (at *Via Dietro le Mura A1/5*) and Villa Madruzzo (at *Via Ponte Alto 26*).

Is there anything tourists do that locals find rude or strange? What can we do to better fit in with the culture?

I think Italians are generally curious about new people and different cultures and they enjoy showing off the goods of Italy. At the same time, this may lead them to behave like "we do everything the best way."

Why should people make sure to visit Trento?

For the surrounding Dolomites and the many mountain lakes.

Where can we go to take beautiful photos?

Piazza Duomo is wonderful. Also, from the back of the Buonconsiglio Castle you can have a nice view of the town and the old rooftops.

Bolzano

This German-speaking city ranks high for its quality of life.

TRENTINO-ALTO ADIGE

Klaus Sparer
Winery Owner. Cyclist. Hiker.

First, tell us about you.
I live in a little village near Bolzano and every day (for the past 25 years), I go into Bolzano for work. In my free time, I like cycling, books, and mountain excursions.

If someone is visiting Bolzano for the first time, what do you recommend they see or do?
Bolzano is a nice little city with a lot of possibilities. There are museums, the cathedral, *Piazza delle Erbe* (with its daily market full of fruits, vegetables, flowers, and groceries), *Via Portici* (the most ancient street here, full of shops), churches...We are very proud of our Museum of Archeology with *Ötzi*, the ice man who was found in 1991 near the Tisa Pass in Val Senales; his life period was about 5,300 years ago.

What neighborhoods or parts of town are best to stay in?
There are a lot of little villages near Bolzano in the valley and the hills (in particular, I like San Genesio and Renon). Inside Bolzano, I recommend *Gries* or the historic part of the city.

Let's talk about day trips...what nearby places should everyone make sure to visit?
I recommend Renon, which is reachable via cableway from Bolzano and from which you have a wonderful view of the city and the Dolomites. Also, Oltreadige and Bassa Atesina with their expansive apple orchards and vineyards.

Tell us about the local dishes. What should people try?
Our dishes are a mix of light Italian dishes with fish and vegetables and the traditional Austrian dishes (meat, sauces, and side dishes). In Bolzano, you should try *canederli* (balls made of old bread, eggs, milk, etc.), *schlutzkrapfen* (beef and potato ravioli), and *bauerngröstl* (fried potatoes with beef).

65

TRENTINO-ALTO ADIGE

What are your top three favorite bars and restaurants?

Hotel Mondschein, in the historical part of the city at *Via Piave 15*, has a nice garden restaurant. Hotel Laurin (at *Via Laurin 4*) has a great piano bar. Restaurant Vögele (at *Goethestreet 3*) is the best place for typical side dishes. And Restaurant Hopfen, at *Piazza dell'Erbe 17*, is a great place for beer (they brew their own).

Is there anything tourists do that locals find rude or strange? What can we do to better fit in with the culture?

White sport socks with sandals is a little bit strange.

What is the best way to meet locals and make friends?

Go out during happy hour for a glass of wine and some finger foods in the different wine bars around the city and you will know a lot of people!

Why should people make sure to visit Bolzano?

Because it is a nice, little, and clean city full of traditions!

Where can we go to take beautiful photos?

In the historical part of the city: the *Piazza Walther*.

Anything else you want us to know?

Alto Adige is a particular little region and in every valley you will find varying traditions and dialects (we've got three languages spoken widely in the region: German, Italian, and Ladin, an old Rhaeto-Romanic language spoken in the northeastern part of South Tyrol).

Find Klaus at: www.kellereibozen.com/en/.

Dro (Lake Garda)

Just minutes from Lake Garda, this little town is a gateway to mountain adventures of all kinds.

TRENTINO-ALTO ADIGE

Matteo Principe Biondo
Sports Enthusiast. Restaurant Owner.

First, tell us about you.

I'm Matteo. I'm 30 years old and have lived in Dro my whole life. I love doing sports outdoors and this place is ideal. In just a few miles, we have lots of sports and geographic diversity.

For example, there are wonderful trails for mountain biking enthusiasts, incredible walls for climbing and canyoning, and, of course, *Il becco dell'Aquila* (a BASE jumping exit famous worldwide). We also have a motocross circuit, where every year the most important riders in the world come and ride.

If someone is visiting Dro and Garda for the first time, what do you recommend they see or do?

If someone was visiting for a day in Dro, I would advise him to take a ride to the *Marocche*—the site of an impressive postglacial landslide. A walk through the interior of this unique landscape is an experience in emotions and energies. Many come here just to do yoga or meditation or to see the dinosaur footprints.

What neighborhoods or parts of town are best to stay in?

This is a very small place, so geographically your choices of where to stay are pretty much the same. The old town has some traditional, unique B&Bs.

Let's talk about day trips...what nearby places should everyone make sure to visit?

There are many great climbing routes that are nearby. A short walk from the center, you can climb a waterfall or go through wonderful places by bridges. The view from our area is unique, from the magnificent Medieval castles to the views on the lake.

Tell us about the local dishes. What should people try?

67

TRENTINO-ALTO ADIGE

The traditional dishes of Dro and the area are *la carne salada* (cuts of meat, cleaned of all fat, sprinkled with a mixture of salt and spices, and placed in a container for two to five weeks depending on the size) and *li strangolapreti* (a typical dish of cucina povera—the poor kitchen—*strangolapreti* are stale bread dumplings with spinach, eggs, and *Grana Trentino* served with melted butter and sage). The town of Dro is also famous for its cultivated plums—*la susina di Dro*.

What are your top three favorite bars and restaurants?
Obviously, my restaurant—Alfio (*www.ristorantealfio.it*)—tops my list. As for bars, I recommend La Parete Zebrata (*www.barparetezebrata.it*).

What is the best way to meet locals and make friends?
During the summer, it is easy to find people and make new friends in places where you can practice sports, on the beautiful beach on the river Sarca, or in the lovely oasis of peace, *Ponte Romano*. The *Basso Sarca* (which is the area from Dro to Lake Garda) offers an infinite number of places to play outdoors and, without a doubt, the shore of Lake Garda is the place to meet new people.

Why should people make sure to visit Dro and Garda?
The simple answer is that this place is truly unique, with varying landscapes, all pleasing to the eye, and the thousand-year history that you can still feel when you visit today. Then there's *Marocche*, with its particular energy.

Another reason is the climate. Lake Garda offers mild winters and summers that aren't too muggy. It is the farthest north place in the world where olive trees are grown.

Find Matteo at: www.ristorantealfio.it.

MILAN & LOMBARDY

Italy's fashion capitol is just minutes from some of the most popular, charming coastal towns.

In this section: Milan / Bergamo / Cremona / Mantua / Cremia (Lake Como) / Lierna (Lake Como)

Milan (Milano)

The second most populous city in Italy, known for its devotion to fashion, design, and hard work.

Andrea Vid
IT Engineer. Hiker. Local.

First, tell us about you.
I was born in Milano and practically always lived here (save for the summer months, when I travel). I work as an IT engineer and am constantly inside an office from Monday to Friday, so I prefer spending my free time outside. I enjoy tennis, hiking, and traveling.

If someone is visiting Milano for the first time, what do you recommend they see or do?
The historical center has a beautiful cathedral (the *Duomo di Milano*) and a full-fledged castle (*Castello Sforzesco*). If you come in the summertime, you should take part in a guided tour of *Castello Sforzesco*, as you'll be able to appreciate it better (for example, there's a huge maze of dungeons underneath, which provided an exit for escaping into the countryside; on a tour, you'll hear all about this history).

During the evening, the areas of *Navigli* and *Brera* are picturesque and welcoming (cars are forbidden to enter them). Especially *Navigli*, since it's the district with the channels that, until the past century, made it possible for Milano to be

69

one of the biggest commercial ports in Italy (despite the city being far from the sea).

Last but not least, the opera house (*La Scala*) is world-renowned and, yet, tickets to an opera or ballet are usually easy to find, even on the same day of the show (especially on a rainy/snowy day).

What neighborhoods or parts of town are best to stay in?

It depends on the purpose of your stay. *Brera* and *Navigli* can be quite welcoming for the aforementioned reasons. If you're looking for nightlife, *Isola* and *Garibaldi* become really lively after sunset. If you plan on doing day trips out of Milano, then your best bet would be to stay close to the central station.

In general, I would stay close to a metro station; the metro system is quite efficient and can take you to any district in a matter of minutes.

Let's talk about day trips...what nearby places should everyone make sure to visit?

Milano is strategically located between the Alps and the seaside, so there are countless possibilities when it comes to day trips. In less than an hour, you can reach many lakes; the Alps and Switzerland are one hour away; and it takes around 90 minutes (by train) to reach the seaside.

If I were to suggest just two places, they would be Bellinzona in Switzerland and Genoa, a port town here in Italy.

If you're looking for an even shorter trip, a half-hour train ride can take you to Vigevano (where the dukes of Milano used to live) and Certosa di Pavia (where the dukes of Milano are buried).

Tell us about the local dishes. What should people try?

Risotto alla Milanese (saffron rice) and *cotoletta alla Milanese* (a variant of the wiener schnitzel) are the two most famous dishes. If you aren't faint of heart, try ordering *cassoeula* (a dish with plenty of cabbage and pieces of the less noble parts of pig, like the head, the feet, and the skin).

What are your top three favorite bars and restaurants?

Tempio d'Oro (located on *Via Delle Leghe*, near MM1 Pasteur) offers a very tasty *aperitivo* that includes lots of vegetarian dishes. Sabbioneta (located on *Via Tadino*, near *MM1 Lima*) has tasty cuisine from Cremona and makes you feel at home. Go there on your name day and you'll get a free glass of wine. The only catch: they suffer from amnesia and may forget what you ordered.

For pizza, try Di Gennaro, at *Via S. Radegonda 14* near the *Duomo*.

For *gelato*: Bottega del Gelato (on *Via Pergolesi*, MM2 Loreto).

Is there anything tourists do that locals find rude or strange? What can we do to better fit in with the culture?

Ordering a cappuccino after noon is considered a crime. That said, we'll frown, but we'll also forgive you if you do it (as long as you don't order a pizza together with a cappuccino, in which case we'll secretly think you deserve to go to our city jail).

What is the best way to meet locals and make friends?

Social networks work quite well in Milano, so you'll find plenty of events and opportunities to socialize on sites like Couchsurfing.org, Internations, and Meetup.com.

Why should people make sure to visit Milano?

Because its cathedral and castle are extraordinary and because it's a good base for exploring northern Italy.

Where can we go to take beautiful photos?

Mt. Stella, an artificial hill that was built with waste from WWII. You can easily get there by catching a metro to QT8 (on the red line). During the day you'll find many hikers and joggers;

however, beware of the evenings...it transforms into a sort of "red light district" after sunset.

Anything else you want us to know?

Most tourists spend, at most, two nights in Milan. However, there are so many things to see in and around the city that you might consider staying one week, one month, or even a lifetime here...and you won't be easily bored!

Find Andrea at: liguriah.wordpress.com.

Alessio Re
Entrepreneur. Marketer. Ski Enthusiast. World Traveler.

First, tell us about you.

I originally come from a small city in the Italian Alps. From there, I moved to study and work in Milan; I've now been living here for over 13 years. Most of my free time is spent traveling, skiing, and drinking beer.

If someone is visiting Milano for the first time, what do you recommend they see or do?

I maintain that Milan's a great place to live, but not as good for a visitor, due to the damage that occurred during WWII (over half of the city was annihilated) and the badly planned reconstruction that followed. Even so, there's plenty to see...but it takes a bigger effort than it would take in other European cities.

In general, I recommend that the average visitor check out the area between Duomo Square and the *Castello Sforzesco*, the *Brera* district (the only one in town with narrow streets), the *Sant'Ambrogio* area, and the canals district, *Navigli* (best suited for the first part of the night). On top of that, I'd add the new *Porta Nuova/Garibaldi* area, which has some of the finest modern architecture in Italy.

Two hidden, lesser-known gems are the Monumental Cemetery and the impressive Ossuary of San Bernardino.

What neighborhoods or parts of town are best to stay in?
I'm a bit biased here, as I prefer the northern part of the city by far. I'd recommend staying in the area between the *Moscova* and *Garibaldi* subway stations.

Let's talk about day trips...what nearby places should everyone make sure to visit?
The lakes (Como and Maggiore) and the Alps shouldn't ever be missed, especially during summer and winter. I'd heartily recommend a day trip to Bergamo as well.

Tell us about the local dishes. What should people try?
Milan's traditional food is pretty hearty, rich in meat and butter and, thus, it is best during the cold months. I adore *ris giald* (yellow rice), *cassöla* (a heavy stew with pork meat and cabbage), and Milan-style *osbüs* (veal shank).

What are your top three favorite bars and restaurants?
Bars: Frida (at *Via Pollaiuolo 3* in *Isola*), Chiesetta (at *Via Paolo Lomazzo 12* in *Moscova*), and Atomic (on *Via Felice Casati*). Restaurants: Da Luigi (at *Via Savona 20* in *San Agostino*), Osteria dei Vecchi Sapori (at *Via Carmagnola 3* in *Isola*), and Da Cecco (at *Via Solferino 34* in *Brera*).

I'll add a mention for Circolo Magnolia (*circolomagnolia.it*), possibly the best place for concerts in town.

Is there anything tourists do that locals find rude or strange? What can we do to better fit in with the culture?
Strange: ordering cappuccino after lunch (which I also do, by the way).

What is the best way to meet locals and make friends?
I'd definitely say using Couchsurfing.org, hitting expat bars (mostly Irish pubs) during *aperitivo* time, and attending summer open-air concerts in smaller venues if you're into

73

rock/alternative music. Milan's not a super easy city to make acquaintances.

Why should people make sure to visit Milano?

To get the feel of a different, less-touristic, and not traditional Italy. At the same time, that is not what most tourists are after, so their mindset should be more about checking out a nice European city as opposed to something distinctly Italian, whatever that means.

Where can we go to take beautiful photos?

The Monumental Cemetery and the *Monte Stella* park, the only hill in town.

Anything else you want us to know?

Milan and Lombardy have long been called the engine of Italy, and that reflects a lot on the way people think here. Work is not something that ends after the office hours; most of the social occasions are also a chance for networking and it's not taboo to talk about the subject when you're chilling out with a beer. No *dolce vita* here (though the restaurant scene and nightlife are quite brilliant). Whether that's a positive or negative thing is up to you.

Yasha Mohammadi Aghdam
Multi-Passionate Philosopher. Student.

First, tell us about you.

I've lived in Milan for 18 years, more or less. I spent my early childhood in Iran, between Rasht and Teheran. Then, in second grade, my family came back to Italy for political reasons.

I still study Philosophy at my local university and work part time in a variety of jobs, from manual to social work. I'm rather eclectic in my passions: astronomy, juggling, martial arts, and a little bit of everything really.

MILAN & LOMBARDY

If someone is visiting Milano for the first time, what do you recommend they see or do?

If it's sunny, climb to the top of the *Duomo* with something to eat, sit on the marble sealing for a while, and talk with a friend or a stranger. If the weather is not good and you love art, go visit an exhibit; there are many different ones every year, generally well organized.

If it's sunny, climb to the top of the Duomo for a picnic.
Photo by: Alberto P. Veiga on Flickr.

What neighborhoods or parts of town are best to stay in?

This really depends on you. Like to go out and find streets full of students? Try *CittàStudi*. Want elegance and aesthetic sophistication? Go somewhere between *Porta Venezia* and the *Duomo*. Looking for nightlife? *Brera*. Bohemian and dirty streets-type nightlife? *Navigli*.

Let's talk about day trips...what nearby places should everyone make sure to visit?

Go to Como for a stroll on the lake, Bergamo if you want to visit something typical of northern Italy, and Pavia for that cozy feeling.

Tell us about the local dishes. What should people try?

Typical of Milano, I'd say, is the *risotto*, a creamy rice dish that comes in different forms. The most Milanese one is the saffron and *Parmesan* one. If you want to try the "poor" dishes of the tradition, we have the *cassöla*, a dish with savoy cabbage and different meats. They also invented the *panettone* here in Milan, a typical Christmas sweetbread with raisins.

MILAN & LOMBARDY

What are your top three favorite bars and restaurants?
Typical: Osteria di Porta Cicca (at *Ripa di Porta Ticinese 51*).
Pizza: La Tradizionale (at *Via Bergogone 16*). Snacks: Bello e
Buono (at *Viale Sabotino 14*).

Is there anything tourists do that locals find rude or strange? What can we do to better fit in with the culture?
To fit in with Italian culture, you should pay attention to
nuances, irony, and discretion. Also, having patience for long
discussions won't hurt.

What is the best way to meet locals and make friends?
To go to the university or at *San Lorenzo* at night.

Why should people make sure to visit Milano?
Milan has a lot to offer in terms of art, taste, people, and
events. It is the most active city in Italy, but still has some secret
charms you can find out. It is a city for exploring.

Where can we go to take beautiful photos?
For unique pictures and atmosphere, you can go to *Galleria
Vittorio Emanuele*. Also, the *Castello Sforzesco* has good views.

Anything else you want us to know?
People in Milan can look just as the city itself: a bit cold and
unattractive. But once you spend some energy to go behind
the surface, both the city and its people have some unique
beauties.

Bergamo

*This picturesque city with its Venetian walled old town is just
below the foothills of the Alps.*

MILAN & LOMBARDY

Stefano Puccio
Dreamer.

First, tell us about you.
Originally I was born in the beautiful city of Lecco, the place where Leonardo da Vinci came for his holidays to paint. It's situated in the Alps on Lake Como, the deepest and most beautiful lake in Europe (which is now famous because of George Clooney or Versace, but has always been the place where artists from all over the world chose to spend their time—a place of legend and mystery). Now I live in Bergamo and have for three years.

My passions include writing poems, painting, and writing songs. I love history and art and, most of all, nature, especially the mountains and the sea. I also hike, travel, read classic Italian literature (by classic, I mean more than 2,000 years old, before Jesus), listen to classic music, go to the opera, create new recipes, and discover new traditional foods (in Italia, there are more than 35,000 different typical foods—every small town had completely different food than the others, so it's beautiful to discover them).

If someone is visiting Bergamo for the first time, what do you recommend they see or do?
Bergamo is divided in two: *Bergamo Alta* and *Bergamo Bassa*. I recommend ignoring *Bergamo Bassa* (the modern part of Bergamo) and not even missing one corner of *Bergamo Alta*, one of the most untouched cities in the world.

The spirit of the people here is very independent and you can feel it throughout the old city, from the strange style of the churches and palaces to the original, too-big walls (too big for a small city), which are a UNESCO World Heritage Site.

Forget maps or places to see and just walk around in the old city, discovering hundreds of interesting corners.

MILAN & LOMBARDY

Let's talk about day trips...what nearby places should everyone make sure to visit?

Start with Como; it's beautiful (though one day is enough for Como if you don't have many days). Take the boat on the lake and go to Bellagio and Varenna, small towns with thousands of years of history and then to Lecco, where the lake becomes the deepest lake in Europe and where the Alps meet the water. If you like to hike, this is paradise. (Interesting side note: many of the most intense mountains around the world, including the Alps, Andes, and Himalayas, were reached for the first time in history by men born in this area.)

Also, don't miss Mantova (the birthplace of Virgilio, the most famous writer of old Roma), a city that it is almost 3,000 years old, with more than 20 beautiful churches (my particular favorite is the *Rotonda*, built in the 11th century). While you're there, make sure to visit the palaces: *Ducale*, *Palazzo Te*, and *Palazzo delle Erbe*, in particular, which are over 900 years old and showcase dozens of ancient bridges, towers, etc.

On the way from Bergamo to Mantova, stop in Brescia, another city with almost three millenniums of history, where you can find from the Roman theater and temples of the period before Jesus up to Renaissance buildings arriving to the period of Baroque (not to mention castles and palaces).

Tell us about the local dishes. What should people try?

As you probably know, every Italian city, town, and village has very different typical foods. The traditional foods of Bergamo are many, and I suggest *casoncelli* (similar to ravioli with a mix of salami, raisins, amaretto, pears, cheese, and many spices), *polenta cunciada* (traditional *polenta* made with five different cheeses), *brasato d'asino* (donkey pot roast), and frogs.

You'll also need to try some of the traditional local cheeses. I recommend *formai de Mut* and the *taleggio*.

Finally, make sure to try our dessert: delicious *polenta e usei* (it looks like polenta, but that's just a joke. Inside it's sweet!) made with traditional ingredients plus chocolate and nuts.

What are your top three favorite bars and restaurants?
Cantiere Cucina (located at *Via Borgo Santa Caterina n. 5*) and Enoteca Zanini (*at Via Borgo Santa Caterina 90/a*) are the best in Bergamo and Nicolin (at *Via Amilcare Ponchielli 54*) in Lecco is the best of the entire region.

Is there anything tourists do that locals find rude or strange? What can we do to better fit in with the culture?
It always seems so strange when you hear strangers talking in wrong way about being Latin. They talk about it as though it's the people-music-food of South America or some European countries that had Roman influence in their language (Spain, Portugal, France), but Latin it means "from Latium" and Latium is the central part of Italia.

What is the best way to meet locals and make friends?
Going to a concert or to one of the many events around in Bergamo during the year.

Why should people make sure to visit Bergamo?
It is one of the few untouched cities on this planet. You can walk in the ancient times while walking in the streets of *Bergamo Alta*.

Where can we go to take beautiful photos?
Walk from the train station up to *Bergamo Alta*, passing through the walls, and, when you arrive at the top, the balcony in front of you shows the whole city and the land until Milano. I suggest taking photos there at sunset.

The main square of the old city is also really beautiful.

Anything else you want us to know?
I want to finish with something curious: every day thousands of tourists arrive in Bergamo. But most of them take the first bus

from the airport to Milano, ignoring that just 10 minutes from them there's such a treasure. Don't let that happen to you.

Cremona

Located on the River Po, Cremona's history is a musical one.

Flavia Vighini
Literature and Heritage Student. Blogger.

First, tell us about you.
My name is Flavia. I'm 30 and I was born in Cremona. I've always lived in Cremona, and I work in the International Relations office of a local bank (which is why sometimes I go abroad). In my free time, I study Literature and Heritage at the Faculty of Musicologia of the University of Pavia. Often I go out with my friends and then I write my experiences on my blog, Bustling Town.

If someone is visiting Cremona for the first time, what do you recommend they see or do?
Visit the workshop of a violinmaker. Stradivari and Amati, two of the most famous violinmakers in the world, were born in Cremona. The Museum of Violin is also a beautiful experience for tourists. *Ponchielli Theatre* is a beautiful theatre, reminiscent of La Scala in Milan.

What neighborhoods or parts of town are best to stay in?
The city center is the best place to stay. The second best, in my opinion, is the neighborhood near *Viale Po*; it's green and near the city center.

Let's talk about day trips...what nearby places should everyone make sure to visit?
I recommend visiting two little towns in the province of Cremona: Soncino and Isola Dovarese. The Palio of Isola

Dovarese, which happens the second weekend in September, is a Medieval commemoration; it's amazing.

Tell us about the local dishes. What should people try?
Typical Cremonese dishes are boiled meat with *mostarda di Cremona* (mustard and fruit), *marubini ai tre brodi* (meat-stuffed pasta), and *torrone* (Italian nougat).

What are your top three favorite bars and restaurants?
My three favorite bars are Tisaneria in *Piazza della Pace*. (My boyfriend works there!) The second one is Chocabeck in *Piazza Stradivari*. The third one is Chocolat at *Piazza Roma n. 30*.

For restaurants, I suggest Osteria Garibaldi (located at *Corso Giuseppe Garibaldi 38)*, Il Violino Restaurant (which is a little expensive, but worth it at *Via Sicardo 3*), and Osteria Il Bissone (at *Via Pecorari 3*). If you love gelato, please try Grom's at Galleria XXV Aprile in *Piazza Roma*.

What is the best way to meet locals and make friends?
Piazza della Pace is the place where everyone meets. But, sadly, people from the north are not very warm. It's difficult to make friends.

Why should people make sure to visit Cremona?
Because it's a little jewel in the north of Italy and it's a beautiful place to stay and live.

Where can we go to take beautiful photos?
Take some pictures of *Piazza del Duomo* with its tower and go on the Po River to take some photos during the sunset.

Find Flavia at: www.bustlingtown.it/en.

MILAN & LOMBARDY

Mantua (Mantova)

With a UNESCO World Heritage Site for a city center, lakes on every side, and a major role in the history of opera, this city is a must-see.

Lorenzo Bonoldi
Art Historian & Tourism Professional. Writer. Researcher. Licensed Tour Guide.

First, tell us about you.

I was born in the hills of the Mantuan province. I still live there, but I commute to Mantua every day. I usually describe myself as an art historian on loan to the tourism profession. With my degree in History of Art, I am constantly studying, researching, and writing essays. But—at the same time—I love to share my knowledge of Mantua (Mantova) with visitors coming here from all over the world. I strongly believe that knowledge is nothing when not shared. So, being a licensed tour guide for several years, I am having a lot of fun showing tourists around Mantua.

When I manage to have a day off, I love to relax in spas. When I have more time for myself, I turn myself into a tourist, passionately traveling to art cities, museums, and galleries. My favorite destination is London. My secret dream? A tea with the queen at Buckingham Palace!

If someone is visiting Mantua for the first time, what do you recommend they see or do?

Mantua was one of the capitols of the Italian Renaissance. Most of the historical monuments of the city are connected with the Gonzaga, the family who ruled the city for almost four centuries from 1328 to 1707 (much longer than the Medici in Florence or the Tudors in England).

The headquarters of the Gonzagas was the Ducal Palace, which covers an area of more than 35,000 square meters.

Frescoes by Pisanello, paintings by Rubens, and tapestries by Raphael are all to be found. And, of course, the Bridal Chamber (*camera degli sposi*) frescoed by Andrea Mantegna.

Another stunning palace belonging to the Gonzagas is *Palazzo Te*, the leisure villa of the Dukes of Mantua. This sumptuous residence was designed, built, and decorated by Giulio Romano, the best pupil of Raphael.

Of course, we have also religious buildings: the Basilica of St. Andrea, by Leon Battista Alberti, is one of the masterpieces of the Renaissance architecture. Just a stone's thrown away, you can also find the oldest church still existing in town: the Romanesque round church known as the Rotunda of St. Lorenzo.

If you are in love with theaters, you'll love the Bibiena Theatre, also known as The Scientific Theatre—a baroque hidden gem in Mantua. Mozart performed here in 1770 when he was just 13 years old!

If you are more interested in nature, don't miss a boat trip on the three lakes that surround the city. The best time of the year to have this experience is July to August, when the Lotus flowers bloom.

What neighborhoods or parts of town are best to stay in?

Mantua is surrounded on three sides by lakes. If you are planning to have after-dinner walks in the main *piazzas* or *porticos*, don't trust the distances provided by your GPS system; a place that may look pretty close the city center can actually be on the other side of the lakes. If you are looking for a central accommodation, check the correct locations on maps.

Please, be aware that the most of the old town is a ZTL zone (controlled traffic zone), so, when choosing the place you want to stay in, try to find out if you can reach it using your car. Many hotels provide their clients with ZTL passes.

MILAN & LOMBARDY

Public transportation is not widespread in the city, but you can call a taxi on weekdays from 5 a.m. to 1 a.m. and anytime on weekends and bank holidays.

If you don't mind staying in rural accommodations (or if you love it!), look for a nice *agriturismo* (farm holiday) or a B&B in the countryside. If you are looking for something really special, I suggest the Reading Retreats property (*corteeremo.com*), based in Corte Eremo. Here, a few miles from Mantua, you can find a paradise for bibliophiles, garden-lovers, and people interested in art and music.

Let's talk about day trips...what nearby places should everyone make sure to visit?

In the province of Mantua, there are two UNESCO sites: the Old Town of Mantua itself and Sabbioneta, often described as the little Athens of northern Italy. Sabbioneta is a perfect example of a Renaissance ideal city, where, amongst many palaces and historical buildings, you can also find one of the oldest modern theaters in the world.

In the surroundings of Mantua, you'll find some of the 100 most beautiful Italian villages, including San Benedetto Po (with its impressive Benedictine abbey and monastery), Grazie (a hamlet built around a gothic church, filled with interesting votive offerings, including a crocodile from the Nile), and Castellaro Lagusello (a walled Medieval village overlooking a heart-shaped lake).

Another great idea for a day trip would be a river cruise; you can have a boat trip on the lakes around Mantua or follow the Mincio River.

Being at the very center of the Po Valley, Mantua is a great location if you are planning to visit other art cities of northern Italy. Within a 100-kilometer radius, you can easily reach Verona, Vicenza, Padua, Ferrara, Modena, Bologna, Parma, Cremona, and Brescia. Lake Garda—the biggest lake in Italy—

is only 45 kilometers away from Mantua and a cycle-path connects the city to Peschiera del Garda.

Tell us about the local dishes. What should people try?

The main signature dish of Mantua is the *tortelli alla Mantovana*, a ravioli-style pasta filled with pumpkin, apple mustard compote, and *amaretti*. The local *risotto* is called *riso alla pilota* and its recipe includes pork sausage. The local fish dish is the *luccio in salsa* (pike with green sauce). If you are into meat, you should try our *stracotto* (literally "overcooked meat") with *polenta* (cornmeal mush).

The Mantuan culinary art finds its divine glorification in desserts and cakes. From the very simple *sbrisolona* (almond crumble cake) to the more elaborate *torta delle rose* (a bouquet of pastry roses with buttercream) and, my favorite one, *torta helvetia* (a dessert cake made with layers of almond-meringue, buttercream, and sabayon).

The local Christmas dessert is the *anello di Monaco* ("the ring of Munich"), whose recipe was actually invented in Mantua at the end of the XVIII century by a family of pastry chefs who moved into Mantua from the central Europe. This festive deliciousness is a ring-shaped doughnut filled with cream made from hazelnuts, walnuts, and candied chestnuts with an icing of sugar on the top.

What are your top three favorite bars and restaurants?

My favorite bar in the old town is the Caffè Modì (at *Via San Giorgio 4*) where you can have a drink, breakfast, or a light meal in a place dedicated to art. The name of this café is in homage to the painter Amedeo Modigliani and nice concerts are often performed here. Into art and music? This is not to be missed.

A great restaurant is Ristorante il Cigno (located at *Piazza Carlo D'arco 1*). You can taste and appreciate the typical Mantuan dishes in a refined atmosphere here.

MILAN & LOMBARDY

If you don't mind driving for about 30 minutes, I'd suggest a wonderful place in Gazzuolo (halfway between Mantua and Sabbioneta) called ArteGusto (address: *Via San Pietro 20, Gazzuolo*). It's an ancient convent turned in a very modern and special restaurant.

I have an additional tip about restaurants, bars, and cafés: avoid every place with a waiter standing at the door to invite (or, in most cases, push) you in. These are tourist traps. The really good places don't need this sort of aggressive advertising.

Is there anything tourists do that locals find rude or strange? What can we do to better fit in with the culture?

The Mantuan summer is really hot and damp. Everybody would love to go around the city almost completely naked. But this is not advisable. Please, don't be half-undressed and avoid bare-chested walks.

Gentlemen are expected to remove their hats when entering churches and ladies should cover their shoulders. It's a matter of respect and good manners. If you really can't cope without going around the city wearing a tank-top or a sleeveless chemise, make sure you have a shirt with you to cover up when entering churches. The same would be advisable for museums.

At restaurants, you can order and eat what you want, but if you are having a pizza and drinking a cappuccino, don't be surprised if the locals look at you in a strange way. Usually Italians don't take cappuccino in the afternoons. (Of course, you can, but people will immediately recognize you as strangers.)

On the other hand, there are things the locals do that tourists find rude or strange. For example, we eat horse meat. Please, don't blame us for following our traditions.

What is the best way to meet locals and make friends?

86

MILAN & LOMBARDY

In the old town, we have two main squares really close each other: *Piazza Sordello* and *Piazza delle Erbe*. While the first one is almost completely a tourist trap, the second is more frequently visited by locals. One of the most ancient bars in town, Bar Caravatti (located at *Via Broletto 16*), is here under the porticos.

Two cafes that are very "in" are Bar Venezia (at *Piazza Marconi 10*) and Caffè Borsa – Antoniazzi (at *Corso della Libertà 6*).

In the summertime, the locals meet on the lakeshores, sunbathing, running, fishing, or just walking. Two very "in vogue" spots here are Papa's Cafè (at *Lungolago Mincio*) and Zanzara (at *Giardini Barbato 2*), which is commonly described as "the best sunset-place in Mantua." By the way, *zanzara* means mosquito, so have your bug spray with you every time you are in Mantua from May to October.

Why should people make sure to visit Mantua?
The cyclists love this place because we have many paths connecting the city with natural parks and Lake Garda. Art-lovers arrive here to visit the Gonzaga family's palaces and villas and the other historical buildings. Of course, we do have great food and wine, so gourmet travelers are more than welcome.

People in love with music often visit Mantua because the city was chosen by Giuseppe Verdi as the set of his famous opera, *Rigoletto*, and also because the very first opera in history, the *Fabula di Orpheo* by Claudio Monteverdi, was first performed in this city on the night of Carnival of 1607.

We also have tourists arriving from Verona, following the footsteps of William Shakespeare; Mantua is the city where Romeo escaped when he was banished from Verona.

Where can we go to take beautiful photos?
Great pictures of the city skyline facing the lakes can be taken from the opposite shores. The best place to shoot panoramic

photos is an area known as *Campo Canoa*; try to find it on your maps or your GPS (it's near the T-junction between *Via Legnago* and *Strada Cipata*). A free car park is nearby, so you can leave your car while shooting.

Great scenic views of the historical buildings can be taken from *Piazza Concordia* (behind the Rotunda of San Lorenzo) and *Piazza Leon Battista Alberti* (behind Sant'Andrea's Basilica). The most photographed corner of the city includes the dome of Sant'Andrea's Basilica and the *Torre della Gabbia* (tower of the cage) as they are seen by the arches of the portico of the Ducal Palace in *Piazza Sordello*.

Anything else you want us to know?
Yes, I'd like to share three more tips:

1. On Thursdays, we have the weekly market in the old town. The city gets crowded and it's impossible to have a peaceful walk and find a place for your car at this time. Be aware of this when planning your visit.

2. Mantua is often described as "the sleeping beauty of Italy." As soon as the sun goes down, the old town falls asleep, most of the locals and tourists disappear, and many bars and shops close. But in the tranquility of the night, the city is even more fascinating. So, don't miss the opportunity for a late evening walk in the city center.

3. Most of the old town still has its original cobblestones. Make sure your shoes are comfortable. Ladies: no stilettos here (unless you are an acrobat). And this is the secret trick to recognize the local ladies: the Mantuan women are able to walk on the cobblestones and pebbles in their high heels!

Find Lorenzo at: www.visitmantua.it.

Cremia (Lake Como)

Walkers, boaters, and those passionate about small towns will love this little lakeside hamlet.

Silvia Cazzola
B&B Owner. Hiker. Sailing Enthusiast.

First, tell us about you.

I am 43 years old. I have been living in this wonderful part of the world for 10 years, although I knew the area very well before I moved. My family used to rent a house here for holidays since I was seven.

I like sailing, trekking, skiing, skating, and traveling. But I also like spending the evenings with friends, enjoying a good dinner with good wine.

About 10 years ago, I had the opportunity to buy a house that was too big for me. When I saw the house, I immediately understood that it would be a perfect bed and breakfast. Built at the beginning of the 20th century with two or three rooms per floor, big stairs in the middle, and three floors, it is a place where you stay and become part of the family.

If someone is visiting Cremia for the first time, what do you recommend they see or do?

The churches of *San Michele* and *San Vito* are a must, but the whole village is lovely. My best advice is to wear comfortable shoes and go for a walk. For instance, walk along the *Antica via Regina* or visit San Domenico in the mountains.

What neighborhoods or parts of town are best to stay in?

The lakefront is perfect if you like some wind and watching wind- and kite-surfers. That said, there are no dangerous places to stay in Cremia, so just choose the house you like best.

MILAN & LOMBARDY

Let's talk about day trips...what nearby places should everyone make sure to visit?

It's easy to visit both the north and south of Lake Como from here. From Cremia to Como, the most southern city on the lake, it is less than an hour by car or, even better, a couple of hours by boat (and public transportation is pretty cheap).

In the north, you can visit Dongo, Gravedona, Sorico, and Gera Lario, which are interesting cities with a lot of historical spots. It's pretty typical Italy: everywhere you turn, you will find 600-year-old buildings, churches, etc.

The north is also known for the *Antica Via Regina*, a Roman street that used to connect Como (and Milano) with Chiavenna via the Spluga or Maloja passes in Switzerland. Medieval churches are everywhere.

In the south, visit the more modern Menaggio, Tremezzo, Lenno, Argegno, and Laglio. These are some of the places where, at the end of the 19th century, rich families from Milan and other large European cities used to spend their summers. Rich palaces are everywhere. If you have an interest in Medieval history, you'll love the area.

The bottom line is that no matter which way you go, you'll find something different and unique. The shape of the coasts, the mountains, the light...they change meter by meter and minute by minute.

If you take a boat across the lake, you can visit Bellano, Dervio, and, in particular, Corenno Plinio, Varenna, and Bellagio. From Cremia, head to Menaggio and from there, head to any of these lovely cities.

Finally, to the west we have the mountains. With every meter you hike into the hills, the lake takes on a new color, a new shape. The views are beautiful and never the same.

MILAN & LOMBARDY

In the mountains, you still can find small villages (*monti*) where farming families used to house their cows in the summer until the early '60s. In these places you can find bunches of small houses (mainly one stable with one room on top) that now are being renovated and are used as summer holiday homes. And when you reach the altitude of about 1,000 meters, you have a fantastic view of the lake.

For serious hikers, walk north or south along the *Via dei Monti Lariani*, a four- to six-day walk along an ancient path that connects the *monti*.

If you do choose to hike up into the mountains (whether for a day or for six), head to the area of Cremia known as San Domenico (there is a small chapel named after San Domenico here) and take the hiking trails north or south. Or even climb the Monte Bregagno.

Of course, the most important thing is to enjoy the view of the lake, especially at sunset.

Tell us about the local dishes. What should people try?
Risotto con persico (risotto with perch fish) is something you cannot miss. *Missultin* (dried lake fish) is also something you should try. You might also enjoy cheese bought directly from the farmer. Irene and Alex in Cremia (whose shop is called Ezio & Irene, though everyone just knows it as Alex and Irene's place, and is close to *San Michele* church) and the Azienda Agricola San Martino in San Siro are wonderful.

What are your top three favorite bars and restaurants?
I love Ristorante La Baia (on *Frazione San Vito*) and Ristorante Hotel Lumin (at *Via S. Vito 10*) in Cremia and La Vecchia Pira, at *Via Cassia 3* in Stazzona. If you are interested in family-driven *agriturismos* in the mountains (not far from Cremia), I recommend San Martino (which has an amazing view, particularly at sunset), Aldora (recently opened) in Montuglio, and Agriturismo Labbio (*www.agriturismolabbio.it*).

In Cremia, you can walk to Rifugio la Canua (*www.rifugiocanua.it*) where you can rest during your hiking tours. (They are normally open between June and September, but check before you go.)

Is there anything tourists do that locals find rude or strange? What can we do to better fit in with the culture?

Having a cappuccino after dinner is strange, but we do not find it rude. You should also know that the restaurants are usually closed before noon and between 2 – 4 p.m.

What is the best way to meet locals and make friends?

Bars are the best place.

Why should people make sure to visit Cremia/Lake Como?

It is fantastic mix of nature and culture, sports and traditions, modern architecture and historical buildings, good food and good wine. And Cremia is a very convenient point to start from for visiting Lake Como.

What is the best place to go take beautiful photos?

The lakefront and the mountains. Also, San Domenico.

Anything else you want us to know?

If you need to know anything else...ask George Clooney.

Find Silvia at: www.ilmotto.it.

Lierna (Lake Como)

Welcome to a small hamlet known for fish dishes and lakeside walks.

MILAN & LOMBARDY

Liu Lamperti
B&B Owner. Culturist. President, Association of B&Bs.

First, tell us about you.
I live in Lierna near Varenna. I come from Milan and I like change in my life. I have a lot of interests: cinema, art, exhibitions, gardening, card games, and organizing cultural meetings on the lake (to name a few). I live with my daughters, my husband, and my cat, Max.

If someone is visiting Lierna and Lake Como for the first time, what do you recommend they see or do?
I suggest an old village named Castello, with its ancient history, and Riva Bianca, which has a really nice beach (this is where my B&B is located).

What neighborhoods or towns are best to stay in?
In addition to Lierna, I suggest Varenna, Corenno Plinio, and San Giovanni (which is near Bellagio, but not so touristy!).

Let's talk about day trips...what nearby places should everyone make sure to visit?
Take a daily cruise on the lake or visit *Il sentiero del viandante* (translated: the path of the wanderer), a pretty walk along the eastern shore of Lake Como.

Tell us about the local dishes. What should people try?
In Lierna and in this part of the lake, try *risotto con pesce persico* (risotto with perch fish), *spaghetti con sugo di pesce di lago* (spaghetti with lake fish), *bresaola* (air-dried, salted beef), *misultit con polenta* (dried fish and porridge), and *pizzoccheri* (ribbon pasta with greens and potatoes).

What are your top three favorite bars and restaurants?
Ristorante Sottovento (at *Via Imbarcadero 3*) and Bar Riva Bianca (at *Via Riva Bianca 10*) in Lierna and Bar Amerigo in Mandello del Lario at *Piazza della Repubblica 10*.

What is the best way to meet locals and make friends?
On the beach and in the bars in Castello, a little ancient place.

Why should people make sure to visit Lierna and Lake Como?
To climb (some of the best climbing in Italy is here). To enjoy panoramas of mountains and the lake. To play sports. To go swimming. To rent a boat. To experience lakeside culture.

What is the best place to go take beautiful photos?
Anywhere! Just take a walk or a boat ride.

Find Liu at: www.leortensiebedandbreakfast.com and www.ospitipercasa.com.

PIEDMONT & VALLE D'AOSTA

Surrounded by Alps and dotted with castles, this region attracts an outdoorsy, adventurous crowd.

In this section: Turin / Casale Monferrato / La Salle / Alba / Stresa (Lake Maggiore)

Photo by Eric Borda on Flickr.

Turin (Torino)

The capital of Piedmont is bursting with culture, architecture, art, and big-name car manufacturers.

Ferruccio Pizzolato
Traveler. Lab Technician.

First, tell us about you.
Hi! I'm Ferruccio. I'm a 45-year-old native of Torino (born here and lived here all my life). Traveling is a big passion and interest for me. And during the week I work at university as a lab technician.

If someone is visiting Torino for the first time, what do you recommend they see or do?
I recommend at least a five-day holiday in Torino. Spring and early autumn are the best seasons because summer is too hot and winter is too cold.

In my opinion, the most interesting museums are the Egyptian Museum (it's the second best in the world after the one in Cairo) and *Museo del Cinema*, (my personal favorite). The *Museo del Cinema* is inside the *Mole Antonelliana*, an extremely tall tower (170 meters) that is also the symbol of the city. (I also recommend going up the elevator as high as you can and enjoying the amazing views from the balcony up there.)

Piedmont (*Piemonte*), the region where Torino is, literally means foothills (*ai piedi del monte*). The Alps are not that far and you can almost touch them when the sky is clear. On the east side of town, there is a very beautiful hill you can climb.

Palazzo Madama is another place to visit. It was the first senate of the Italian Kingdom. Right next door, you'll find *Palazzo Reale*, the royal palace of the House of Savoy.

La Venaria Reale, just outside the city, is another palace absolutely to see. It was renovated a few years ago.

Finally, check out the *Museo dell'Automobile* and don't miss the *Museo del Risorgimento* (National Museum of the Italian Renaissance) or the GAM (modern and contemporary art gallery).

If you want a full list of local museums (we have so many), you can find it here: *www.comune.torino.it/musei/en/elenco/*.

What neighborhoods or parts of town are best to stay in?
Generally, people stay in the center or (for the young or young at heart) *San Salvario*, an area just a few steps from the center. In the last 10 years, it has gone through a very big and nice renovation. It used to be a rough area (though I've never ever had any kind of problems, even when it was considered dangerous), but now it's so lively with many small restaurants and cafes.

Also, the *Quadrilatero Romano* was considered a rough area and that's the old town. Just like *San Salvario*, so many small restaurants and cafes popped up and now it's rather lively.

Let's talk about day trips...what nearby places should everyone make sure to visit?

PIEDMONT & VALLE D'AOSTA

The surrounding mountains are perfect in winter (for skiing) and summer (for long walks).

Personally, I would absolutely go to Alba, a town almost an hour by car. It's beautiful. It's in the Langhe area, which I think is as beautiful as Tuscany. And it's the capital of Italian food. Plus, the best red wine comes from that area (*Barolo, Barbaresco, Nebbiolo, Dolcetto*, and so on).

Tell us about the local dishes. What should people try?

Personally, I tend to mix different regional cuisines. My mom is from Taranto (south Italy) and my dad was from Treviso (close to Venice) and I tend to eat a lot of fish and vegetables (which it's not typical cuisine from here).

That said, the typical Piedmont dishes I adore are *agnolotti* (roast beef ravioli), *tajarin* (egg pasta), raw beef (steak tartar with lemon juice and olive oil instead of an egg), and *bollito* (stew).

These days, in 2014, what was true 30 years ago about Piedmont cuisine is not true anymore. I thought it was a bit poor (always meat, meat, and meat again), but it's not like that anymore because our cuisine has been influenced so much by the southern cuisines since there are so many people from the south here. I'd say now it's a good mix.

Finally, Torino is probably the best in Italy for *pasticcini* and *torte* (pastries and cakes). They're delicious, beautiful, and elegant—a real art.

What are your top three favorite bars and restaurants?

Torino has the most interesting and historic cafes of Italy, but I don't think tourists would be interested in my personal favorites, since they are my favorites because they're where I meet up with my friends (not because they are particularly charming).

Apart from ethnic restaurants, my favorite place to eat in Torino is Eataly (*www.eataly.it*). It's an ex-factory where you can buy and eat food. The quality is very good. It was born in

Torino eight years ago and has since expanded into Japan, the US, Turkey, etc.

Is there anything tourists do that locals find rude or strange? What can we do to better fit in with the culture?
Good manners are the same wherever you go.

What is the best way to meet locals and make friends?
I think Couchsurfing.org is the best way to discover the city and find friends here.

Why should people make sure to visit Torino?
Torino has always had a low profile. In my opinion, it has been underestimated for too long, even though it's a beautiful city. It's a Baroque city (I mean the center), very interesting, with so much green and parks.

Where can we go to take beautiful photos?
To have a nice view of the city, you better go to the *Monte dei Cappuccini,* which is just on the other side of the river. From that balcony you have a wonderful view of the whole city and the Alps.

Anything else you want us to know?
You shouldn't miss the flea markets in town: Balon and Gran Balon.

Casale Monferrato

On the bank of the River Po, this ancient city features a town center full of palazzi.

Cristhian
Tourism Professional. Native Italian.

First, tell us about you.

I grew up in Casale Monferrato, in a family from the south of Italy. For work, I do small jobs as a freelancer and I love to travel to other cities or countries to discover the local culture.

If someone is visiting Casale Monferrato for the first time, what do you recommend they see or do?

Casale is a small city, but her richness makes her one of the best spots to visit in the north of Italy and to use as a base for further excursions (because of its strategic middle position between Milan, Turin, and Genoa). It was also a capital of the ancient state of Monferrato.

In Casale, you can find many churches (there are 55!) that deserve a short visit, but the main one is the *Duomo*, a cathedral over 1,000 years old. The Jewish Synagogue is one of most beautiful in all Europe (with its Jewish Museum and one hundred Hanukkah lamps made by famous artists).

Also, you can find many palaces and courtyards. One of them is a museum with the unique *gipsoteca* (plaster cast gallery) with hundreds of gesso sculptures.

As a capital of Monferrato, Casale is a perfect place to see all the beautiful, vast hilly area with its ancient villages, castles, vineyards, and typical food. It's like Tuscany, but more real!

Finally, check out the Po River, the longest river in Italy, with its natural park and bio-diversity.

What neighborhoods or parts of town are best to stay in?

The best place is the center of the town. I recommend avoiding hotels and, instead, taking advantage of the local hospitality. In some cases, you can even volunteer for accommodation.

Let's talk about day trips...what nearby places should everyone make sure to visit?

PIEDMONT & VALLE D'AOSTA

Day trips should include villages such as Rosignano, Cella Monte (with its *infernot*—an ancient excavated stone used to preserve food and wines), and Moleto (a town built with ancient sandstone from the sea, with its eco-museum dedicated to the material).

During the trip, stop by the many wine producers along the road to enjoy the panorama and taste the special, original wine varieties.

Another good spot is the Crea Sanctuary with its natural reserve, its walk through the chapels, and, on the top, a breathtaking view.

Tell us about the local dishes. What should people try?

I always suggest a vegetarian menu, but the *agnolotti* (roast beef ravioli, sometimes with donkey meat) and the *bagna cauda* (hot garlic, anchovy dip), which is served so that every person at the table has their own small burner to warm the sauce and into which you can dip a variety of veggies, are also great.

With all this, try the local *Barbera* or *Grinolino* wines!

Rice with truffles is delicious, as is *fritto misto* (a big, strange dish with fried, crunchy fruit, entrails, and meat).

If you love food, come to Casale in the second half of September, when the wine festival takes place. There are about 25 villages that offer their local food and, of course, the wine that makes the event unique, special, and crazy!

What are your top three favorite bars and restaurants?

For the local, organic, and true experience in a wonderful, green place, try Cascina Trapella in Rolasco (at *Strada San Martino 38/40*). For a more conventional restaurant, try Il Melograno in Terruggia (at *Piazza Vittorio Emanuele 9*), which offers menus for vegetarians, vegans, and celiacs.
For a coffee, head to the Riviera Cafe (at *Via Roma 128*).

PIEDMONT & VALLE D'AOSTA

What is the best way to meet locals and make friends?

There is a special cafe' in town called Pantagruel (located at *Via Giovanni Lanza 28*); it serves drinks, *aperitivos*, lunch, and dinner. Everything there is organic and local and every week they hold concerts and other events. The locals are very nice and it is very easy to make friends (just start toasting, saying *cin cin*, which is our version of cheers).

If you don't see people when you walk in, look behind the small door; there is a courtyard and they might be there!

Also, on weekends, many people hang out in the cafes in the early evening. It is easy to talk with locals if they have had a few cocktails, but be careful, some old grandmother might throw water from her window if the noise is too much!

Why should people make sure to visit Casale Monferrato?

Casale and the Monferrato *are* Italy—tourism has not spoiled the place and never will, as there are not any leaning towers or Romeo and Juliet stories. You can find all the unique traditions here and if you stay a little while and get to know the locals, you will definitively find yourself pampered by the locals, invited to eat with Italian mammas until you explode, and falling in love with the area, as so many expats have.

Where can we go to take beautiful photos?

You can just walk to *Salita Sant'Anna* and from there you can see all of Casale Monferrato. On the second weekend of every month, you can find the Civic Tower and other monuments open. Up inside the tower, the view is great.

Anything else you want us to know?

Keep in mind that in July and August there are many mosquitos, produced from the east area of Casale Monferrato, where rice grows. They don't bring any disease and they "go to sleep" at 10 p.m.

Also, it might seem like nobody speaks English here, but that's not true. People are shy about it and many just need to be encouraged.

Find Cristhian at: monferratodelights.blogspot.it.

La Salle (Valle D'Aosta)

In the highest wine producing area in Europe, Mont Blanc serves as a backdrop for charming towns and mountain lakes.

Magdorys Velasquez
Craftswoman. Expat. Walker.

First, tell us about you.
I'm Magdorys Velasquez. Originally from Venezuela, I have lived in the Aosta Valley since 1990. I am a housewife and in my spare time I like to do manual things with wood or with fabric. When spring comes, I like walking.

If someone is visiting the Aosta Valley for the first time, what do you recommend they see or do?
The Aosta Valley is a mountainous area and there are many things to do, such as going to see Mont Blanc, which is the highest mountain in Europe. In winter, you can ski or hike with snow shoes. In spring, summer, and autumn, explore the lakes and mountain refuges. If you're brave enough, you can do some mountain biking. And you can visit Aosta, a small Roman town

What neighborhoods or parts of town are best to stay in?
Courmayuer, Saint Vincent, Aosta, and La Thuile are the most prestigious locations (and the most expensive), but I recommend, instead, going to Morgex, La Salle, Valgrisenche

Rhêmes Valley, and Val di Cogne (which are less expensive and also lovely).

Let's talk about day trips...what nearby places should everyone make sure to visit?

From here to La Salle, there are: Val Veny, Val Ferret, Arpy Lake, Bonatti Refuge, and Refuge Bertone. From June to September, there are walks with the priest of each locality, feasts of patron saints, etc., but it all depends when you come.

Tell us about the local dishes. What should people try?

The specialties of Aosta are fontina cheese fondue and dumplings, Aosta Valley ribs, *polenta* (porridge with cheese), *soupe valpellineintze* (bread, cabbage, fontina cheese, and broth), wild game, chamois and ibex stew, trout, dried meat of chamois *carbonade* (meat sauce), and *panna cotta* with blueberries (for dessert). *Genepy* (traditional liquor) is characteristic of the valley.

What is the best way to meet locals and make friends?

As in most places, you can always meet people at bars. Though, here in the valley, people come, above all, for sport, to live a healthy life, and to get outdoors, so they tend to go to bed early.

Why should people make sure to visit the Aosta Valley?

The spectacular Mont Blanc range. The beauty of being in the heart of the highest wine-producing area of Europe, wandering through the vineyards, villages, and streets. Bordered by Switzerland and France. And for the many Roman ruins in Aosta (which gave it the title of "Rome of the Alps").

What is the best place to go take beautiful photos here?

The higher you climb into the mountains, the more stunning the scenery. There are so many places.

Anything else you want us to know?

Crossing the three countries of Mont Blanc—Italy, France, and Switzerland—on foot is a unique and unforgettable

PIEDMONT & VALLE D'AOSTA

experience. The Tour du Mont Blanc is a multi-day trek (7/8 days) between cliffs, looming glaciers, pastures, and grasslands. Along the 170-kilometer route, there is a whole world to discover. In Italian territory, the undisputed protagonists are the *Val Veny* and *Val Ferret*.

Crossing the three countries of Mont Blanc on foot is a unique, unforgettable experience.
Photo by: Alain Wibert on Flickr.

The Valle d'Aosta is also interesting for the presence of some ancient buildings, castles, and fortifications full of charm and character. In particular, I must mention the Fenis Castle, dating back to 1200 A.D.; the Castle of Verres, located in the Val d'Ayas and built around the thirteenth century; *Castello di Savoia*, connected with a large nineteenth century villa; the Bard Castle, built in the 1800s at the behest of the Savoy family; and the Issogne Castle, built during the twelfth century on the ruins of an ancient building of Roman origin.

Alba

Famous for its white truffles, peaches, and wine, hilly Alba will charm you with its ancient towers and Baroque churches.

Daniel Blair
Expat. Newbie Runner & Cyclist.

PIEDMONT & VALLE D'AOSTA

First, tell us about you.

I'm from Bethesda, Maryland, and I've lived in Alba since 2008. I'm actually a reserved and lazy person, but the landscape is so nice around Alba that I'm trying to take up running and cycling. I like music and computers, too.

If someone is visiting Alba for the first time, what do you recommend they see or do?

Alba is in a region that prides itself on food and wine. So anyone who visits Alba needs to see a few restaurants and vineyards (either in Alba or the region). Most Americans have heard of *Chianti*, but that's a different region. Wine buffs know about *Barolo* and *Nebbiolo*, considered top wines around the world and all from the region where Alba is.

What neighborhoods or parts of town are best to stay in?

Just to clear some things up: Alba is in the region of Piedmont, but the area where it is located is referred to as the Langhe. It's not a big city (31,000 people). If anyone wants to stay here, I recommend the historic city center or one of the bed and breakfasts in the hills in the area. If you stay in the center, you are immersed in the daily city life. If you stay outside the city, you're in the middle of the countryside with rolling hills and views of countless vineyards.

Let's talk about day trips...what nearby places should everyone make sure to visit?

Turin is the biggest city in the region and worth the 1.5-hour train ride. You can find a variety of museums (including an Egyptian museum), an opera house, and a very tall cinema museum.

The Langhe has a lot of castles. You could spend a day driving around to each one. Some are empty; others have been transformed into museums or restaurants. Some names (off the top of my head): Grinzane Cavour, Guarene, and Barolo (it's a town *and* a wine).

Tell us about the local dishes. What should people try?

105

PIEDMONT & VALLE D'AOSTA

Wow. Uh...that's a long list. Here's it is common to have three or four appetizers, then a first and second course followed by dessert...then maybe coffee...and then maybe some *grappa*. Of course, not everyone eats like that every day!

Appetizers: *carne cruda* (raw meat). Piedmont prides itself on the quality of their meat and it is common to find an appetizer that consists of thin slices of raw meat. Sometimes it's ground up instead of sliced. Don't worry about bacteria, but for some people the concept is unappetizing. I have bravely tried it. The taste is nice with a bit of lemon and pepper, but I've never been able to get over the fact that it's raw. I've seen other Americans simply *love* it.

Another appetizer is Russian salad, which is basically potato salad. Still another is *vitello tonnato* (literally "tuna-ed veal"), which is slices of veal with a tuna/mayo sauce. The combination seems strange, but it is very, very good.

First courses: obviously pasta. A common noodle here is *tajarin* (ta-ya-*reen*). It's fresh pasta (made from egg) often served in a meat *ragu*. A type of ravioli called *agnolotti* is very popular and can be filled with meat or veggies.

Second courses: meat and veggies. *Brasato al Barolo* is a thin steak (usually veal) cooked in a *Barolo* wine sauce. It's very good. Rabbit is also common.

What are your top three favorite bars and restaurants?
VinCafe (located at *Via Vittorio Emanuele 12*, on the main street) triples as a restaurant, cafe, and wine bar. Their food is good and the waiters are fun. They get a lot of business and, in nice weather, you can sit outside on the street.

I also like Osteria del Teatro (located at *Via Generale Govone 7*), a small restaurant with simple, good food.

If you want pizza, I recommend La Ducchessa (located at *Via Ospedale 5*). These guys (from Naples) have been around forever and their pizza is very good (and very filling).

Is there anything tourists do that locals find rude or strange? What can we do to better fit in with the culture?

Piedmont people are more closed compared to other parts of Italy, so they can seem angrier than they really are. Alba is touristy, but it's still small enough that tourists are stared at. It's not meant to be menacing or angry, that's just how some of the people look. Tourists should always be friendly. I've found that I can get a lot of smiles and make a lot of friends in the area by being nice and polite and courteous.

The nightlife isn't too crazy in Alba, so loud, drunk tourists are frowned upon. There are a couple bars and one can easily have a good time. Just don't overdo it and don't bring chaos into the streets.

The only other thing I can think of isn't a problem, just a difference: Italians don't typically drink a cappuccino beyond breakfast...and tourists do. It's not insulting. It's just different, but in this area, food is important. If you want a cappuccino after dinner, you can have it. The locals wouldn't, but it's your meal, so who cares?

To fit in, try following some of the local rhythms, living how the locals live. Between 12:30 and 3 p.m., shops close and people eat/relax. In the evening, everyone goes home or goes out. No reason to work (or shop). They have small espresso and brioche in the morning for breakfast. Simple. They eat a big lunch and smaller dinner.

What is the best way to meet locals and make friends?

Talk to the shop owners, in English or Italian (it doesn't matter if neither one of you can speak the same language). It's fun to communicate and people appreciate it. If there are special events, talk with some of the people managing things. Go to bars and sit at the counter and chat with the barman.

PIEDMONT & VALLE D'AOSTA

Why should people make sure to visit Alba?

People often want to see something authentically Italian. Alba is large enough that it offers some nice touristy things, but it's small enough to avoid the feel of a huge tourist city. It's closer to being Italian than other places. Also, the wine is good. And if you come in October/November, there's a truffle fair. That gets big and touristy, but there are some fun events (including a donkey race and Medieval games).

If you want a taste of truffles, I recommend coming mid-November or even December (after the fair). You'll still find them in restaurants...and maybe you'll get a bit of snow.

Where can we go to take beautiful photos?

From the hills surrounding the city (Alba is in a small valley by a river with hills all around it). You can drive up these hills if you want, but cycling and walking are best. If you do it the day after rain, in the morning, the sky is perfect.

Anything else you want us to know?

Honestly, the area is out of the way. People who come here are usually looking for the place. They don't necessarily stay long, but they eat and drink well when they do. If time is short, there are many other bigger places to see in Italy. If you just want to relax and enjoy beautiful scenery, Alba and the Langhe are a good choice (especially in May...the weather is great today). If you want to practice your Italian, you can find families willing to host you. Many locals love the opportunity to host people. The cultural exchange is fun and it's an excuse for more food.

Stresa (Lake Maggiore)

This well-touristed lakeside city is a mecca of historic villas and breathtaking lake views.

PIEDMONT & VALLE D'AOSTA

Dana Kaplan
Holiday Rental Owner. Blogger. Former New Yorker.

First, tell us about you.

Who would ever think this girl born and bred in Brooklyn, New York would now be living in the magical little town of Stresa, Italy, on the shores of beautiful Lago Maggiore? Yet, here I am!

I've been coming to Stresa for about 10 years, but as an American it was necessary for me to obtain a *Permesso di Soggiorno* to stay in Italy for more than 90 days out of every 180 and, now, having obtained my *Permesso*, I plan to live here almost full-time.

What I do here in Stresa is manage guest apartments in a lovely building we call *La Lombarda*. I get to meet our guests, who arrive from all over the world and I have the opportunity to help them make the most of their stay here in Stresa.

In my spare time, I love to walk around these beautiful towns, taking photos and, of course, trying wines and foods.

If someone is visiting Stresa for the first time, what do you recommend they see or do?

First-timers really need at least two nights here—just to get a sense of the town. The very first sites they must see, apart from the natural beauty of the lake, are the Borromean Islands. These three islands dominate the lake in front of Stresa and each is fascinating in its own way.

Isola Bella, the iconic island of the three, contains a 16th century palace and gardens, lived in by the Borromeo family since the 1500s. The island is both whimsical and baronial and offers several memorable surprises.

On Isola Madre, the entire island is a botanical garden and villa of the same royal family.

PIEDMONT & VALLE D'AOSTA

And Isola Pescatore, the Fisherman's Island, is just that—a 500-year-old fishing village that still functions today.

What neighborhoods or parts of town are best to stay in?

I would break this down to three general choices. The most elegant (and expensive) choice is to stay in one of the old-world-style hotels that line the lake. These have hosted many celebrities and VIPs over the years. For example, The Grand Hotel des Iles Borromees is where Ernest Hemingway convalesced during World War I and where Winston Churchill honeymooned!

Second, some people choose to stay at one of the many small hotels, B&Bs, and rental apartments here in the center of Stresa. This way they are in the center of everything.

Third, some people choose to rent apartments high up in the hills in the charming Medieval towns, such as Someraro and Campino, that are above Stresa. This works best for those arriving with cars and who really want to enjoy relaxing with the breathtaking views and cool air that the altitude provides.

Let's talk about day trips...what nearby places should everyone make sure to visit?

One nice thing about Stresa is that you can reach many other places from here. We're on a good train route and there are several good tour companies.

That said, the best way to take day trips is with the wonderful ferries that traverse the lake every day. They can bring you to the islands or all the way to Locarno, Switzerland, Villa Taranto (the famous gardens in Verbania), and so many charming towns that line the lakeshore. What's best about traveling this way is that the journey is part of the adventure!

Another must-do trip is to take the gondola from Stresa up to the top of Mt. Mottorone. From here you can see seven lakes.

110

PIEDMONT & VALLE D'AOSTA

Other places you can visit as day trips are Milan, the Matterhorn, Lake Orto, and even Venice!

Tell us about the local dishes. What should people try?

Stresa is part of the region of Piemonte and is very close to Switzerland and the Alps and just 30 minutes north of Milan. So, we have all these different influences.

You might want to try traditional Piemontese dishes such as *vitello tonnato* (cold, sliced veal in creamed tuna sauce with capers), *ravioli plin* (meat and veggie-filled small ravioli), and *bagna cauda* (warm anchovy and garlic dip). Or mountain dishes such as *brasato al Barolo* (beef braised in red wine), *polenta* (porridge), or *raclette* (potatoes covered in raclette cheese).

We have Milanese influence here as well, seen mostly in the traditional *risotto zafferano* (saffron risotto) and the chicken/veal Milanese (thin, breaded slices of veal or chicken).

When it comes to wine, we are surrounded by, arguably, some of the best wines in Italy. Some Piemontese specialties to try are *Barolo*, *Barbaresco*, and *Nebbiolo*. And don't forget to try our favorite bubbly drink, *Prosecco*.

What are your top three favorite bars and restaurants?

Ah, I can send you to three wonderful places for *aperitivo* drinks. First, Buscion (located at *Via Principessa Margherita 18*), which always has a happy, mixed crowd of locals and visitors. The proprietor, Massimo, is constantly finding new, interesting bottles to open.

You should also try Enoteca da Gianinno, located in the central *piazza* in Stresa at *Via Luigi Cadorna 10*, which has a more contemporary vibe, cool lounge music, and a great selection of wines by the glass.

To enjoy your wine, cocktail, or beer while taking in a full view of the lake, visit the Sky Bar (at *Lungolago Umberto I n. 33*) on the rooftop of the La Palma Hotel. Bring your camera for that.

Is there anything tourists do that locals find rude or strange? What can we do to better fit in with the culture?

Stresa is so international during the summer months that we are accustomed to so many different languages, manners of dress, and culinary customs. But if I would generalize a thing that might annoy locals a bit, it could be tourists who drive along the lake much too slowly because they are taking in the view or snapping photos while they drive. This holds up traffic behind them and locals find this rude (as well as dangerous). To fit in, just be a courteous guest who loves and respects Stresa as much as we do and take your photos while you are walking, not driving.

What is the best way to meet locals and make friends?

The best way to meet locals here is to patronize their shops and restaurants and speak to them about Stresa. Some of these restaurants and businesses have been in the same family for generations and, like many small towns, people work long and hard. Search out local businesses (rather than temporary kiosks run by people who don't live here) and then talk with them. Many speak some English and will be happy to use it with you and give you advice about Stresa.

Why should people make sure to visit Stresa?

Although still a bit under the travel radar for many people, Stresa is very touristic in the summer season. The reason it is so touristic is because it is so worth seeing. We are nestled between the Alps and the lake with natural beauty of rare comparison, high-quality accommodations and restaurants, excellent services, and a variety of very unique sights. For these reasons Stresa surprises many and many return over and over.

Where can we go to take beautiful photos?

There is the afore-mentioned Sky Bar atop the La Palma Hotel. That is an excellent spot.

PIEDMONT & VALLE D'AOSTA

From the summit at Mt. Mottarone, at 1,492 meters with a 360° view, is another. Or take a ferry out on the lake and take pictures of Stresa from the water. Or sit in *Piazza Cadorna* and people-watch.

But I believe the best way is just to walk along the lake, wander on the streets, and climb the old stone staircases into the small villages in the hills. In other words, it's all gorgeous here. You could close your eyes and take beautiful photographs. Perhaps this is the main reason people come here. There are specific, fascinating sights to see, yes, but you are surrounded by beauty all the time and it is very soothing for the soul.

Anything else you want us to know?

Stresa is a place with many layers. Yes, you can come for two nights, see the islands, and say you've been to Stresa. But I think one should stay at least a week and, even better, return often. Use it as a base for some day trips so that you can return here each evening. In this way, you can really start to appreciate the magic of this little town and you can slowly, in between glasses of *Barolo* and plates of risotto, discover all her little secrets.

Find Dana at: www.stresasights.blogspot.ch and www.stresaapartments.com.

THE ITALIAN RIVIERA (LIGURIA)

With colorful cliffside towns, bustling
port cities, and a famously mild climate,
relaxation is this region's middle name.

In this section: Genoa / La Spezia /
the Cinque Terre / Rapallo

Genoa (Genova)

*A bustling port city full of hidden art, significant monuments,
and the largest aquarium in Italy.*

Matteo Noris
Traveler. Bicyclist. Airbnb Host. Outdoor Enthusiast.

First, tell us about you.

My name is Matteo and I am 22. I was born in Santa
Margherita, Liguria and I grew up in Recco, a small town near
Genoa. As soon as I finished high school, I moved to UK where I
completed my university studies. In January, I will move to
Stockholm where I have been offered a job.

I am passionate about traveling and I have already visited
many countries (from China to Guatemala to Qatar). I also
travel by bike and I have cycled last May from Manchester
(UK) to Genoa. I am passionate about Couchsurfing.org and I
also host people through Airbnb. I am the proud owner of a
Fiat 500r (1973 model).

In my spare time, I enjoy the beautiful surroundings that this
region offers. I am a cyclist, swimmer, and runner.

THE ITALIAN RIVIERA (LIGURIA)

If someone is visiting Genoa for the first time, what do you recommend they see or do?

Well, the historical center of Genoa and the *caruggi* or *vicoli* (alleyways and narrow streets) are a very interesting spot in town and they offer a lot from the historical/art point of view while also being the center of the nightlife.

Also, the Porto Antico—the area that faces the sea in front of Genoa—offers a great number of bars and things to do (including the Genoa Aquarium).

If you are coming in spring or late summer, I would suggest a walk along *Corso Italia*, a three-kilometer long promenade facing the sea and surrounded by beautiful villas. Another must for first time visitors is a visit to Garibaldi Street, the street that takes you past most of the important palaces in Genoa.

What neighborhoods or parts of town are best to stay in?

The city center, most of the *vicoli*, and the eastern part of the city are all safe and generally nice. The western part of the city (where the airport is) tends to be a more complicated place to be, although there are exception like *Pegli* and *Arenzano*, which are beautiful areas.

I would also recommend, if you are not too concerned with going out at night and don't need to be right in the city center, staying in Nervi, Bogliasco, Recco, or even Camogli. They are very nice towns located along the coast, very well connected to Genoa through trains and bus lines.

Let's talk about day trips...what nearby places should everyone make sure to visit?

You should make sure to visit Camogli, Nervi and it's promenade, Portofino, Sestri Levante, the Cinque Terre, Porto Venere, Final Borgo, and Alassio.

Tell us about the local dishes. What should people try?

Well, in Genoa you will find some very typical *osterias*, which will serve incredibly good food. Some of them will look older, while others might have enjoyed some renovation lately and be more attractive. Either way, you're in for a treat.

The very typical dishes in Genoa are: *pesto* (a sauce that we put with a special type of pasta called *trofie*), *farinata*, *focaccia*, many different vegetable pies (*torta di bietole* for example), *focaccia con il formaggio di Recco* (very special), *pignolini* (very small fried fish that can be found in the small traditional take-out places in Porto Antico area), *ripieni* (filled vegetables), *ravioli*, and much more.

What are your top three favorite bars and restaurants?

The best pizza in Genoa, in my personal opinion, is found at Edo Bar, at *Via Mazzini 5*. It's not very fancy, but, trust me, the take-away pizza is amazing (and very well priced!).

The best restaurant, which is divided in two parts (a fancy and more expensive one and a *trattoria*), is Da o Vittorio (address: *Via Roma 160*).

The best *gelato* is at Gelateria Priaruggia (at *Via Quarto 1*).

For a different experience, try Trattoria della Maria, which is very traditional. (Address: *Vico Testadoro 14*.)

A brand new place with great sandwiches and a beautiful bar can be found at *Via Colombo 56 r*. The bar is simple, but simply great. Finally, for great sandwiches (but avoid the bar itself; it's awful), check out Gran Ristoro. (Address: *Via Sottoripa 29*.)

What is the best way to meet locals and make friends?

People from Genoa are not famous for being the most open population in Italy. However, Couchsurfing.org might be a good shot. Also Piazza delle Erbe will be the place to be for aperitivo or late in the evening; it's usually very crowded with university students and young people in general.

Where can we go to take beautiful photos?

Spianata Castelletto is the best spot in the Genoa city center.

THE ITALIAN RIVIERA (LIGURIA)

Why should people make sure to visit Genoa?

Genoa it's a very peculiar city. Unlike Florence or Venice, where art is right in front of your nose and you can't miss it, in Genoa, art and history are hidden and it takes a long time to discover and notice things. Genoa is a city that enjoyed different golden periods and crisis. Because of this, the city has no one prevalent architectural style, but there are many different styles that coexist.

Find Matteo at: www.airbnb.it/rooms/1982240.

Paolo Perrotta
Gardener. Painter. Local.

First, tell us about you.

I was born and have lived my whole life in Genoa. In my free time, I like to dedicate myself to the house, to paintings, to a garden, to the sea, to dine in the old taverns of Genoa, to going out to the movies, and to being with friends.

If someone is visiting Genoa for the first time, what do you recommend they see or do?

It's nice to visit the old town, the ancient churches of Genoa, the old port, and, if you have a little time, cross the harbor by boat and see the Abbey of St. Fruitful (located in Camogli).

What neighborhoods or parts of town are best to stay in?

I think the center is the best option. You could also stay in the old town (though in the old town there are some areas that are a little dangerous). *Strula* or near the sea is also nice.

Let's talk about day trips...what nearby places should everyone make sure to visit?

As I mentioned above, the Abbey of St. Fruitful is a great place to visit. I also recommend Portofino. Then there is the *passeggiata di nervi*, a long walk along the ocean that is beautiful even when the sea is rough.

117

THE ITALIAN RIVIERA (LIGURIA)

Tell us about the local dishes. What should people try?

The Genoese cuisine is simple and quite poor. There is the typical *pesto* pasta (which can also be served with potatoes and green beans), *la cima* (veal stuffed with vegetables, meat, and cheese), *stoccafisso accomodato* (Genovese stockfish), *torte di verdure* (vegetable pies), *focaccia*, *farinata* (a thin, unleavened pancake or crepe), and pretty much any type of fish.

What are your top three favorite bars and restaurants?

I'm not really a bar person, but I do love restaurants. My favorites are Ugo (located at *Via dei Giustiniani 86 R*), Trattoria Vegia Zena (at *Vico del Serriglio 15 R*), and Infernotto (at *Via Giuseppe Macaggi 64*).

Is there anything tourists do that locals find rude or strange? What can we do to better fit in with the culture?

Normally tourists behave well (sometimes better than the Italians). To fit in, always have a smile in your pocket (as we say).

What is the best way to meet locals and make friends?

This is a tough one. Even locals have trouble meeting new people sometimes. That said, the Internet helps.

Where can we go to take beautiful photos?

The *la Spianata di Castelletto* (a tower with a fantastic panorama of the city and an elevator to take you there), the roof of the *Palazzo Rosso* (red palace) museum, Genoa's elevated road, and the old port are all spectacular for views.

If you take your camera out in the right light (sunset is particularly amazing), you'll have great photos wherever you go.

Why should people make sure to visit Genoa?

There are certainly cities that deserve to be seen before Genoa—Venice, Rome, and Florence. That said, Genoa also has its own charm. It is an ancient seaside town and is very traditional and Italian.

La Spezia

This hub of museums, art shows, and exhibitions is also just minutes from the Cinque Terre.

Ari Lopez Nunes
Artist. Theater Buff. Milanese.

First, tell us about you.
I was born in Milano and now I live in a little village eight kilometers from La Spezia (where I've been for 15 years). I'm an artist and I practice art in everything I do.

If someone is visiting La Spezia for the first time, what do you recommend they see or do?
La Spezia has a lot of museums, a nice castle, exhibitions, many art shows in summer, but not a beach. It isn't a town for young people and La Spezia's youth prefer to go and enjoy themselves at the pubs, fun little shops, and dance clubs of Sarzana (a little town 15 kilometers from La Spezia). Versilia Coast in Tuscany is also popular with the young crowd.

What neighborhoods or parts of town are best to stay in?
In La Spezia, *Via Prione* and the surrounding area have some nice, typical restaurants and the best shopping. Near La Spezia, there are many little and amazing villages on the sea, including Lerici, San Terenzio, and Portovenere, which you can reach by city buses (€2.50). Then, of course, there is the Cinque Terre, which are easily reachable by train or boat (don't try to go to the Cinque Terre by car; the cost of car parks is very high).

Let's talk about day trips...what nearby places should everyone make sure to visit?

119

THE ITALIAN RIVIERA (LIGURIA)

You can visit the Cinque Terre in a day, walking from one village to the next, especially when the weather isn't too hot.

Tell us about the local dishes. What should people try?
In La Spezia, you can snack on *focaccia* (bread with olive oil and salt), *focaccia al formaggio* (with cheese), and *farinata* (focaccia made with chickpeas).

For lunch or dinner, try *testaroli* (the most ancient type of spaghetti), *panigacci* (a sort of Indian chapati with sliced salami or nutella), and *trenette al pesto* (tagliatelle with a typical Ligurian sauce with basil, garlic, pine nuts, and olive oil).

Is there anything tourists do that locals find rude or strange? What can we do to better fit in with the culture?
Don't walk on the streets of La Spezia in your swimsuit, even if the weather is hot.

What is the best way to meet locals and make friends?
It's very hard to make local friends in La Spezia, but people are courteous in general.

Why should people make sure to visit La Spezia?
Because of the wonderful and amazing villages on the sea, visited in past centuries by Goethe, Shelling, Mann, and many European intellectuals.

Where can we go to take beautiful photos?
From around and in the castle and on the sea-walk.

Anything else you want us to know?
It's better to visit the region in spring and autumn when the weather isn't too hot and there aren't too many tourists.

THE ITALIAN RIVIERA (LIGURIA)

Vernazza (Cinque Terre)

Walk the cliffside paths between the five towns, try a limoncello, and enjoy a complete lack of modern development in this five-town UNESCO World Heritage Site.

Miriana Rovaron
Travel Agent. Cinque Terre Enthusiast & Promoter.

First, tell us about you.
I was born in La Spezia and have lived here all my life, but we are so close to Cinque Terre (just a few minutes by train) and I have been visiting them since I was a child—first as a day-tripper, then for longer holidays, and now as a travel agent.

I have been working with Cinque Terre, promoting them and renting properties, since 2005 through my agency, originally located in La Spezia. Then, last year, we opened our office in Vernazza, right on the main street, *Via Roma 24*.

If someone is visiting the Cinque Terre for the first time, what do you recommend they see or do?
First of all, stay a bit longer than a few nights; that way you can relax, visit all the villages (Vernazza is our favorite, but they are all nice and each has its own charm), and try a lot of different area activities, including boat tours, wine tasting, and cooking classes. This way you'll really get the most out of the region.

Cinque Terre is actually a national park and trails connect each of the five major villages. The views you experience while walking the trails will be amazing. One interesting fact: until about 50 years ago, the trails were the only roads that locals used to get around (apart from riding in their boats).

There is a hike for everyone. The shortest is 25 minutes; the longest can take about two hours. When you review the trail maps, you'll see that there are two different types of trails that connect the villages: the trails that run closer to sea level

121

THE ITALIAN RIVIERA (LIGURIA)

(easy/intermediate trails) and the trails that run along the tops of the hills (a bit more difficult). While you are hiking the high trails, you can find a spot to jump into the sea.

What neighborhoods or parts of town are best to stay in?

Vernazza is the most visited village of the five. So, for those who want a relaxing holiday, especially during the day, staying in *San Bernardino* or *Fornacchi* areas (just 4.5 kilometers from the village center) above the village, might be a better choice.

Monterosso is the biggest of the five villages, as well as the most accessible and the only one with an amazing, almost sandy beach (the other Cinque Terre beaches are smooth pebble beaches). Here, apartments are a bit larger, so it's a great option for families on vacation.

Corniglia is the hiker's paradise. Manarola is a simple village that slopes uphill and tends to have great sea views. And Riomaggiore is the easternmost town, with a steep slope and beautiful sunsets.

The locals call Cinque Terre the land between sky and sea.

Let's talk about day trips...what nearby places should everyone make sure to visit?

From here, you can visit easily Tuscany and Piedmont. For really nice closer spots, try lively La Spezia, scenic Portovenere and Lerici, Medieval Sarzana, and the Luni Roman ruins, plus all the Cinque Terre countryside, including the Val Di Vara.

Tell us about the local dishes. What should people try?

THE ITALIAN RIVIERA (LIGURIA)

My top choices? Handmade pasta with *pesto* (which originated in this region), seafood, and fish and vegetable pies.

I'd also recommend *acciughe al tegame* (fried anchovies), *coniglio alla Ligure* (Ligurian-style rabbit), *pesto lasagna*, *ravioli alla Ligure* (Ligurian ravioli, featuring beets, meat, and pine nuts), *spaghetti allo scoglio* (seafood spaghetti), mussels in marinara sauce, baked white fish, *stocafisso In umido* (stockfish in sauce), fried *triglie* (red mullet), *mesciua* (bean soup), *cima* (stuffed veal breast), *minestrone* soup, and *spaghetti* with mussels.

What are your top three favorite bars and restaurants?
Taverna del Capitano at *Piazza Guglielmo Marconi 21/24* in Vernazza, Micky Restaurant (at *Via Fegina 104*) in Monterosso, and A Pie de Ma (at *Viale Giovanni Amendola*) in Riomaggiore.

Is there anything tourists do that locals find rude or strange? What can we do to better fit in with the culture?
The only things we ask are that you respect nature, do not leave garbage all over, do not ask for air conditioning, which is often not necessary for this kind of architecture (thick stone walls keep houses cool in summer and warm in winter), do not invade villages in huge day trip groups (it is mostly an area for individual visitors and small groups, not 100-person groups), and do keep quiet at night (it is not a disco-type region).

What is the best way to meet locals and make friends?
Stay longer, learn basic Italian words, go shopping at local stores, and talk to locals, even in simple Italian or basic English.

Why should people make sure to visit the Cinque Terre?
It is still an unspoiled region, extremely natural, not yet invaded by McDonalds and other fast food chains or big brand luxury stores.

There are no cars and no traffic in all the villages.

Anything else you want us to know?

When you imagine the Cinque Terre, imagine century-old vineyards built onto the sides of steep rocks by fishermen. It's like the Amalfi Coast of the north. *Pesto*, grapes for white wines, and anchovies (served about two dozen different ways) here are king and a deep source of pride.

Italians refer to the Cinque Terre as *"terre tra cielo e mare"* (the land between sky and sea). When you see it, you'll know what they mean.

Find Miriana at: www.cinqueterreriviera.com.

Volastra (Cinque Terre)

Located in the Cinque Terre national park, this tiny town is just outside the tourist bustle.

Andrea Capellini
B&B & Holiday Apartment Owner. Winemaker.

First, tell us about you.

My name is Andrea and I run the Il Vigneto B&B in Volastra, along with my wife Patrizia. We're two kilometers from Manarola and three kilometers from Riomaggiore. Our B&B is a small 6-room place with a wide terrace (where we serve breakfast in the morning) and an amazing sea view. We also have holiday apartments here. The house has been in my family for a very long time and we rebuilt and started the B&B in 2003.

The name *"Il Vigneto"* means vineyard, because my family has cultivated vineyards and produced white wine for many years. We have a very nice, small cellar with a very old mill where we produce our wine and where my clients can taste it.

THE ITALIAN RIVIERA (LIGURIA)

If someone is visiting the Cinque Terre for the first time, what do you recommend they see or do?

From Volastra, the best thing to do is walk with path n. 6d to Corniglia (it should take about one hour and 15 minutes) or path n. 6 to Manarola (about 30 minutes). Taking these walks, you can appreciate the magnificent sea views and terraces with vineyards held up by dry stone walls.

From there, visit the rest of the villages by boat, path, or train.

What neighborhoods or parts of town are best to stay in?

Volastra is our favorite because is very natural and true. It only has two hotels and two B&Bs, all very well managed, new, and with amazing sea views.

Let's talk about day trips...what nearby places should everyone make sure to visit?

You cannot lose with Manarola and Vernazza.

Tell us about the local dishes. What should people try?

Pasta al pesto, acciughe salate e fritte (friend anchovy salad), *frittura mista di paranza* (mixed fried fish), *spaghetti allo scoglio* (seafood spaghetti), *lasagne al pesto, pesce al forno con patate* (fish and potatoes), *vino doc Cinque Terre* (local dry white wine), and *Sciacchetrà* (local dessert wine).

What are your top three favorite bars and restaurants?

Trattoria L'Arcobaleno in Volastra (located at *Via Montello 270*), Trattoria dal Billy in Manarola (located at *Via Aldo Rollandi 122*), and Ristorante Cappun Magru in Groppo (located at *Via Volastra 19*).

What is the best way to meet locals and make friends?

Go to Cantina dello Zio Bramante in Manarola (located at *Via Renato Birolli 110*).

Why should people make sure to visit the Cinque Terre?

Because the landscape is unique and unforgettable and from May to September you can swim in the warm sea.

THE ITALIAN RIVIERA (LIGURIA)

What is the best place to go take beautiful photos?
Path n. 6d from Volastra to Corniglia.

Find Andrea at: www.ilvigneto5terre.com.

Rapallo

Part of the Parco Naturale Regionale di Portofino, Rapallo is known for its picturesque castle and world-class seafood.

Fern Driscoll
Expat. Blogger. Retiree.

First, tell us about you.
My husband and I moved to Rapallo from the U.S. after retiring and have lived there on and off for 13 years. We both enjoy playing golf (the world's second oldest golf course is in Rapallo and it's beautiful). We also swim and boat with friends and enjoy looking after our house and gardens.

If someone is visiting Rapallo for the first time, what do you recommend they see or do?
Just walking around Rapallo is a pleasure, particularly along the *Lungomare* (waterfront walk). The town hugs its little bay and a walk to the port will reward you with views of some pretty special boats. There are two main pedestrian walking areas, one along the coast (*Lungomare*) and the other a block inland (*Via Mazzini*). The former tends to be for the older folks, the latter for the younger. *Via Mazzini* is a mad bustle at five o'clock during the *passeggiata*, as people window shop, have an *aperitivo*, or just people-watch.

A *funivea* (cable car) runs up to the pilgrim church, Montallegro. The view from the church is tremendous and the history of the church and why it's there is fascinating. There are several adequate restaurants and lodges up there as well. It is

126

THE ITALIAN RIVIERA (LIGURIA)

really worth the effort to see it. For hikers, it is on a system of trails that runs through the mountains behind Rapallo all the way to Chiavari, down the coast 15 kilometers.

The *Castello* in the center of town was built in the 16th century to discourage marauding Saracens. For a time it served as a prison; now it is host to exhibits of various types. There are elaborate fireworks July 1st, 2nd, and 3rd, around the festival of the Madonna. After an evening procession the *Castello* goes up in smoke every year.

Several lovely churches in town are worth a visit: the 16th century *San Francesco* is right in the middle of town; the Basilica of Saints Gervasio and Protasio gives Pisa a bit of competition in the leaning tower division. There are other lovely churches to visit in San Michele and Caravaggio, just down the road.

On the western side of town, a bit more difficult to reach, is the ancient ruin of the Monastery of Valle Christi, which hosts an outdoor series of dramas in the summer.

Fans of mini-golf and/or books will find both in the *Parco Casale*. The International Library has books in French, German, Spanish, and English, as well as Italian. The mini-golf is in the same park. The Lace Museum is also found in the *Parco Casale*.

Being a Riviera town, swimming and sunbathing are must-do activities in the summer. There are plenty of places to rent a cabana and a chair for the day. As well, Rapallo has two excellent swimming pools: one indoor, one outdoor (also a championship water polo team), though they are several kilometers from the center of town.

Sports lovers will not want to miss Rapallo Golf and Tennis Club. The 18-hole golf course spreads itself along the hills on the western side of town (near the autostrada entrance) and is meticulously maintained. One hole gives a long view down the fairway to Valle Cristi. The tennis center is well maintained and popular. The club has one of the better restaurants in town.

There is ample opportunity for scuba diving from various nearby scuba shops and there is a protected zone along the coast where you can still see some interesting fishes.

A stroll around the old downtown will bring visitors to The *Polipo*, the octopus fountain that is Rapallo's mascot, the band shell, and an underground peek at a bit of the old port (right near the band shell) that was dug up when the *Lungomare* was rebuilt.

What neighborhoods or parts of town are best to stay in?

There are many fine hotels in Rapallo. The prettiest places to stay are on the seafront, are certainly the most convenient for getting around, and offer the best views. The hotel Italia has rooms that offer a view of the harbor without an intervening street. The Excelsior Hotel is a 5-star spot with a health club/spa and a pool set in the rocks above the sea. The Hotel Bristol is a Grand Old Hotel, about one kilometer from the center of town. It, too, has a spa.

Let's talk about day trips...what nearby places should everyone make sure to visit?

Rapallo is a convenient 40-minute train ride from the famous Cinque Terre, so many visitors go to hike the trails there (though, those who like to hike should not overlook the Portofino Peninsula which has trails that rival the Cinque Terre for beauty). A ferry ride will carry visitors to Santa Margherita, Portofino, and *San Fruttuoso*, all of which are *musts*. *San Fruttuoso*, a 15th century monastery, is still accessible only by foot or ferry; entry into its wee harbor on the ferryboat is an adventure all its own.

For those with time, Zoagli and Chiavari are two lovely towns just down the coast from Rapallo. Camogli, in the other direction, is still a fishing town and is a famous tourist destination for Italians.

THE ITALIAN RIVIERA (LIGURIA)

Genova is a city rich in history and full of beautiful places to visit. It's worth a vacation visit of its own, but one can get a feel for the place with a day trip from Rapallo, also about 40 minutes by train.

Tell us about the local dishes. What should people try?

Focaccia! Focaccia is the famous Ligurian flatbread. *Farinata* is another Ligurian specialty, made from chickpea flour. It is much more delicious than it looks or sounds. The pasta specialties of Rapallo are *trofie al pesto* (small irregular pastas with the famous Genovese basil sauce) and *pansotti* with walnut sauce (little hats of pasta stuffed with mixed greens). Yum! True *pansotti* must be made by hand and most still are.

Fish! Rapallo no longer has a fishing fleet, but Santa and Camogli do; you can't find fresher fish than what you'll be served in a Rapallo restaurant.

What are your top three favorite bars and restaurants?

Coffee bars: Bar Cristallo (located at *Via Agostino Giustiniani 12*) and Bar Roma (located at *Via della Libertà 14*). There are great pastries at both and both are frequented by locals.

Caffe Canepa (located at *Piazza Garibaldi 41*) dates from the late 19th century and is just a stone's throw from Rapallo's famous octopus mascot.

There are several restaurants/bars (Bar II Castello—at *Lungomare Castello 6*—and Bar Sole, at *Lungomare Castello 10*) on the little *passeggiata* by the Castello; it's very pleasant to sit outside and watch the water and the passing scene.

Locals congregate at Ristorante Nettuno on the *Lungomare* (*Lungomare Vittorio Veneto 28*). Seafood and pizza are excellent there.

There are a handful of other good restaurants along the *Lungomare*. If you have a car, don't miss Ristorante U Giancu, on *Via San Massimo*, where you will eat Chef Fausto's delicious creations surrounded by cartoon art. Beloved by locals, Fausto

129

is also well known in the US, where he gives infrequent and over-subscribed cooking classes.

Is there anything tourists do that locals find rude or strange? What can we do to better fit in with the culture?

Italians are, by and large, a very courteous people. They find loud talk, sloppy dress, and undue haste rude (patience is absolutely requisite to get along in Italy). But on the Riviera people are used to these things, as there are so many visitors from other countries. As in most places, simply being pleasant, patient, and polite will do the trick.

Why should people make sure to visit Rapallo?

Rapallo is one of the original Riviera resort towns; over the years, it has grown to be quite large (30,000 or so), unlike neighboring Santa Margherita, Zoagli, and Camogli. (Portofino is in a class by itself; with a population of only about 500 full-time residents, it is almost purely a tourist attraction.)

While Santa, Zoagli, and Camogli retain their rather upper-crust characters (and they are charming and delightful), Rapallo has continued to grow and develop as a real town, with a wide variety of people pursuing a variety of occupations, not all of them tourist-related. There was an unfortunate surge of construction in Rapallo in the 1960s as the town spread out from its old center. A lot of large block apartments were constructed to accommodate the growing population. This gives Rapallo a different personality than its near neighbors, a personality we find authentically Italian.

Where can we go to take beautiful photos?

Anywhere along the *Lungomare*, on the ferry boat rides, *Montallegro*, *Parco Casale*, golf course, and on the road that leads from Rapallo through San Michele and Santa Margherita to Portofino.

Anything else you want us to know?

It is great fun to visit during the annual *festa* for the Virgin, July 1-3. There are fireworks morning, afternoon, and evening all three days, a procession of crosses, a conflagration of fireworks on the *Castello*, and a fair. Every weekend in the summer, there is music from the kiosk, and weekend evenings the *Lungomare* is closed to traffic so it becomes one big party.

There is a system of bus routes around the town and plenty of taxis at the train station. Ferries, buses, and trains will take you to neighboring towns or down to the Cinque Terre.

Market day is Thursday and markets carry mostly clothing and housewares, as well as some food.

Rapallo has an excellent website in Italian and English (*www.comune.rapallo.ge.it*). Choose *Canale Turistico* for a listing of the many events going on around town.

Find Fern at: farfalle1.wordpress.com.

EMILIA-ROMAGNA

This lesser-known region is a foodie's paradise, original home of lasagna, Bolognese sauce, and Parmesan cheese.

In this section: Emilia's Countryside / Bologna / Parma / Ferrara / Ravenna / Modena

Emilia's Countryside

When it comes to Emilia, all you need to do is eat.

Mariana Pickering
Architecture Studio Owner. Texpat.

First, tell us about you.

I'm a "Texpat," originally from Dallas, but I've been moving around the world since I left for college at 18. I went from St. Louis to Copenhagen to Los Angeles to Sydney. That's where I met my future husband and the reason I find myself here in Emilia. He tamed my big city ways and kidnapped me to his little hometown just outside of Reggio Emilia almost six years ago.

We have an architecture studio together, so we have basically no free time. Luckily, we love our work! When we do get a day free, we like to head into the Apennines with our Labrador, Saba, and walk through the hills. I also blog a bit about my life here in Emilia, mainly venting about culturally shocking and hilarious stories.

If someone is visiting Reggio Emilia for the first time, what do you recommend they see or do?

Put on some stretchy pants and EAT! That's what they do best here. Food. And they do it well. In fact, they do it SO well that

EMILIA-ROMAGNA

even Italians from other regions exclaim, "Ooooh! Emilia, *si mangia bene lì!*" (Emilia, boy do they eat well!)

What neighborhoods or towns are best to stay in?

Generally speaking, if you're traveling by train you'll want to stay in the historic center (*centro storico*) of one of the main towns of the region: Reggio Emilia, Parma, Modena, Piacenza, Ferrara, or Bologna. However, to get a real taste of rural Emilia, you'll want to head out into the countryside. You'll need a car or a local guide for that, though.

Let's talk about day trips...what nearby places should everyone make sure to visit?

Again, those major towns I mentioned before each have beautiful city centers. The central location of Emilia, however, allows for a day trip to include most of northern Italy. And now that the new high-speed train station is open in Reggio Emilia, you can even get to Rome in a couple hours. Within two hours from my house, I can get to Florence, Bologna, Mantova, Venice, Cinque Terre, or Rimini. There are *a lot* of options.

I also love love *love* the Apennines. Honestly, I can't understand why tourists spend so much money to go stay in Tuscany when the other side of the ridge here in Emilia is just as gorgeous, with excellent food, and a fraction of the costs. There are tons of castles to visit, as well as several beautiful parks with hiking trails. When I have family and friends come to visit, we usually recommend a day trip to the hills as a nice pause between the busy city center trips.

Tell us about the local dishes. What should people try?

As I said before, Emilia-Romagna (and Emilia especially) has some of the best food in Italy. Every 10 kilometers, you pass into an area famous for a different kind of food, whether it is the balsamic vinegar of Modena, the *Parmigiano-Reggiano* cheese of Reggio Emilia, or the *prosciutto* of Parma.

Depending on which side of the River Enza you're on, there are *capelletti* (on the Reggio side) or *anollini* (on the Parma side): little stuffed pasta pockets served in broth (and a splash of

133

EMILIA-ROMAGNA

Lambrusco for true locals). There are my all-time favorite *tortelli*, which are similar to what Americans call *ravioli*. On this side of the Enza (Reggio Emilia side), they are made from *biettola*, which is like a Swiss chard or kale, with a bit of *ricotta*. On the Parma side, which was historically a wealthier dairy area, they stuff theirs with more *ricotta* and less greens. On the *padana* (the plains), anything from the pig is fantastic. And, up in the hills, wild boar and *caprioli* (deer) are my favorite.

What are your top three favorite bars and restaurants?
Well, the best restaurant would be my mother-in-law's house. Seriously, if you visit Emilia, find a way to meet some locals. Nothing beats mamma's cooking.

The next best thing is to find a restaurant with a mamma in the kitchen! My husband and I are long-time patrons of Osteria della Capra (at *Via Rivasi* 94) and Cantina Garibaldi (at *Piazza Garibaldi* 16 in Cavriago). We also love La Rupe at the foot of the Canossa Castle (address: *Localita' Canossa 12, Canossa*). It's very difficult to pick three out of the whole region, though. There are at least three within walking distance of my house that are amazing!

Is there anything tourists do that locals find rude or strange? What can we do to better fit in with the culture?
Here in rural Emilia, there, frankly, aren't many tourists. So when one does show up, most people are quite interested. It's important to remember that a small town is a small town...Sometimes Americans on a whirlwind tour of the country forget to slow down and absorb the personality of a place. That can seem arrogant sometimes to locals. But, in general, Italians are pretty forgiving and love to practice their English (even if it's only five words).

What is the best way to meet locals and make friends?
Food. Did I mention food is important here? I always bring back little gifts from Texas...pecans, pralines, beef jerky, chili spices, and other food items that they probably won't eat but will find fascinating and endearing. Gift exchange is a lovely

134

tradition here and coming prepared for that would be quite impressive.

Why should people make sure to visit Emilia?
Ok, I'll set food aside for a minute. The people here are just fantastic. This region was historically a poor agricultural area. Even though it is now one of the wealthier parts of Italy, the people here are incredibly down to earth and genuine.

What is the best place to go take beautiful photos?
The Apennines. Take the *Strada dei Vini e Sapori* (Road of Wines and Tastes) that winds through the hills past several castles and excellent traditional restaurants.

Find Mariana at: emuarchitects.com.

Bologna

Italy's other food capitol—famed for the invention of lasagna and Bolognese sauce.

Alessandro Ferin
Traveler. Foodie. Native Bolognese.

First, tell us about you.
I am a native-born Bolognese and have lived in Bologna almost my entire life (with the exception of one year where I lived abroad in the UK and Denmark). In my spare time, I like to meet friends, talk with people, read books, see movies, take long walks, and travel.

If someone is visiting Bologna for the first time, what do you recommend they see or do?
They should, EAT! Bologna is one of the best cities for food in Italy (I think it is one of the capitals of food in Italy, alongside Naples). So eat, eat, and eat some more.

135

EMILIA-ROMAGNA

In between eating, go out and see *Piazza Maggiore* and *Statua del Nettuo* (the Fountain of Neptune), walk in *Via Indipendenza* (the main street of Bologna), or go out at night to drink (and eat, obviously) in *Via del Pratello* or *Via Zamboni*.

What neighborhoods or parts of town are best to stay in?

I recommend staying in the historical center (*il centro*) because it is the most interesting, but also go to *Fiera* District if there are some *fiera* (fairs). The best area to live in is surely *Zona Mazzini*.

Let's talk about day trips...what nearby places should everyone make sure to visit?

Outside the city, there are many small towns on hills or the plains around Bologna. I like Marzabotto or Pianoro on the hills and Medicina or Budrio on the plain.

If you go bit farther, there are bigger nice cities like Ferrara, Modena, Parma, and Imola.

Tell us about the local dishes. What should people try?

Italian food is famous throughout the world and all cities have good food...but there are two cities that have the best of Italy. One is Naples, with its world-renowned pizza, spaghetti, and mozzarella. The other is most definitely Bologna, home of the Bolognese sauce (a yummy meat sauce known around the world).

There are two cities that have the best food in Italy: Naples and Bologna.
Photo by: Sebastian Mary on Flickr.

136

EMILIA-ROMAGNA

So, you should definitely eat pasta with *Bolognese* sauce (we call it *ragu* and it's usually served on *tagiatelle* pasta, which is a flat spaghetti made with eggs).

Other very famous dishes are *mortadella* (a nice kind of ham, originally from Bologna) and *tortellini* (Bologna and Parma share this kind of dish), which is a kind of dumpling with meat inside and is very good in broth or sauce.

Of course, you can also find *Parmesan* and *prosciutto* here; they are originally from Parma, but very good here too.

Then there's the most famous of our dishes: *lasagna*. Here you can find the best *lasagna* in the entire world, just as in Naples you will find the best pizza in the world!

Finally, if you can, try *zuppa imperial* (a hearty egg soup in meat broth), *passatelli* (pasta made with bread crumbs, parmesan, nutmeg, and eggs), *bollito* (a northern Italian stew, which you should try at Da Bertino Restaurant, located at *Via delle Lame 55*, if you can – absolutely amazing), and *cotoletta alla Bolognese* (a fried meat dish with ham and cheese on top).

What are your top three favorite bars and restaurants?
The best restaurant in Bologna (and, really, in the world) is surely Da Tony (located at *Via Righi 1/B*). It's a small place, very good, not too expensive (though not cheap), and traditional (a *trattoria*). You can find all the Bolognese traditional dishes here.

Second is surely Da Bertino (another traditional restaurant, at *Via delle Lame 55*).

And third is Osteria La Fondazza (at *Via Fondazza 35*). Go late in the evening to drink and eat.

Is there anything tourists do that locals find rude or strange? What can we do to better fit in with the culture?

EMILIA-ROMAGNA

Some of us are not great with our English and would love it if people would try to speak a little Italian with us.

What is the best way to meet locals and make friends?
Bologna is a city of 300,000 Bolognese, plus 100,000 university students, so when you go out to drink or have fun you will always run into students. The best way to meet new people is to go out to drink in a pub or *osteria* in the evenings. Couchsurfing.org is also very useful.

Why should people make sure to visit Bologna?
Bologna is not famous and is less touristy. We are not Florence or Venice or Rome, even if Bologna is bigger than both Florence and Venice. The city isn't crowded with tourist traps, giant monuments, and throngs of tourists. We just have some small hidden charms, the best food in the world, and a university-town feel.

Where can we go to take beautiful photos?
Piazza Maggiore, San Luca on the hill, *Ospedale Rizzoli,* and the many narrow alleys of the center (*il centro*).

Nicholas Montemaggi
Digital PR Lead for Emilia-Romagna Tourism. Public Speaker.

First, tell us about you.
I lived in Bologna for one year, but have spent most of my life living nearby. My hometown is a one-hour drive from Bologna, so it's pretty close and I also come to Bologna during the week for work and often to spend weekends in the city.

If someone is visiting Bologna for the first time, what do you recommend they see or do?
There is, of course, a lot to see and do in Bologna, but if you are there for the first time I suggest you to follow the two-hour itinerary that you can find on the map of the local tourist office.

EMILIA-ROMAGNA

Personally, I also love to get lost walking under the many miles of porticoes that allow you to see the city and do some shopping, even if it rains (they'll keep you dry).

What neighborhoods or parts of town are best to stay in?
The city center, for sure. It is really fascinating and, since it houses the oldest university of the western hemisphere, you can really feel the culture, the knowledge, and the student vibe in every corner.

I also like the hills surrounding Bologna; it seems like you're in the middle of nowhere, but you are just 15 minutes from the city center.

Let's talk about day trips...what nearby places should everyone make sure to visit?
Bologna is the capital of the Emilia Romagna region, located in the middle of one of the most ancient roman roads, the *Via Emilia*, and there are a lot of cities and towns that are really worth a visit, including:

Parma, located one hour by train from Bologna, home of the famous *Parmigiano-Reggiano cheese* and the *Parma ham*, and where the world-famous opera composer Giuseppe Verdi was born.

Reggio Emilia, also just one hour by train from Bologna, home of the Italian Tricolor Flag and a city in which I personally like to shop, with many Made in Italy clothing shops.

Modena, located only 30 minutes from Bologna, the city of Ferrari, Maserati, and the traditional Italian balsamic vinegar. (It is also one of the UNESCO sites of the region and was the birthplace and home of Pavarotti.)

Ferrara, located just 40 minutes by train from Bologna, the second UNESCO site of the region with its wonderful, well-kept Renaissance historical center.

EMILIA-ROMAGNA

Ravenna, located one hour by train from Bologna, with its world-famous mosaics dating back to the Byzantine Empire (this is another of our UNESCO sites).

Rimini, located one and a half hours by train from Bologna, with a great historical center dating back to Roman times—the perfect place if you want to relax on wide, sandy beaches facing the Adriatic Sea.

There are also many little towns surrounding Bologna itself that are really worth a visit, like Dozza, a city known for its painted wall festival, where famous artists come and paint works on the walls twice a year, and home of the regional wine cellar (with the best wines from the region, including *Sangiovese*, *Pignoletto*, and *Lambrusco*).

Another small town worth visiting is Sant'Agata Bolognese, where you can visit the Lamborghini factory!

Tell us about the local dishes. What should people try?
Bologna and the Emilia Romagna region are home of the best Made in Italy food products and Italian pasta dishes.

For example: *Parmigiano-Reggiano cheese*, *Parma ham*, *traditional balsamic vinegar* of Modena and Reggio Emilia, *mortadella of Bologna* (a type of Italian sausage), *piadina* bread (typical flat bread of the region), the white truffle of the Apennines, and pasta dishes like *tagliatelle al ragù* (NOT Spaghetti Bolognese, which is a phrase that doesn't exist here), *cappelletti* (meat-filled pasta) in broth, *ravioli*, and many more.

What are your top three favorite bars and restaurants?
My list of favorite restaurants is long, but if we want to choose a category, pasta dishes, for example, in Bologna my top three are: Osteria dell'Orsa (at *Via Mentana 1*), Trattoria Annamaria (at *Via Belle Arti 17/A*), and Trattoria del Rosso (at *Via Augusto Righi 30*).

140

EMILIA-ROMAGNA

A good suggestion for coffee (espresso) is Caffè Terzi (at *Viale Ilic Uljanov Lenin 9*).

Is there anything tourists do that locals find rude or strange? What can we do to better fit in with the culture?
Ordering a cappuccino after 11 a.m.

What is the best way to meet locals and make friends?
Because of the university, Bologna is a city with a good vibe and loads of friendly people. So, just walking around under the porticoes or in the bars and restaurants or parks in the city, you have the chance to meet new friends.

Why should people make sure to visit Bologna?
Because it's perfectly located on the main Italian tourist route, just 30 minutes by train from Florence and one hour from Venice, and since it's not overcrowded by tourists, you can still experience the Italian *dolce vita* lifestyle and meet loads of locals.

Find Nicholas at: www.emiliaromagnaturismo.it.

Parma

Prosciutto, cheese, and architecture—need we say more?

Chiara Carta
Linguist. Teacher. Cat-Lover. Travel Dreamer.

First, tell us about you.
I was born in Sardinia and, after high school in Sassari, I went to live in Bologna, where I studied German and Finnish. I lived in Berlin for a while, but my love for Emilia Romagna was too big, so I returned.

Today, I live in Parma with my boyfriend and a lovely cat called Harley Quinn. I teach Italian to foreigners and my

141

EMILIA-ROMAGNA

biggest dream is to live in Los Angeles for a few months. I love translating, watching movies, and reading.

I think Bologna is the best city in Emilia Romagna when you are young and free, but here in Parma you can have a lot of good things, too. Nothing is too far away, especially if you have a bicycle (and everyone here does).

If someone is visiting Parma for the first time, what do you recommend they see or do?
First of all, Parma is popular for food (and who doesn't love food?). You can find little shops with the best *Parmigiano* and *prosciutto* in the center and sometimes there are cool sales.

Parma is also popular for music. You can visit *Il Teatro Reggio* for ballet and music, and in September/October there is the show in memory of Verdi.

The best places in Parma: the river (*la Parma*), the bridges full of flowers, and *la pilotta* if you like old history. *Il Duomo* is an old church and it's so pretty, and nearby is the *battistero* (baptistery), where you can find some handsome art.

If you like green spaces, visit *Il Giardino Botanico* (the botanic gardens) and *Parco Ducale*.

What neighborhoods or parts of town are best to stay in?
I chose to live in the center because I can go to the train station in five minutes and find all the shops I want. In the center, there are some small, old streets called *borghi*; they are not in the principal streets, but close, and they are quieter, but close to the night life.

Let's talk about day trips...what nearby places should everyone make sure to visit?
Parma is just 90 minutes from Milan and 60 minutes from Bologna, so if you want to go to the best events it could be easy for you!

142

EMILIA-ROMAGNA

Tell us about the local dishes. What should people try?
Parmigiano is the best cheese ever! I'm vegetarian, but if you want to taste other typical food from Parma or Emilia Romagna, there is *prosciutto di Parma*, *salame di Felino*, *tortellini* from Bologna, and *la piadina* (thin flatbread) from Romagna.

And if you are curious, since Barilla is from Parma, you can go to see the big blue factory of Barilla. It's like a giant box of pasta.

What are your top three favorite bars and restaurants?
I don't have favorite bars, because I'm more a fan of food than drinks, but you can find a popular bar for young people in *Via D'Azeglio*. On weekend nights this street is closed to cars and there are a lot of people walking in the street. In *Strada Farini* there are also some good bars.

The best pizzeria on earth is called La Pizzeria da Luca; it's close to the train station (at *Viale Fratti 24/bis*) and you can choose so many different kinds of pizza. You MUST try this pizza.

Misterpizza (on *Via Abbeveratoia*) is our second favorite. We also found a good Asian all-you-can-eat restaurant called Mishi Mishi (located at *Viale Antonio Fratti 28*), which is cheap and good!

Is there anything tourists do that locals find rude or strange? What can we do to better fit in with the culture?
In Germany or north Europe, people walk around with a beer. Here, we just drink close to or inside the bar.

What is the best way to meet locals and make friends?
Italian cliché says that we are not shy and since most clichés are true, I guess it's not hard to get to know Italian people in a bar or just walking around. But since we are in the internet era, you can use Couchsurfing.org or Facebook and search for some events.

EMILIA-ROMAGNA

Why should people make sure to visit Parma?
If you love food, classic music, art, old churches, and history, there is everything you like here!

Where can we go to take beautiful photos?
I love taking photos under the bridge, *Ponte di Mezzo*, but if you go to the *Duomo* you can get a good old-style photo (it reminds me of Florence).

Anything else you want us to know?
Parma was a rich city before the economic crisis; now you can (sadly) find some old shops closed. If you want to taste the old Parma, don't buy food in the supermarket; try to patronize an old food shop. They will be kind and you will have the best food ever.

Valentina Sardella
Concert-Lover. Musician. Architect.

First, tell us about you.
I was born in Parma and lived there until I was 19 years old, when I went to university in Florence. In Parma, I liked to go to concerts and have long happy hours with my friends with good food and good wine.

If someone is visiting Parma for the first time, what do you recommend they see or do?
Visit the museums, *Galleria Nazionale*, *Teatro Farnese*, *Teatro Regio*, and the dome—and eat a dish of *tortelli*!

What neighborhoods or parts of town are best to stay in?
For a tourist, it is better stay in the center because all the best things to see are there...or in villages outside the city.

Let's talk about day trips...what nearby places should everyone make sure to visit?

EMILIA-ROMAGNA

The castle of *Torrechiara* is one of the best places to see out of the city; it has an amazing setting and seems to go back in the time. Another amazing place is the village of Fontanellato—home of another amazing castle with a moat. There's also another important museum outside the city, called *Fondazione Magnani Rocca*. They have a permanent exhibition with famous paintings by Goya, De Chirico, Matisse, Monet, Manet, Cezanne, and others.

Tell us about the local dishes. What should people try?

Probably Parma is one of the best places in the world to eat; it is the birthplace of *Parmigiano* cheese, *Parma ham*, prestigious *culatello* (a kind of ham—really delicious!), and *salami Felino*.

One of the typical dishes of Parma is *tortelli* (a kind of ravioli); there are three different kinds: *tortelli* filled with cheese and herbs, *tortelli* filled with potato, or *tortelli* filled with pumpkin. *Tortelli* is a dish for all seasons.

A typical dish for the winter is *cappelletti*: another kind of ravioli filled with meat and *Parmigiano* cheese and served with meat broth.

Finally, a typical dessert is *sbrisolona* cake (which literally means crumble cake), which is made with almonds and hazelnut.

What are your top three favorite bars and restaurants?

Cafè le Bistro, located in the main square of the city, *Piazza Garibaldi*, serves all kinds of traditional dishes like *cappelletti* and *tortelli*, as well as fine cuisine. This is the restaurant with the best location in the city!

Bacco Verde is a tavern located in the center of the city (located at *Strada Felice Cavallotti 33*). They make typical dishes like *tortelli* and entrees with local ham and salami. They have a really good homemade wine and prices are cheap.

Sorelle Picchi (located at *Strada Farini 27*) is the best place to eat Parma ham and other dishes with ham and salami.

EMILIA-ROMAGNA

What is the best way to meet locals and make friends?
Locals like go to the opera, so one of the best places to meet locals is at the bar of the main opera theater—*Teatro Regio*—or, if you want meet young people, a pub crawl in *Via d'Azeglio*. In Parma, *aperitivo* time starts at 7 p.m. and many people go to the bars to drink a glass of wine and eat something.

Why should people make sure to visit Parma?
Parma is a little city, but hides a lot of treasures. It is the hometown of Giuseppe Verdi, the famous opera composer, and is very famous for its culinary specialties. For this reason, it was chosen as the headquarters of the EFSA (European Food Safety Authority).

It is a very musical city, where people love opera, but also jazz and blues. A lot of bars in the center organize live music with local bands. It is definitely one of the many jewels of Italy.

Where can we go to take beautiful photos?
The dome's square and the main park, *Parco Ducale*.

Anything else you want us to know?
Emilia Romagna might just be the best place for food in all Italy. I think that the best cities of this region are Bologna, Ferrara, and then Parma.

Also, the countryside of this region merits a trip; there are a lot of beautiful little villages, like Sabioneta.

Ferrara

This UNESCO World Heritage Site is full of ancient palaces, broad streets, and the non-competitive Buskers music festival.

146

EMILIA-ROMAGNA

Mattia Rimessi
Bicyclist. Musician. Student.

First, tell us about you.

I have lived in Ferrara my whole life (24 years). For the past three years, I have been using my vacations to travel the world by bike with my close friends. We had traveled through Slovenia, Croatia, Serbia, Bosnia, Austria, Germany, Denmark, Sweden, and Norway. The next trip we're planning? India and Nepal. I also really like music. I play trumpet, harmonica, and piano. And I love playing sports as well.

If someone is visiting Ferrara for the first time, what do you recommend they see or do?

First, I would take them to my favorite place to relax: *Piazza Ariostea*. It's a square like an arena with a statue in the middle.

Then I would bring them to a hidden place called Terra Viva (located at *Via dell'Erbe 29*, really close to *Piazza Ariostea*), where there is a sacred vegetable garden; it's a magic place with a restaurant that only uses food that they produce themselves. I particularly love that it's inside the town walls.

Finally, I would take them to the Medieval wall and we'd walk along the top to help with our digestion. Along the way, we would visit one of the most beautiful, interesting jazz clubs in Europe, which is inside a circular medieval tower.

The other well-known parts of the city are the castle and the cathedral.

What neighborhoods or parts of town are best to stay in?

Every part inside the wall is a good place to stay. There are a lot of restaurants and pubs and the most beautiful thing is to lose yourself wandering the city streets. It's a small city, so you won't really get lost.

EMILIA-ROMAGNA

Let's talk about day trips...what nearby places should everyone make sure to visit?
Near the city, you'll find the longest cycle path of Italy, which starts from Bondeno and follows the Po River down to its delta (about 123 kilometers). You can rent a bike and have a great day away from the city and its crowds.

Tell us about the local dishes. What should people try?
In Ferrara, try typical dishes like *cappellacci di zucca* (butternut squash pasta), *pasticcio di maccheroni* (a sweet pastry with béchamel sauce, mushrooms, nutmeg, and truffle), and *salama da sugo* (pork with spices and wine, aged and cooked) with a local wine called *Lambrusco*.

What are your top three favorite bars and restaurants?
Due Gobbi (located at *Adelardi 7*), Brindisi (located at *Via Guglielmo degli Adelardi 11*), and Xi Comandamento (located at *Via Carlo Mayr 57*) are three nice bars near the cathedral.

The three best restaurants are Osteria delle Volte (located at *Via Delle Volte 37/a*), Balebuste (located at *Via della Vittoria 44*), and Pizzeria Orsucci (located at *Via Giuseppe Garibaldi 76*).

What is the best way to meet locals and make friends?
I think that if you are an open-minded person, you won't find it difficult to meet people. The most difficult thing is finding people who speak English.

Why should people make sure to visit Ferrara?
It's an old and unique city.

Where can we go to take beautiful photos?
Under and over the wall.

148

EMILIA-ROMAGNA

Elena Zucchini
Traveler. Native.

First, tell us about you.
I have lived in Ferrara since I started college in 2009. Originally, I'm from Bologna. In my free time, I like going out with my friends, going to concerts, or just chilling out.

If someone is visiting Ferrara for the first time, what do you recommend they see or do?
I recommend that they see *Il Castello Estense e Piazza Castello*, *Palazzo Diamanti*, *Palazzo Schifanoia*, *Il Duomo*, *Piazza Trento-Trieste*, *La Certosa*, *Parco Urbano*, and *Terraviva* (a rural place inside the Medieval city, where people can eat and drink organic products or just take a nice walk). I also recommend a walk on *Le Mura* (the main street).

In the evening, visit *Arci Bolognesi* (a good local concert venue) and the Jazz Club (one of the most famous in Italy: *www.jazzclubferrara.com*).

What neighborhoods or parts of town are best to stay in?
The city center is the best. Hotel Touring and Ostello della Gioventù are good choices.

Let's talk about day trips...what nearby places should everyone make sure to visit?
Comacchio, the lakes of Gambulaga, Bologna, Padova, and Ravenna.

Tell us about the local dishes. What should people try?
Cappellacci di zucca (butternut squash pasta), *salama da sugo* (pork with spices and wine, aged and cooked), *farinata di ceci* (bread made with chickpea flour), *panpepato* (round, sweet cake), *zia ferrarese* (aged pork sausage), *tenerina* (dark chocolate cake), *coppie* (tipical Ferrarese bread), and products made with pumpkin.

EMILIA-ROMAGNA

What are your top three favorite bars and restaurants?
Bars: Due Gobbi (located at *Adelardi 7*) and Brindisi (one of the oldest wine bars in Italy, located at *Via Guglielmo degli Adelardi 11*), Cambusa (located at *Via Carlo Mayr 147*), Xi Comandamento (located at *Via Carlo Mayr 57*), Clandestino (located at *Via Ragno 35*), and Korova (on *Via Croce Bianca*).

Restaurants: Osteria Tri Scalin (located at *Via Darsena 52*), Osteria Balebuste (located at *Via della Vittoria 44*), Ristorante Via Vignatagliata (located at *Via Vignatagliata 61*), La Brasserie (located at *Via Ortigara 24*), and Piadineria Mordicchio (located at *Piazza Sacrati 3*).

What is the best way to meet locals and make friends?
Usually, young people meet in front of the *Duomo* on Wednesdays to drink something in one of the bars in the city center. Also, Couchsurfing.org groups are a good way to meet people.

Why should people make sure to visit Ferrara?
It's a nice small city with the typical Medieval architecture.

Where can we go to take beautiful photos?
Near the castle at dusk.

Anything else you want us to know?
We are very likable and friendly people.

Ravenna

With eight UNESCO World Heritage Sites, a world-class opera, and a top Italian music festival, this pretty little city is an Emilia-Romagna must-see.

EMILIA-ROMAGNA

Francesca Manzoni
Cyclist. Reader. Humanitarian. Hiker. Local.

First, tell us about you.
I was born and lived in Ravenna for 20 years. Then I moved away, but I kept on coming and going. In my free time, I love walking along the sea or in pine forests and villages nearby, cycling, reading, and going to the theater.

If someone is visiting Ravenna for the first time, what do you recommend they see or do?
Basilica di San Vitale and *Mausoleo di Galla Placidia* are a must. Also, I would suggest visiting *Mausoleo degli Ariani* and *Mausoleo Neoniano*. A stroll in the city center is worthwhile.

What neighborhoods or parts of town are best to stay in?
Ravenna city center is really pretty; I think would be lovely to stay in a B&B in the center to have a real taste of the town itself.

Let's talk about day trips...what nearby places should everyone make sure to visit?
On the artistic side, the *Basilica di Sant' Appollinare* in Classe should be visited. I think would be also nice to arrange a trip to *Delta del Po* where is possible to walk, ride a bike, or take a boat trip. I also recommend Cesenatico or Cervia, which are both full of little canals and lovely, narrow roads.

Tell us about the local dishes. What should people try?
In Ravenna, people should try *piadina*; there are two lovely places for it: Ca' de' Ven (located in a beautiful old building at *Via Corrado Ricci 24*) and Piadineria Magnani (a small, family-run place at *Via Romolo Ricci 13*). For those who love cheese, *squacquerone* is a must-taste, while meat-lovers should have *ciccioli*. Another very traditional dish is *cappelletti al ragout* (traditional, local pasta with meat sauce) or, for the vegetarians, *burro e salvia* (local spinach ravioli).

151

EMILIA-ROMAGNA

What are your top three favorite bars and restaurants?

My favorite bars in the area are Caffe' Alighieri (located at *Via Gordini 29*), which has a lovely and friendly atmosphere (the owner sometimes entertains people by playing his guitar), Caffe' Corte Cavour, located in a beautiful square along *Via Cavour* (address: *Via Cavour Camillo Benso 51*), and La Casa del Caffe (located at *Via Gioacchino Rasponi 14*), which is not a bar, but has must-taste, fantastic coffee at the counter.

My favorite restaurants are L'Osteria dei Battibecchi (a little, hidden place near *Teatro Alighieri*, address: *Via della Tesoreria Vecchia 16*), Pizzeria La Mia Patria (located at *Filippo Lanciani 6/B*, near the *Duomo*; the place itself is a bit rough, but the pizza is wonderful and the atmosphere very friendly), and Ristorante /Pizzeria Babaleus (located at *Vicolo Gabbiani 7*).

Is there anything tourists do that locals find rude or strange? What can we do to better fit in with the culture?

Shouting and screaming. Spitting on the road.

What is the best way to meet locals and make friends?

Alighieri Caffe' (located at *Via Gordini 29*) is a nice place where people tend to gather.

Why should people make sure to visit Ravenna?

Ravenna is peculiar. In some aspects, it is similar to other small, narrow-roaded Italian towns, but its Bizantine styles and mosaics give it a unique image.

Where can we go to take beautiful photos?

Just behind the *Basilica di San Vitale*, there is a little square where there are concerts in summertime. From there, you can take beautiful pictures of the church from outside.

Anything else you want us to know?

Generally speaking, Emilia Romagna is a very friendly region, especially in summer, where you can enjoy the beach and get a great welcome during your stay. Moreover, it offers a variety of activities from cultural heritage to sports to natural environment and, last but not least, tasty food!

Modena

Welcome to the home of balsamic vinegar, sports cars, and the second oldest athenaeum in Italy.

Mirco Grandi
Motorbike Enthusiast. Photographer.

First, tell us about you.
I'm 35. I was born in Modena and always lived, studied, and worked here (I'm mechanical engineer). I have lots of interests, but my greatest passion is my motorbike (I ride in winter, too). I'm a photographer (only film cameras!) and a home-brewer, making traditional balsamic vinegar in my attic. I play soccer with friends for a local team.

If someone is visiting Modena for the first time, what do you recommend they see or do?
I recommend the cathedral, the civic tower, and *Piazza Grande* (the major square). They are UNESCO World Heritage Sites.

There are two different Ferrari museums—one in Modena and one in Maranello (20 kilometers south). I really love both.

If you are unconventional tourists, maybe you are interested in *Salse di Nirano*; it is a natural park in the hill area with strange post-volcanic activity (I read somewhere that it's the only place in the world with its particular phenomenon).

What neighborhoods or parts of town are best to stay in?
It depends on your taste. Many people love the historical center because everything's close and it's a pedestrian-only area (aka. not noisy). I'm a countryside man, myself, so I prefer

153

the suburbs, especially in the south because of the views of the hills and mountains.

Let's talk about day trips...what nearby places should everyone make sure to visit?

Bologna is very close and you can reach the coast or mountains. A little bit closer, you'll find the *Via dei Castelli*, a walking path between Modena and Bologna (where you can visit Medieval castles).

You can also visit Nonantola, a little town with a very old abbey (6th century) and a pilgrim path to Rome from the Middle Ages. It was a kind of *Camino de Santiago*.

Tell us about the local dishes. What should people try?

If you visit Modena, you *must* try *tortellini in brodo* (handmade pasta stuffed with meat and cheese and boiled in meat broth); this really represents our culture.

Other suggestions include *zampone* (pork meat boiled inside a pig's leg) and *gnocco* (fried bread to eat with ham, salami, or whatever you want).

I must also suggest that you try the traditional balsamic vinegar, but it's better to have a local guiding you, because it's becoming very hard to find the real balsamic, even in restaurants.

If you have enough time, you can visit the town of Vignola, where there is a bakery called Café-Pasticceria Gollini (located at *Via Giuseppe Garibaldi 1/n*), which makes our traditional cake, the *torta barozzi* (which is a lot like a brownie), following the original recipe from the 17th century.

What are your top three favorite bars and restaurants?

The most famous restaurant is Osteria Francescana (at *Via Stella 22*); its chef, Massimo Bottura [whose interview you can find in the Plan by Interest section of this guide], was voted the best chef in the world in March 2014, so I have to suggest it

EMILIA-ROMAGNA

(but remember it's really expensive, at least by Italian standards).

In addition to that, I prefer the ones preparing the traditional dishes in the authentic way like Enzo (located at *Via Coltellini 17*) and Osteria Carducci (located at *Via Canalino 73*).

My favorite, for sure, would be Trattoria Ermes (located at *Via Ganaceto 89*). It's the real Modena old-style tavern (50 years old and with the original owner). The owner is constantly shouting at the customers (he never speaks Italian, only local dialect, so you will need an help from other customers). You will eat sharing long tables with other people. It's an amazing experience—trust me!

As far as bars go, I love beer, so my favorite is Goblet in *Piazza Pomposa*, where you can find local beers. Caffè dell'Orologio in *Piazza D'Ova* (named best bar in Italy few years ago) and Embassy (*located at Via Bellinzona 1* and best for *aperitivos*) are also very good.

Is there anything tourists do that locals find rude or strange? What can we do to better fit in with the culture?
Be patient and try to speak some of the language. Young people often speak English, but older people usually do not. We find it strange when tourists ask for tea or even cappuccino at lunch.

What is the best way to meet locals and make friends?
From 6 – 8 p.m. you can find many people at bars for *aperitivo*. You can find people everywhere that time, but mostly in *Via Gallucci* or *Piazza Pomposa*.

Why should people make sure to visit Modena?
There is lot of history everywhere (there is also the oldest shop in the world, Salumeria Giusti, located at *Via Farini 75*). You can eat very well and, if you are a car fan, it's your place for sure (not only Ferrari, but also Maserati and Pagani are here).

EMILIA-ROMAGNA

Where can we go to take beautiful photos?

According to your taste, the best places can be *Piazza Grande* (if you walk to the top of the tower, you can take good landscape picture), or perhaps the open market days in the historical center, where you can take journalist-style photos (the most important market days are January 31st, which is Patron's Day, and the first weekend in June, which is when we have the international markets).

Anything else you want us to know?

I really hope you meet a local and get to know our mentality. On the town's coat of arms, it says *avia pervia*, which means "we make possible what is impossible." That's us: maybe a little arrogant, but also stubborn enough to make the impossible possible.

FLORENCE & TUSCANY

Birthplace of the Renaissance and home of some of the world's most well-known wines, it is no wonder Tuscany is one of Italy's most popular destinations.

In this section: Florence / Pisa / Siena / Montepulciano

Florence (Firenze)

Ranking among the prettiest cities in the world, the capitol of Tuscany is famed for its pretty Duomo, its UNESCO-recognized old town, and its high-ranking fashion.

Stefania Saba
Student. Artist. Linguist. Vegan.

First, tell us about you.
I've been living in Florence for five years. I came when I was 18 and I chose the city for its perfect mix of dynamism and tranquility. Florence is, in fact, famous for the historical center, which is very active, but at the same time small, so you have everything at your fingertips.

I am a college student, so I like to spend my free time with college friends in the many "hidden" pubs Florence sets aside. There are many cafes where you can have an *aperitivo* (aperitif), drinking and eating appetizers usually from 6 to 9 p.m. These tend to be more than a snack, but lighter than supper. They are common when you want to meet somebody right after work or school before going home.

On sunny days (which are quite common!), I like to have a walk in one of the many parks in the city, such as *Villa Vogel* or *Fabbricotti*, which is delightful.

157

FLORENCE & TUSCANY

If someone is visiting Florence for the first time, what do you recommend they see or do?

When my friends come here for the first time, I feel obliged to show them first the built-up area in the center. The most famous monuments are all near the station. So, we have a little trip including the visit to the *Duomo*, *Piazza della Repubblica*, *Piazza della Signoria*, and the inevitable, famed *Ponte Vecchio*.

When we get there and admire the wonderful view of the River Arno, I always suggest that we continue in the direction of *Piazzale Michelangelo*, where we have the best scenery in the whole town, beautiful both in the afternoon or, with the soft lights, at night.

You can easily get everywhere by foot, but, if you need to, you can take the bus with a specific daily ticket for tourists. Just ask at the central station.

What neighborhoods or parts of town are best to stay in?

If you are just visiting, I'd suggest finding a place right in the center, so you will not miss the nightlife (the last bus leaves at 1 a.m.).

If you are planning to stay a bit longer, for work or study reasons, the best area is *Campo di Marte – Le Cure*. It is not far from the center, so you can still rely upon your feet (as a traveller I feel always safer when I know I have the option of getting where I need by walking, because of possible delays or transportation strikes or just me running late!), and it is a really calm and safe neighborhood. You have all the facilities and there is no limited traffic zone (which means you're allowed to drive there anytime). You can easily park a car here (which you can't do in the center; it's forbidden).

Rents can be a bit expensive in *Campo di Marte – Le Cure*, so if you need something cheaper you can try *Novoli*. Still a nice neighborhood, with all you need, but a bit farther. Since it's a university area, you can go out there in one of the many

158

student pubs and you won't need to change areas at night, so no bus problems.

Let's talk about day trips...what nearby places should everyone make sure to visit?

I definitely wouldn't miss Fiesole, the countryside town up on the hill. You have the view of Florence, the quiet of the countryside, but on a hill. It is about 20 minutes with the bus n. 7 from *San Marco* Square.

It's not as easy to get there and it's a less usual thing to do, but Tuscany has a lot of natural thermal baths that I highly recommend. Saturnia or Petriolo, situated in the middle of woods, are natural hot baths and both are public and free.

Florence is also directly connected by train with Siena, Pisa, and Livorno. Siena is a must-see and, if you get there, there is a little shuttle that can bring you to San Gimignano, a very striking medieval town with historical streets and little museums. Since both little towns are saturated with tourism, they can be a bit expensive, though.

Pisa is worth a day trip, but no more. It's small and you can see the attractions (Pisa tower) in one morning. Everything is close and you can see it all by walking.

If you are here in summer and feel like seeing the sea between a monument and a nice *gelato*, go to Livorno. I highly recommend it, with its nice, welcoming people and awesome seascapes. (And I am from Sardinia...I know what a good beach should look like!)

Tell us about the local dishes. What should people try?

I am vegan and I am happy to say I can suggest a lot of traditional dishes that don't include meat. Tuscany gastronomy is based on the old, poor recipes of farmers mostly.

I'll start with the appetizers: *crostini* and *bruschette* are very common in every restaurant. Slices of toasted bread covered in tomatoes and basil or just olive oil (but you can find the liver-

159

topped too). It's a simple food that intensifies the flavors of those Mediterranean ingredients.

Ribollita, the legume and bread soup, is a must. They cook it for days, a long preparation time, and it's worth it. I am not a soup lover, but I totally love this one.

Pici is a homemade pasta (which rarely contains eggs) dressed with garlic and tomatoes or fried bread crumbles!

If you are sightseeing and need to eat something to-go, try one of the thousand kinds of *schiacciata*, a typical short bread, stuffed or simple, you chose. A typical one is with grapes!

The *pan di ramerino*, a sweet-salted focaccia with raisins and rosemary, or the *cecina*, an omelet made with chickpea flour, are also wonderful.

And if you have a sweet tooth, try *cantuccini* (biscotti) with *vinsanto* (straw wine) or *castagnaccio* (chestnut flour cake)!

What are your top three favorite bars and restaurants?
It is hard to make a list of only three favorite places, but I'd put the Brac Libreria Cafè (located at *Via dei Vagellai 18*) at first place. It's a nice and cozy restaurant-bar in the center, with an inside garden decorated with wicker sofas, plants, and curtains. They have international breakfast, lunches, drinks, free Wi-Fi, and books for reading while having a coffee.

Second place goes to Nabucco (at *Via XXVII Aprile 28*), a café in the student area (but it's a place for everybody, not just students). Well-groomed and warm-colored, it is the perfect spot for a drink or a snack while visiting the museum area. Also: good prices.

I think I should mention at least one for the nightlife. The Trip per Tre on *Via Borgo Ognissanti*, two steps from the Arno and easy to find, is a hard-rock pub owned by three friendly men. They have a large selection of beers and spirits and the kitchen is open until 11 p.m. with hamburgers (vegan options available), pizzas, and paninis stuffed with typical Tuscan ingredients.

Is there anything tourists do that locals find rude or strange? What can we do to better fit in with the culture?

Not really. The only thing Italians usually complain about is the habit of having a cappuccino while having spaghetti or using ketchup as pasta dressing. I don't really care, but some might!

What is the best way to meet locals and make friends?

Pubs, restaurants, and cafes in the center are popular with everybody. There, people of every age are friendly, used to seeing tourists, and glad to have a chat with them. Or you can always take one of the hundred cooking classes in the city. You'll definitely meet people that way.

Why should people make sure to visit Florence?

As the popular proverb says, *"Firenze la bella, Padova la dotta, Ravenna l'antica, Roma la santa,"* which is "Firenze the beautiful, Padova the smart, Ravenna the ancient, Roma the holy one!"

Florence is stunning. Just come and you'll see!

Anything else you want us to know?

People in Firenze might seem a bit rude, yelling or being sarcastic, but they don't mean anything by it. It's their so-called *umorismo Fiorentino* (Florentine humor). So don't get offended; just follow suit!

M.E. Evans
Humorist. Blogger. Future Book Author. American Expat.

First, tell us about you.

I moved to Florence in the fall of 2009 to do a graduate year in painting. I have no idea why, since I doubled in sociology and English in college. I've lived in Italy ever since. I met my husband only a few months after I arrived. He wasn't the only reason I stayed, but he was definitely a large reason. I write, paint, hang out with my poodle, and make fun of how my husband pronounces "cloves," in my free time.

If someone is visiting Florence for the first time, what do you recommend they see or do?

In my opinion, the best thing a tourist can do is to simply spend a day or two like a local. It tells you a lot more about a culture and place than a building that was constructed hundreds of years before. I studied art and I love it; Florence is amazing, but what makes it different from the rest of the world is the culture.

With that in mind, in Florence, I'd recommend strolling the city and shopping, going to Due Fratellini, located at *Via dei Cimatori 38*, for lunch, grabbing a *gelato*, sitting at the park, going home and changing into night clothes, grabbing an *aperitivo*, and then having dinner at Giuggiolo, located at *Viale Righi 3*.

What neighborhoods or parts of town are best to stay in?

That depends entirely on your age, what you enjoy doing, etc. If you like to go dancing, stay out late, drink, or do touristy things all day, stay in the center near *Santa Croce*. If you want to stay in a calm area surrounded by locals, I'd pick *Campo Di Marte*. It's an eight-minute train ride to the center, but it's what living in Florence looks like for most locals.

Let's talk about day trips...what nearby places should everyone make sure to visit?

The Chianti area is gorgeous, all of it. I'd recommend staying in a little *agriturismo* anywhere in Chianti in both summer and winter.

Tell us about the local dishes. What should people try?

I'm about to get myself killed, but I am not a Florence foodie. The most famous dish is the *bistecca alla Fiorentina* and everyone is always impressed with it, but honestly I'm not huge on typical Florence dishes served in restaurants. I've been spoiled by my friends' mothers.

I like the more modern Florentine cuisine when I eat out, stuff you can find at Giugello or Alle Murate (it's very authentic, but not what people read in tour guides usually). Truly, the best restaurants in Florence tend to offer fusion dishes or a "modern twist" on the traditional dishes. I've yet to eat something at a restaurant that claims to be a typical Florence dish and be blown away. Part of this is because the typical dishes are just not for me: I don't do entrails or liver pate. I'm not a fan of horse or wild boar. I'm probably just weird.

Rather, my favorite thing to do is get a glass of *Chianti* wine and a few different *antipasti* outside somewhere in the summer. The olive oil in Tuscany is amazing. You have to try a bunch of olive oil and some *Chianti*.

What are your top three favorite bars and restaurants?
I love Due Fratellini (*Via dei Cimatori 38*) for lunch; it's where a lot of locals go during the workday. I also love Giuggello (*Viale Righi 3*). They do the *bistecco Fiorentina* (my husband's favorite) very well. And one of my favorite pubs is Finnegins Pub, at *Via San Gallo 123R*.

Is there anything tourists do that locals find rude or strange? What can we do to better fit in with the culture?
There are many things that tourists do that Italians find rude and weird. A simple list would be: wearing flip-flops outside (Italians do not wear these unless they are at the beach), expecting the same things that you'd find in your home country (this is especially a problem with American tourists; Italians don't eat in 30 minutes, for example, so the waiters are not going to be fast to get you in and get you out), and screaming and/or crazy, drunk behavior (Italians start drinking in their teens, so they're pretty good at handling their alcohol. It's considered trashy and disgusting to get screaming loud drunk in public).

What is the best way to meet locals and make friends?

That's not the easiest thing to do. Florentines are famous even among Italians for being very socially closed. However, if you want to meet locals, go where locals go and avoid tourist spots. Go to the *Oltrarno* and hang out at a pub. That's probably your best bet.

Why should people make sure to visit Florence?

Florence is my favorite city in Italy. It's beautiful, it's the perfect size, and it just feels like home somehow. Most of my friends who have visited would say the same. Florence is like a magical city that traps people with a weird form of Stockholm syndrome.

Where can we go to take beautiful photos?

It's Florence. I have pictures of dog crap that look pretty rad.

Anything else you want us to know?

Florence is incredibly dog friendly. You'll see dogs in shops, in restaurants, and out on the street at all hours of the day/night. It's perfect for us and our demonic poodle, but weird people who dislike animals might be bothered. Florence is a very fashionable city, but it's different from Milan or Rome. The style is sort of elegant-bohemian. If you're considering packing all of your pastels for summer, don't and, guys, leave the basketball shorts at home.

Find M.E. at: survivinginitaly.com.

Georgette Jupe
Copywriter. Blogger. Social Media Strategist. American Expat.

First, tell us about you.

Ciao! My name is Georgette. I am a 29-year-old Tuscan Texan, originally from San Antonio, Texas, and now living in Florence, Italy, which has been my home for eight years. It doesn't feel that long, but that's also why I love it here. Time flies when you're having fun (or working a lot).

FLORENCE & TUSCANY

I work as a freelance social media strategist, copywriter, and blogger. It's a lot of work, but I absolutely cherish sharing what I love most about this city and, really, the world.

If someone is visiting Florence for the first time, what do you recommend they see or do?

Get oriented to the city on foot: take an hour or two to walk around the historical center and just immerse yourself in the beauty of your surroundings.

Personally, I get excited about a place by reading about it. There is nothing like the first time you see the famous façade of the *Duomo* cathedral in the center of town and a good book to read before you go is *Brunelleschi's Dome* by Ross King. This landmark is like going home for many of us "locals," as is, of course, visiting the famous squares around town—*Piazza della Repubblica, Piazza della Signoria, Piazza Santa Croce*.

Don't forget to cross the river at the famous *Ponte Vecchio* (old bridge) and come to the more authentic Italian side, the *Oltrarno*, to see the majestic *Palazzo Pitti* and Boboli gardens. Wander around the small streets in the area, stretching from *Palazzo Pitti* to *Piazza Santo Spirito*, to pop your head into tiny artisan shops and pretty cafés. There is so much to see and do in this city, the history is a protagonist in itself.

Another good book recommendation is *The House of Medici: Its Rise and Fall* if you want to get to know the most famous historical family in Florence, The Medici family, which held such an important role in shaping Florence into what it is best known for even today.

Also, sunset at *Piazzale Michelangelo* (or better yet the Church of San Miniato al Monte) is always a good idea!

What neighborhoods or parts of town are best to stay in?

I am pretty biased to the area I currently live in, the *Oltrarno*, or "other side of the river," in the area around *Palazzo Pitti, Piazza Santo Spirito,* and *Borgo San Frediano.* Just a little further away from the chaos by the *Duomo* and surrounding areas (especially during the spring & summer), it's like an oasis, a window into daily Italian life. The opening of small shops, the chatter of locals, artisans working on their crafts, the important *aperitivo* drink taken before dinner...you'll find it all here. It's a great area.

Let's talk about day trips...what nearby places should everyone make sure to visit?

The closest and one of the best is most definitely Fiesole. This hilltop town (about five to seven kilometers from Florence and easily reachable by bus) is home to some impressive Roman ruins and beautiful panoramic views overlooking Florence on a clear day. There are some great hiking paths and markets on some weekends in the main *piazza*. Not to mention the monastery on top of the hill.

Other great day trips include gorgeous Tuscan town, San Gimignano; Florence "rival," Siena; Val d'Orcia Natural Park; and Elba Island if you are here in the summer.

Tell us about the local dishes. What should people try?

Florence is well known for its simple food (which is nothing less than fabulous). The focus here is on fresh, local ingredients used for traditional dishes such as *pappa al pomodoro* (a delicious Tuscan tomato & bread soup), *ribollita* (another hearty soup made with bread and vegetables), Tuscan cured meats & cheeses, the famous *bistecca alla fiorentina* (Tuscan steak and crostini with liver pate or various toppings), and so, so much more.

For the adventurous, I highly recommend indulging in the famous Florentine street food, like *panino di lampredotto* (a round bread roll stuffed with hot *lampredotto* (cow stomach) and topped with salsa verde).

What are your top three favorite bars and restaurants?

Osteria il Buongustai, located at *Via dei Cerchi 15r* (near *Piazza della Signoria*): a tiny hole-in-the-wall lunch spot with three ladies cooking up a Tuscan storm and a cheap daily menu.

FLORENCE & TUSCANY

Osteria Tripperia Il Magazzino in *Piazza della Passera*: for *lampredotto* meatballs that are drool-worthy and more.

Cafe degli Artigiani at *Via dello Sprone 16r* in *Piazza della Passera*: this is my neighborhood go-to bar. Locals and tourists flock here for their morning coffee or, later, a *spritz* or *Prosecco* before dinner. Get a table outside to people-watch on the tiny, gorgeous adjoining street.

Is there anything tourists do that locals find rude or strange? What can we do to better fit in with the culture?
Well, people tend to park ANYWHERE (really, I have seen cars almost vertical for lack of parking space). Also, personal space is less of a norm here and standing patiently in line at a café or busy place isn't going to win you any favors; elbow your way to the front like any seasoned local.

Personally, I would say don't dress like a tourist (aka. bulky tennis shoes, large floppy hats). Wear neutral colors and think business casual. And learn a few basic Italian words, which will help out when you are out and about in the city. Don't try and rush anyone; just sit back relax and (literally) smell the coffee.

What is the best way to meet locals and make friends?
Like any city in the world, it's best to meet people by taking classes or joining a group—like a language exchange.

Why should people make sure to visit Florence?
Well, I can't imagine someone not wanting to visit Florence! It truly is one of the most beautiful cities in the world. Don't believe me? Just read most lists of must-see places and you will see my beloved Firenze on the list. So much important artwork is located in the museums and galleries in Florence. Plus, it has great food, a good location for day trips, walkability—and it's a visual candy land!

Where can we go to take beautiful photos?
Piazzale Michelangelo is probably the most famous vantage point, though I prefer view from Fort Belvedere (which isn't open year-around) and the view from the *Palazzo Vecchio*

tower. Also, there are so many great panoramic views from the terraces on top of hotels, like Hotel Baglioni, Antica Torre di Via Tornabuoni, and even the cafeteria above the Oblate Library, located in *Via dell' Oriuolo* 26. I adore these places and tend to snap away like a tourist any time I go back for a visit.

Anything else you want us to know?

I would say that Florence is always worth a second chance if you find it a bit touristy or chaotic the first time you visit. It's a small city, and hordes of people flood it from spring to the end of summer and then some. So, the best time to visit might be November or December, when the temperature drops and the pretty Christmas lights come out. August is probably the worst time to visit, since many Italians close their stores and head to the seaside to escape the heat of the city center.

I recommend exploring Tuscany in general; this region is really a gem—from thermal springs to historical hilltop towns, you certainly won't be bored!

Find Georgette at: girlinflorence.com.

Melinda Gallo
Blogger. Writer. *Fiorentina d'Adozione.*

First, tell us about you.

I was born and raised in California and moved to Paris to work for a French software company a few months after graduating university. I lived in Paris and Hampton Court (a half hour outside of London) for eight years before moving to Florence.

I have lived in Florence for the last 10 years. I initially moved to Florence for two years in 1997 to learn Italian and find my inspiration to write. Three days into my stay, which was supposed to last only a couple of months, I felt at home and decided to move here permanently.

FLORENCE & TUSCANY

In my free time, I love to bask in my beloved city (which is what I call Florence), soak up its energy, write about it in my blog, and take photos of it. I take great pleasure in experiencing Florence, whether it is visiting a museum or garden or running along the Arno River. As a writer, I am continually being inspired by Florence. Not only is it an aesthetically pleasing city to the eye, but it is also an emotionally gratifying city to the heart and soul.

If someone is visiting Florence for the first time, what do you recommend they see or do?
Put away your maps and schedules and navigate the city by letting Florence guide you. Try to walk down less-frequented streets, enter a museum you've never heard of, sit in a *piazza* to watch passersby, have a drink on a café terrace, and just breathe in the city. Let Florence awaken your senses.

What neighborhoods or parts of town are best to stay in?
To anyone visiting Florence, I would suggest staying in the historical city center. Being in the heart of Florence is a unique experience because you can walk around the city, return to your hotel or B&B to relax, and then go back out to enjoy the city some more. You might not realize how intense Florence can be until you find yourself exhausted after walking around for just a few hours.

Let's talk about day trips...what nearby places should everyone make sure to visit?
In the area just outside Florence, you can visit the winemaking region of Chianti, walk in the natural park of Maremma (*Parco dell'Uccellina*), enjoy many beaches (like Viareggio, Forte dei Marmi, and Castiglione della Pescaia), and stroll in a few other towns like Lucca, Pisa, and Siena.

Tell us about the local dishes. What should people try?
Two of my favorite Florentine dishes are *pappa al pomodoro* (a tomato soup with bread and basil) and *panzanella* (a fresh salad made with bread, onions, tomatoes, and basil). One of the most famous specialties is the *bistecca alla fiorentina*,

which is a large T-bone steak for two. It is grilled and served rare (you are normally not asked how you want it cooked). And don't forget to order one or more *contorni* (side dishes), like *patate arrosto* (roasted potatoes) and *spinaci* (spinach).

One word of advice is to always ask about the specials. Almost always it is a dish whose ingredients are in season. Eating any fruit or veggie in season is enjoying it at its peak. You will definitely notice the difference.

Also, don't be surprised if you take a bite of bread in Florence and find that it's tasteless. Florentine bread (except the *schiacciata* flatbread) does not have salt in it. It's a tradition that dates back to the 12th century. In Florence, bread is used in cooking (like *pappa al pomodoro* and *panzanella*) and is generally only eaten with hearty Florentine dishes (although not pasta).

What are your top three favorite bars and restaurants?
Generally when I go out for a drink, I have an *aperitivo*, which is a pre-dinner drink accompanied by some nibbles. My absolute favorite place is La Terrazza lounge bar (at *Vicolo dell'Oro 6r*), which is the rooftop bar at the top of the Continentale Hotel. If you do end up going to for an *aperitivo* (around 7 p.m.), you will be in one of the best places to admire the sunset.

If La Terrazza is full, go across the street to the Fusion Bar and Restaurant for a wonderful drink and great atmosphere.

Another bar I enjoy is SE•STO on Arno (at *Piazza Ognissanti 3*). It offers some of the most spectacular and unique views of Florence and is situated just above the Arno River.

I have a long list of favorite restaurants in Florence, but for classical Tuscan food, I love Osteria di Giovanni (at *Via del Moro 22*) and Buca dell'Orafo (at *Via dei Girolami 28/r*). Both restaurants serve seasonal Tuscan cuisine and have a great collection of wines to accompany your meal. I take everyone who comes to visit me in Florence to at least one of these restaurants.

For something out of the ordinary, I'd go to Trattoria Cibrèo (at *Via del Verrocchio 8r*). They don't do reservations, so arrive when it opens. In a small room with just a few wooden tables, you'll delight in tasty Tuscan dishes that you won't find anywhere else.

Is there anything tourists do that locals find rude or strange? What can we do to better fit in with the culture?

Generally, the Florentines are quite tolerant of tourists. Most Florentines, however, do find it rude when tourists are loud and/or drunk in public.

One thing that I believe would help with fitting in is to say *buongiorno* and *arrivederci* upon entering and leaving a store, especially if the salesperson says it to you first.

What is the best way to meet locals and make friends?

In Florence, the best way to meet locals is to be kind and sincere with people you meet. If you go to the same bar, café, restaurant, or shop more than once and the same person helps you, he/she will most likely recognize you and quite possibly will strike a conversation with you.

Speaking Italian is a huge benefit to anyone visiting Italy. The Florentines are pleased if you speak their language, because they know that Italian is a language you learn more for the love of it than for its usefulness. Even if you mess up, they'll appreciate that you gave it a try.

Why should people make sure to visit Florence?

Florence is a work of art. Even if you don't want to visit the important museums, you can navigate the city and get a feel for the Renaissance by admiring its buildings, *piazze*, and churches, as well as the Arno River and the lush gardens around the city.

FLORENCE & TUSCANY

If you don't come to Florence for its museums, come just to be inspired. Florence is a city that wakes you up to yourself. You might not become an artist or writer after visiting Florence, but you will certainly be encouraged to follow your heart and do whatever brings you joy.

Where can we go to take beautiful photos?

I'd first suggest *Piazzale Michelangelo*, which allows you to enjoy a spectacular panorama of Florence. You can capture many of the city's monuments and churches as well as the Arno River in one photo. In the summer, you can sit on the steps of the *piazzale* and watch the sunset, which lights up the sky with deep reds and purples.

Another favorite place for me to take photos is along the Arno River and from the *ponti* (bridges) that cross over it. When the water is calm, the reflections and colors of the city and sky are breathtaking.

Anything else you want us to know?

While people know Florence mostly for its art, some might not know how great of an impact the city has had on our modern society. I was surprised to find out that opera started in Florence and that many inventions we use today, like the thermometer, also come from Florence. Two interesting museums you can visit to see some of the discoveries made in Florence are the Museo di Leonardo da Vinci and the Museo Galileo.

Find Melinda at: www.melindagallo.com/blog/.

Mariangela
B&B Owner & Chef. Traveler. Southern Italian.

First, tell us about you.
I moved from the south of Italy (Matera) when I was 12 years old. Now, I live in Florence, running my B&B and offering cooking lessons. For fun, I travel.

If someone is visiting Florence for the first time, what do you recommend they see or do?
Take a walk to *Piazzale Michelangelo* for an amazing view and then another walk in the evening along the river Arno. Go to the Accademia Museum to see the original David and the slaves by Michelangelo. Visit the paintings at Uffizi Gallery. And don't miss a visit to the local open food market of *Sant'Ambrogio* or a cooking lesson with me!

What neighborhoods or parts of town are best to stay in?
I love *Santa Croce* area because it is in the heart of Florence, but it is still genuine.

Tell us about the local dishes. What should people try?
Panino con il lampredotto (a Florentine sandwich made with cow stomach and salsa verde that you can buy on the streets), *crostini Toscani* with chicken liver pate, *ribollita* (a thick vegetable soup made with bread), *panzanella* (a bread salad), *pollo fritto con verdure fritte* (fried chicken with veggies), and *la bistecca alla Fiorentina con i fagioli all'olio nuovo* (Tuscan steak with white beans).

What are your top three favorite bars and restaurants?
Caffé Rivoire (at *Via Vaccherreccia 4r*) is very elegant, though expensive if you sit and eat. Restaurant Il Fagioli (located at *Corso dei Tintori 47r*) is simple, but genuine. Gelato Vivoli (located at *Via dell'Isola delle Stinche 7r*) is the best in the world.

Is there anything tourists do that locals find rude or strange? What can we do to better fit in with the culture?
Don't drink a cappuccino after a meal. It is a morning drink.

What is the best way to meet locals and make friends?

FLORENCE & TUSCANY

It is not easy because there are many tourists here in Florence. But if you travel from November to March, it is easier.

Where can we go to take beautiful photos?
If it is open, *Forte Belvedere* or *Piazzale Michelangelo*.

Find Mariangela at: lestanzedisantacroce.com.

Pisa

After you hold up the leaning tower, stroll along the waterfront walkways and visit the gothic church.

Davide Diolaiti
Tourism Expert. Linguist. Citizen of the World.

First, tell us about you.
My name is Davide and I'm 28. I was born and grew up in Pisa. My father is from Pisa and my mother is from a small town halfway between Pisa and Florence.

During my free time, I like to play sports, read, and listen to music. In summer, my passion is going to the sea. And, when I have the opportunity, I love travelling.

I don't watch TV; Italian television is rubbish.

If someone is visiting Pisa for the first time, what do you recommend they see or do?
Pisa is principally known for the leaning tower and the whole *Piazza dei Miracoli*, but that's a limitation. Pisa is a city with a great history. In fact, the city was founded before the Roman Empire and was re-invented century by century.

FLORENCE & TUSCANY

You can see all the places that made the history of the city: *Piazza dei Cavalieri*, where the *Scuola Normale Superiore*, a school founded by Napoleonic decree in 1810 is located; *Borgo Largo* and *Borgo Stretto*, our busiest, most charming streets; the San Jacopo Cemetery; the *Torre Guelfa*, a 15th century tower with a beautiful view from the top; and an authentic jewel like *Chiesa Della Spina*, the only gothic church in Pisa.

I also recommend the beautiful views from the *lungarni* (walkways along the Arno River).

What neighborhoods or parts of town are best to stay in?
Pisa is quite a safe city; there's not much crime and you can move through the streets on foot or riding a bike.

The only place to avoid, especially during evenings, is *Piazza delle Vettovaglie*.

Let's talk about day trips...what nearby places should everyone make sure to visit?
Pisa's surroundings are very nice! First of all, you have to go to Calci, a beautiful town really close to the city. Calci is famous for the good quality of its oil and vegetables. In Calci, you must visit the *Certosa*—an ancient monastery that houses the Natural History Museum of the University of Pisa, which includes paleontological, mineralogical, and zoological collections.

After Calci, another beautiful town is San Miniato. The lower part of the town is totally historical.

Another important trip is to Lucca. Lucca is a medieval city in the north of Pisa and its historical center is totally surrounded by walls!

Tell us about the local dishes. What should people try?
There are lots of first course soup dishes during the winter months, which are always accompanied by slices of stale bread. These include really tasty bean (or *fatto*) soup, *pappa*

al pomodoro (or Pisan-style cabbage soup), and lots of fish soups.

Another typical dish is *panzanella*, a poor man's dish based on stale bread, tomatoes, and onion. A pasta dish worth a mention is *pappardelle* with duck or hare sauce. *Pallette*, little balls of polenta in meat sauce, are also really tasty.

Pisan cuisine incorporates many types of meat. You can taste typical Pisan beef, wild boar with olives, lamb fricassee, rabbit, and lots of game, including hare, pheasant, deer, and wild boar, prepared in various ways. Obviously, fish is also very much present; there is a lot of dried cod, which you can eat fried or in a sweet and sour sauce.

What are your top three favorite bars and restaurants?
You must go to Pizzeria da Pancino, located at *Via Benedetto Croce 59*, where you can eat the best pizza in the whole city! It's a funny and friendly place with cheaper prices.

If you want to eat some typical food from Pisa and its surroundings, I recommend Osteria del Tinti, located at *Vicolo del Tinti 26*—a really relaxing place.

If you want to pass a nice evening with your friends, the best place is The Wall Pub, close to the leaning tower (at *Via Cardinale Maffi 26*) and rich with events of various kinds.

Is there anything tourists do that locals find rude or strange? What can we do to better fit in with the culture?
The majority of the Italians have a great defect: they think that Italy is the best country in the world for food, art, and clothes. The rest is often seen as something ridiculous compared to the things we are used to in Italy. Anyway, the socks with sandals fashion trend is really strange to us.

I think foreign people must be remain the same and don't change. In my opinion, it's important for the Italians to accept diversity.

FLORENCE & TUSCANY

What is the best way to meet locals and make friends?

This is really a good question! This situation is object of discussion by locals and people who're not from Pisa. People from everywhere often say that local people are closed. Local people are say that foreigners don't want to mix to local population. I think the truth is in the middle. It's not a simple answer, sincerely.

Why should people make sure to visit Pisa?

Piazza dei Miracoli and the *lungarni* are unique in the world!

Where can we go to take beautiful photos?

The most known place of the city: *Piazza dei Miracoli*! Many people like to take a picture of themselves next to the leaning tower. In my opinion, though, pictures of the *lungarni* from different points of view, especially from bridges, are fantastic too.

Anything else you want us to know?

Yes, I want to invite everyone to visit Tuscany. Art, history, culture, and food are the perfect mix for an unforgettable holiday!

Cortona

Right on the Tuscany-Umbria border, this city is best known as the setting for the book-turned-movie, Under the Tuscan Sun.

Tania Von Barkenhagen
Wine Blogger. Holiday Rental Owner. Olive Oil & Balsamic Vinegar Maker.

First, tell us about you.

I grew up in Washington State, but lived in southern California since 1986. In March 2005, I moved to Cortona.

FLORENCE & TUSCANY

In my free time, I like to go for walks in the countryside with my husband and dogs, enjoy a nice glass of wine, discover new restaurants and upcoming chefs, photograph the stunning Val di Chiana countryside, and catch up on my American TV shows!

For work, my husband and I have an olive oil & balsamic vinegar business. (In fact, we just won our third gold medal for our 2013 Tuscany Olive Oil!) I am a wine blogger and do some social media for the local wine industry. We also have a rental apartment in our farmhouse that I manage.

If someone is visiting Cortona for the first time, what do you recommend they see or do?
Park your car outside the walls and, like a true Italian, take a *passeggiata* (stroll) through the city, giving yourself time to take everything in. Start off on our one level street in town, *Via Nazionale*, where you will find many of the shops and eventually see our beautiful town hall in *Piazza Repubblica*. Then, find one of the many little *vicolos* (alleys) leading up and lose yourself in the tiny streets. Since Cortona is small, you can't get too lost, and there are some really beautiful buildings in many of the little streets.

What neighborhoods or parts of town are best to stay in?
It is a small town that you can easily walk through in 10 minutes. There are many nice accommodations in the area. Staying in town is fun and you can walk to everything, although you need to park your car outside the city walls and walk in. Staying nearby in the countryside is absolutely beautiful and you can easily drive up to Cortona, park outside, and walk in.

Let's talk about day trips...what nearby places should everyone make sure to visit?
Le Celle, a tiny little monastery just outside of Cortona where St. Francis stayed in a cell for two months not long before he died, is a special place, set into the hillside and open for visits.

178

Also, go up to the Santa Margherita church above Cortona where our patron saint is laid in the altar.

The *Medici Fortezza*, which is above the church on the highest point of the hill Cortona sits on, has amazing views of all the Val di Chiana and Lago Trasimeno. Lago Trasimeno is also worth driving around, visiting some of the little towns on the edge of the lake, as well as taking the ferry from Tuoro to Isola Maggiore for a day trip or lunch.

Tell us about the local dishes. What should people try?

Depending on the season, wild boar is quite common and worth trying. Also, *pici al fumo*, which is a very large spaghetti noodle in a creamy, smoky tomato sauce that is rich and savory.

What are your top three favorite bars and restaurants?

All our restaurants are pretty amazing, but my top picks are Osteria del Teatro (located at *Via Giuseppe Maffei 2*), Pozzo Antico (located at *Via Ghini 12*), and Locanda nel Loggiato (located at *Piazza di Pescheria*).

For bars, I like Caccio Brillo (located at *Piazza Luca Signorelli 6*), Tuscher (at *Via Nazionale 43*), and La Saletta (at *Via Nazionale 26*).

Is there anything tourists do that locals find rude or strange? What can we do to better fit in with the culture?

Walking in a store without saying hello. Here all the locals expect to say good morning or afternoon and acknowledge you when you walk in; they find it strange when people just ignore them and look around the store and then leave without saying anything.

Also, look people in the eye and smile and try to speak even just one word of Italian. They really appreciate that!

What is the best way to meet locals and make friends?

Don't be shy, smile and say hello, and ask questions. When they find out you are truly interested, they will be happy to talk to you!

Why should people make sure to visit Cortona?
It is one of the most beautiful little Medieval hilltop towns with nice shops, great restaurants, and amazing, award-winning local wine (try some of the Cortona *Syrah*!).

Where can we go to take beautiful photos?
From down below in the valley or up above near Santa Margherita Church, looking down. Also, *Piazza Garibaldi* has great views of the valley.

Anything else you want us to know?
There is a free wine tasting every Thursday night from May to October in *Piazza Repubblica* in front of the Molesini Wine Shop, who I do social media for. Come by and say hello and think about joining up for the dinner that follows!

Find Tania at: www.tuscanwinenotes.com, www.larte.us, and www.casabelposto.com.

Claudia Toppani
B&B Owner. Native Roman. People-Person.

First, tell us about you.
I'm originally from Rome. I lived in NYC for seven years. And, after so many years of city life, I finally decided to change my life and move in the countryside, which is how I ended up here in Cortona.

I have a B&B, called Il Sole del Sodo, in Cortona. I like animals, long walks, traveling as often as possible, and meeting people from all over the world (which makes my job incredibly fun for me).

FLORENCE & TUSCANY

If someone is visiting Cortona for the first time, what do you recommend they see or do?

The must-sees are *Eremo delle Celle* (the Franciscan monastery), *Fortezza del Girifalco* (an ancient fortress), and the small streets around the town center (which are perfect for a stroll).

What neighborhoods or parts of town are best to stay in?

It is nice to be in the center of Cortona, but also outside the city because the countryside is so tranquil and enjoyable.

Let's talk about day trips...what nearby places should everyone make sure to visit?

Within a one-hour drive you can go to Siena, Montepulciano, Montalcino, Pienza, San Quirico, Perugia, Arezzo, Lago Trasimeno, Anghiari, Firenze, and San Casciano—all worth seeing.

Tell us about the local dishes. What should people try?

The *chianina* steak is a special local meat. The homemade pasta is delicious and sauce, like *ragu* (meat sauce) and *fumo* (rosemary and garlic cream sauce), are the best in Italy.

What are your top three favorite bars and restaurants?

Restaurants: Osteria del Teatro (located at *Via Giuseppe Maffei 2*), La Grotta (at *Piazza Baldelli 3*), and Trattoria Dardano (at *Via Dardano 24*).

Bars: Enoteca Enotria (located at *Via Nazionale 81*), Bottega Baracchi (located at *Via Nazionale 78*), and Cacio Brillo (at *Piazza Signorelli 6*).

What is the best way to meet locals and make friends?

Just go to the two main *piazzas* and you will make friends soon, especially if you are a woman.

Why should people make sure to visit Cortona?

Cortona is the grandmother of Rome, an old town full of history, and it gives a unique feeling to all visitors.

181

Where can we go to take beautiful photos?
From the very top of the town.

Anything else you want us to know?
Be prepared to walk on steep roads, to make new friends, and to fall in love with the town and keep coming back here.

Find Claudia at: ilsoledelsodo.com.

Siena

One of Italy's most visited tourist attractions, a UNESCO World Heritage Site, and the site of the world-famous horse race.

Giorgio Sperandio
Student. Musician. Juggler. Bicyclist.

First, tell us about you.
I am a student in Environmental Sciences, originally from Le Marche. I decided to move to Siena to continue my studies here about a year and a half ago. In my free time, I like playing percussion, listening to music from different cultures, juggling, cycling, and visiting natural parks.

If someone is visiting Siena for the first time, what do you recommend they see or do?
Siena is a really nice city. The first thing to see, of course, is *Piazza del Campo*, the main square. The first time you will be shocked. Other nice places include the *Fortezza Medicea* (a fortress near the center), the Dome, and the *Torre del Mangia* (the big tower in *Piazza del Campo*). In every corner, you can also find churches and Medieval architecture. And in July and August, there is the *Palio di Siena*—the famous horse race.

What neighborhoods or parts of town are best to stay in?

FLORENCE & TUSCANY

In the center, you'll probably pay a lot of rent, but it's the best place to stay. And if you stay inside the ancient walls, it's easy to explore the whole city on foot.

Tell us about the local dishes. What should people try?
Siena has a lot of sweets: *cavallucci* (a Christmas pastry with almonds and candied fruit), *panforte* (the Italian version of fruitcake), and *ricciarelli* (almond cookies) are all really good. Also *pici caio e pepe* (pasta with cheese and pepper).

What are your top three favorite bars and restaurants?
The bar L'incontro (located at *Strada di Sant'Abondio 56*) is the cheapest and it's where all the students hang out. The owners are kind and you will find a lot of nice and interesting people.

La Corte dei Miracoli (located at *Via Roma 56*) is a place that organizes a lot of electronic music at night and features cultural shows (photos, drawings, paintings) and activities (yoga, dance, and other kinds of classes that are open to everyone—student or otherwise) on the weekends.

Another place to see is the Bella Vista Social Pub (located at *Via San Martino 31*). Inside, you'll find a lot of strange interior design and good, danceable music.

Is there anything tourists do that locals find rude or strange? What can we do to better fit in with the culture?
The only thing that people who live in Siena care about is the city quarter (or *contrade*). They get really angry if you say something bad about their *contrada*—even to the point of blows sometimes. It is normal see brawls (more in the summer) about this kind of stuff.

What is the best way to meet locals and make friends?
In *Piazza del Campo* in the summer, you can find a lot of nice, crazy people doing everything from running crazy around the square to singing together to playing music. You can pass the whole night there in the square.

FLORENCE & TUSCANY

Why should people make sure to visit Siena?
History. Relaxation. Good food.

Where can we go to take beautiful photos?
Piazza del Campo and *Orto dei Tolomei*—a little garden, busy and beautiful in spring and summer.

Montepulciano

This Medieval hill town is known for its Chianina beef, wine, and pici pasta.

Pamela Sheldon Johns
Author. Agriturismo/Cooking School Owner.

First, tell us about you.
I am originally from California, where I catered, cooked, and ran cooking schools for a number of years. I commuted between the US and Italy, teaching workshops and writing cookbooks from 1992 until, in 2001, my family moved to our farm in Montepulciano, Poggio Etrusco. Luckily the things I do for work are also what I do for fun: gardening/farming, cooking, and hospitality.

If someone is visiting Montepulciano for the first time, what do you recommend they see or do?
Just walking along the main road, there is a lot to take in, such as noble *palazzi* with Renaissance architecture and even one with Etruscan urns built into the wall. Don't miss the many little alleys and *piazzas* in Montepulciano, all worth exploring. There are great little food shops specializing in local products, *cantinas* to visit and taste the *Vino Nobile* of Montepulciano, and some amazing artisans (copper, mosaic, painting). The churches are also plentiful and *San Biagio*, at the bottom of the town, designed by architect Sangallo the Elder, is worth the walk to see.

184

FLORENCE & TUSCANY

What neighborhoods or parts of town are best to stay in?
Some people like to stay in the town and some like to be just outside in the countryside. Inside the town, any area is pleasant. Outside, there are *agriturismos* of all levels ready to accommodate you.

Let's talk about day trips...what nearby places should everyone make sure to visit?
Montepulciano is the perfect hub to see many great hill towns, artisans, and cultural/historic places. Within a one-hour drive, you can visit Pienza, Montalcino, Siena, Cortona, and lots of tiny villages. Florence is only 1.5 hours away, as are Assisi and some of the Umbrian villages.

Tell us about the local dishes. What should people try?
This part of southern Tuscany has deep roots in *cucina povera*, the simple rustic cooking that dates back to harder times. Today's dishes are richer, because we have more abundance, but are still much appreciated. Here are a few you should try:

Pici, the fresh hand-rolled pasta served with a spicy tomato garlic sauce called *aglione*; *ribollita*, a seasonal vegetable soup layered with bread; *tagliata*, sliced grilled beef (usually from the *chianina* breed); and *panzanella*, a summer bread salad with tomatoes, cucumber, and onion.

In the fall, game is prevalent and you won't want to miss *cinghiale* (wild boar) and fabulous fresh *porcini* mushrooms.

What are your top three favorite bars and restaurants?
La Porta in Monticchiello (located at *Via del Piano 1*), La Grotta in Montepulciano (at *Via San Biagio 15*), and Latte di Luna in Pienza (at *Via San Carlo 2*).

Is there anything tourists do that locals find rude or strange? What can we do to better fit in with the culture?
By now, the Italians are used to the cultural differences of tourists. It is always respectful to learn a few words in Italian, especially *grazie* (thank you).

FLORENCE & TUSCANY

What is the best way to meet locals and make friends?

There are a couple of fun bars. One is the Caffe Poliziano (located at *Via Voltaia Nel Corso 27*), a beautiful place to have a glass of wine and meet some people. Others have live music and *aperitivi* to offer...the best thing is to check with the tourist office when you arrive to see what is going on.

Why should people make sure to visit Montepulciano?

Montepulciano is considered a pearl of the Renaissance and is very well-known for wine. The DOCG wine is *Vino Nobile di Montepulciano* and is made from a *Sangiovese* clone called *Prugnolo Gentile*. It is heavenly with the local *pecorino* (cheese made with sheep's milk) and the typical dishes of the area.

Where can we go to take beautiful photos?

There are photo ops in every direction! This is the classic Tuscan landscape of farmhouses, olive groves, vineyards, and cypress trees. One special place that you might like to visit is the estate of *La Foce* (which is only open to the public on Wednesday afternoons), just outside of the nearby town of Chianciano Terme. From the garden terrace, you can see the classic cypress-lined road that shows up on so many postcards and calendars.

Anything else you want us to know?

The area is also known for its thermal waters and there are a number of spas around. Some of my favorites are in Bagno Vignoni and Chianciano Terme. Again, the tourist office will be of great help organizing a spa day if you want one.

Find Pamela at: www.foodartisans.com and www.poggio-etrusco.com.

PERUGIA & UMBRIA

Tuscany's lesser-known neighbor is also a mecca of hilltop towns, sprawling vineyards, and rich wines.

In this section: Perugia / Palazzo d'Assisi / Orvieto / Paciano

Perugia

A hilly university town central to the Umbrian countryside, known for its chocolates.

Sara Necoechea & Angelo Panciarola
A Translator and an Architect. Travelers. Airbnb Hosts.

First, tell us about you.
Sara: I am from Mexico City. I love to travel, live in other countries, and learn new languages. I studied communications in Mexico City and did my social services and thesis in Chiapas working with indigenous women. From there, I fell in love with anthropology and came to do my master's degree in Cultural Anthropology here in Perugia.

I chose to come to Italy five years ago because my grandmother is Italian and always told me tales about this land. I met my neighbor, Angelo, and ended up staying here.

Nowadays, I work doing translations from Italian and English to Spanish. I love meeting people from all over the world and Perugia is perfect because it's a very cosmopolitan town.

Angelo: I was born in Perugia and grew up in a little town called Montepetriolo (25 kilometers from Perugia). I studied

PERUGIA & UMBRIA

architecture in Rome and Florence and then came back to
Perugia, where I've been living for the last 10 years.
Since I was born in a bricklayer-builders family that lived in the
countryside, I grew up loving nature and cultivating olive trees,
making wine, taking care of the vegetable garden and
orchard, and having the passion for creating beautiful places
inspired by nature. That's why I bought and restructured my
house, which I now rent out on Airbnb.

Together, we like to relax, watch films, walk around beautiful
landscapes, discover new little streets that we have never
walked before, listen to music, cook with a glass of wine, and,
of course, be with our friends. A lot of activities in Italy are
related to good food and wine, and we love taking part in
them. When possible, we love going to admire the sea.

If someone is visiting Perugia for the first time, what do you recommend they see or do?

Walk around the city to discover its many hidden secrets. Visit
the panoramic views, the Etruscan places, the Medieval
doors...we particularly like our neighborhood, *Porta
Sant'Angelo*, as well as il *Tempio Sant' Michele Arcangelo*,
Borgo XX Giugno, and the center (of course).

We recommend the little cinemas inside the city for wintertime
and the open-air ones during the summer.

Eat chocolate and have an ice cream at the little store at *Via
Pinturicchio* called Perugina (the chocolatier that created the
famous baci). And try Umbrian wine (one of the bests is
Sagrantino di Montefalco).

What neighborhoods or parts of town are best to stay in?

Corso Garibaldi and *Borgo XX Giugno* are the best two
neighborhoods in town. You can find things to visit and locals
to talk to, especially if you go around visiting the old workshops
(*botteghe*).

PERUGIA & UMBRIA

Let's talk about day trips...what nearby places should everyone make sure to visit?

We love Assisi, Orvieto, Gubbio, Lago Trasimeno, Spello, Trevi, and Montone. If possible, rent a car and drive into little places. Umbria is full of tiny beautiful towns that don't even appear on maps.

Tell us about the local dishes. What should people try?

The best pasta is homemade *tagliatelle, pappardelle,* or *umbricelli* with *ragù* or *cinghiale* (boar) or *lepre* (hare). Also, *lasagne, cannelloni,* and *tortellini.*

A must-try is white *tartufo* (the king of mushrooms, less strong but with a very special aroma) or black (more common, but delicious). If you ever have the chance, try *gnocchi* with pumpkin and *tartufo* or *norcina* pasta.

Another great dish is the very typical *torta al testo,* a dough crust filled with various ingredients. *Torta al testo* was created by farmers when there was no bread. Also, fun fact: bread in Umbria doesn't have salt, because the taxes on salt are too high.

Also, make sure to do the *scarpetta* (bread used to wipe up the last of the pasta sauce on your plate...the Italian way is to never waste one bit!).

A few last things you should try: *lenticchie di colfiorito* (lentil soup), cheeses (fresh *ricotta* and *pecorino*), *tozzetti* with *vin santo* (dessert cookies and wine).

What are your top three favorite bars and restaurants?

Restaurants in Perugia: Brizi, located at *Via Ariodante Fabretti 75,* (I've never seen such good deals), Civico 25, located at *Via Viola 25,* and Locanda dell'Arco (at *Via Ulisse Rocchi 36*).

In Assisi, try Gli Eremi, located at *Via Eremo delle Carceri 32.* In Città della Pieve, try Serenella, located at *Via Fiorenzuola 28.* And at Lago Trasimeno, try Faliero, known as "La Maria" and located at *Via Case Sparse.*

Our favorite bars in Perugia are Enoteca Il Tempio (at *Z. Faina 50*), Giardino Rosso Vino (a must in summer, at *Corso Garibaldi 21*), and Caffè Morlacchi (at *Piazza Morlacchi 6/8*).

Is there anything tourists do that locals find rude or strange? What can we do to better fit in with the culture?

Cappuccino is only for breakfast and with sweet stuff. Don't mix your food (pasta and salad should not be on the same plate at the same time, especially if that mixes flavors).

What is the best way to meet locals and make friends?

Going to a bar, the little workshops, or the markets.

Why should people make sure to visit Perugia?

It's a museum city. The landscape is gorgeous inside and outside the city. The food is great. Perugia is the capital city of Umbria, so you have artistic, industrial, cultural, musical, and gastronomic activities year-round. For example, Umbria Jazz in the summer. Also, it's not crowded, so you can have a comfortable visit and get to know locals.

Where can we go to take beautiful photos?

It's a place rich with culture, quality of life, and food. Even inside the city you will find olive groves; it's very common that people cultivate their own vegetables and produce olive oil or wine, so the quality is very high and not necessarily expensive.

Find Sara and Angelo at:
www.airbnb.com/users/show/3795394.

Palazzo D'Assisi

14th-century castles and a world-famous monastery are just the beginning in this Assisi-adjacent town.

190

PERUGIA & UMBRIA

Gian Domenico Trojano
Photographer. Part-Time Chef. Music Festival Enthusiast.

First, tell us about you.
I moved to Palazzo d'Assisi about two years ago for work, but my mom has lived here for 10 years, so I was already familiar with the area.

I was born in Perugia and lived in a really small village called Mercatello near Marsciano, another big city in Umbria.

In my free time, I love to discover new places in my region. I also love to go and recharge in places like Monte Subasio, Lago Trasimeno, Bosco di San Francesco, and Cibottola with my dog and my reflex camera. If I want to see people, I go in Perugia, where I have friends who manage bars and restaurants.

In the summer, I go to see traditional historic festivals like Quintana in Foligno, Infiorata in Spello, Calendimaggio in Assisi, Gaite in Bevagna, Festival of Colors in Spoleto, Todi International Hot Air Balloon Grand Prix, Corsa dei Ceri in Gubbio, and Palio dei Terzieri in Citta della Pieve, and music festivals like Umbria Jazz in Perugia, Trasimeno Blues at Trasimeno Lake, Music for Sunset in Isola Maggiore, and Dancity in Foligno.

Sometimes I go free climbing in Pale with a friend.

If someone is visiting Palazzo D'Assisi for the first time, what do you recommend they see or do?
Visit Assisi, Santa Maria degli Angeli, Bevagna, Montefalco, and the countryside. If you like the history, make sure to see *Basilica di San Francesco*, where you can see some frescoes of the best 1300 A.D. artists like Cimabue, Giotto, Martini, and Lorenzetti. Under *Piazza del Comune*, there's the roman forum.

PERUGIA & UMBRIA

Rocca Maggiore has a fantastic view of the valley, Eremo delle Carceri gorge, *Duomo di San Rufino*, and *Basilica di Santa Chiara*.

If you like extreme sports, you can do paragliding on Monte Subasio, rafting on the Nera River, and free climbing in Pale.

If you like to walk, there is a lot of trekking around (or you can rent a horse). The only thing you won't find in Umbria is the sea.

What neighborhoods or parts of town are best to stay in?
There isn't bad place to stay.

Let's talk about day trips...what nearby places should everyone make sure to visit?
The places to visit absolutely are Assisi, Monte Subasio, Bevagna, Spello, Foligno, Montefalco, Torgiano, Perugia, and Corciano.

Tell us about the local dishes. What should people try?
The food that definitely represents Umbria is the *torta al testo*, a typical pizza-bread made with flour, milk, yeast, lard, and olive oil and cooked on fire with *testo*, a typical cast iron skillet. You can fill it with sausage, cheese, ham, etc.

Other products to try include Giano dell'Umbria's black truffle, Norcia's cold cuts, Colfiorito's lentils, Trasimeno Lake's *fagiolina* (a legume that is produced just around Trasimeno Lake), Cannara's onion, Colfiorito's red potatoes, Civita di Cascia's *roveja* (wild pea), and Trevi's black celery. Together with Tuscany, we also produce the best extra virgin olive oil in Italy. Most of these products are under the supervision of the Slow Food Association.

Baci Perugina (small chocolates with hazelnut in the center) are very typical and world-renowned.

PERUGIA & UMBRIA

There isn't a typical drink, but you can find some really good wine like *Sagrantino di Montefalco* (an autochthonous vine that you can find only in Montefalco) or some artisanal beer.

What are your top three favorite bars and restaurants?
Magnavino in Bastia at *Via Isola Romana 3* has really good wine and food.

If you want a great sensory experience, you need to go in Nun Relais Spa-Museum Restaurant in Assisi (address: *Via Eremo delle Carceri 1*); you will eat the best products from Umbria with a modern presentation.

If you want a really good pizza, go to Taverna del Maniscalco at *Viale Michelangelo 69* in Palazzo d' Assisi.

In Perugia, my favorite places are Frittole, at *Via Alessi 30*, for really typical cheeses and cold cuts and Civico 25, a fantastic small restaurant with easy dishes and high quality products located at *Via della Viola 25*

Finally, Osteria Stella, located at *Via Narcisi 47A* in Casaglia (five minutes from Perugia) is amazing for both food and wine.

Is there anything tourists do that locals find rude or strange? What can we do to better fit in with the culture?
It's strange to drink cappuccino during a meal and put ketchup and potato chips on pizza.

What is the best way to meet locals and make friends?
The main thing is curiosity, the desire to know and to fit in with the new culture. Try to be open and you will meet locals.

Why should people make sure to visit Palazzo D'Assisi?
For all the places and dishes I mentioned above.

Where can we go to take beautiful photos?
The best places are Rocca Maggiore (the fortress on the hill above Assisi), Monte Subasio mountain, and *Bosco di San*

193

Francesco because you have a good view and you are absorbed in nature.

Anything else you want us to know?
If you go to Trasimeno Lake, you need to eat in Faliero restaurant (at *Località Montebuono di Magione*) where you will try the best *torta al testo* of the region. If you have time, you should to visit Marmore Falls, the Roman remains of Carsulae, and Lake Corbara near Terni (the second largest city in Umbria).

Find Gian at: www.flickr.com/photos/gian-do.

Orvieto

Bustling with university students and locals, this walled Italian hill town is a popular destination in the countryside north of Rome.

Toni DeBella
Freelance Journalist. Blogger. Tennis Player. Expat.

First, tell us about you.
I was born and raised in a quintessentially Italian-American family in San Jose, California. Following university, I relocated to San Francisco, where I lived and worked happily for over 20 years. It was after a visit to Orvieto in 2004, however, that I began to long for the Italian way of life.

In November 2012, after many years of plotting and planning, I sold my car and all my furniture, packed two suitcases, and headed to Italy to begin a new chapter. When I am not writing, you'll probably find me working on my clay court tennis game.

If someone is visiting Orvieto for the first time, what do you recommend they see or do?

First, tour the magnificent *Duomo* containing Luca Signorelli's masterpiece, The Last Judgment. Next, climb to the top of the *Torre del Moro* (the clock tower) for a spectacular 360-degree view of the city below. Third, take a guided tour of the Orvieto Underground—a fascinating labyrinth of Etruscan wells and Medieval caves that lie just beneath the town's surface.

What neighborhoods or parts of town are best to stay in?

Orvieto's *centro storico* (historical center) can be reached by taking the three-minute ride on the *funicolare* (mountain train) from the train station below to the top of the rock. From there, it's an easy 20-minute stroll up the *Corso Cavour* to the main part of town. If you have a lot of luggage, you might want to take the small bus that carries you from the funicular to the heart of the city. Remember, no matter where you stay in the center, you are only minutes by foot to virtually everything.

Let's talk about day trips...what nearby places should everyone make sure to visit?

The town of Civita di Bagnoregio is one of my favorite places in all of Italy! It's perched high atop a pinnacle surrounded by deep canyons. This traffic-free village is a marvel and one that you'll never forget.

Lago di Bolsena is a beautiful and ancient town on the shores of Lake Bolsena, just 20 kilometers away. Stroll the narrow streets and walk down to the lake where you'll find sandy beaches and restaurants serving fresh fish caught in its waters.

Because Orvieto is so well situated on the main train line between Rome (one hour) and Florence (2.5 hours), day trips to these cities (and more) are a breeze. If you want to see some of the many towns dotting the Umbrian and nearby Tuscan countryside, renting a car for a day or two is the way to go.

Tell us about the local dishes. What should people try?

Eating well in Orvieto is like shooting fish in a barrel—you can't miss. The most typical Umbrian dishes are *cinghiale* (wild boar), *tartufo Nero* (black truffles), *porcini* mushrooms, pigeon, dove, and *umbricelli* (a strand pasta that is a thicker, chewier version of spaghetti). Butter is rarely used in Umbrian cooking. Instead, the region's smooth and peppery olive oil is a daily staple. Be sure to try a glass (or two or three) of *Orvieto Classico*—the town's world-renowned white wine—and, after dinner, take an evening walk while eating Pasqualetti's award-winning *gelato*.

What are your top three favorite bars and restaurants?

Ristorante al Saltapicchio (located at *Piazza XXIX Marzo 8*) is a bright and contemporary restaurant that's slightly off the main drag near the Church of San Domenico. Young Chef Valentina prepares dishes that are classic Umbrian, but with a slow food, artistic, and modern twist.

Trattoria Del Moro Aronne (located at *Via San Leonardo 7*) is always filled with locals and savvy foodies. On weekends and during the high season, be sure to make a reservation ahead of time because Cristian and his mother Emiliana serve food and wine that are a cut above. I guarantee you won't be disappointed. (Note that it's closed Tuesdays.)

Pizzeria Charlie (located at *Via Loggia dei Mercanti 14*) is an Oriveto institution. Pizza can be had any time of the year, but in the warmer weather sit outside in the courtyard and enjoy the best pizza (and beer) in town *all'aperto* (open air). (Closed Tuesdays.)

As for bars, FEBO - Officina del Gusto (located at *Via G. Michelangeli 7*) is a warm and cozy place to sip your cappuccino and have a quiet lunch or dinner in its upstairs café.

Caffe ClanDestino (located at *Corso Cavour 40*) serves coffee and pastries in the morning, light lunches in the afternoon, and cocktails (*aperitivi*) in the evening. Take a table underneath the umbrellas on the main drag for prime people watching.

Scarponi Pasticceria (located at *Pizza Del Popolo 7*) makes the best pastries, cakes, cookies, and interestingly-shaped chocolates. This spot hasn't changed one iota since it's opening in 1975...and that's a good thing. (Closed Mondays.)

Is there anything tourists do that locals find rude or strange? What can we do to better fit in with the culture?

Social formalities are very important in Italian culture, therefore it's considered disrespectful and even downright rude to ask for help or directions without first offering a polite greeting. Saying *buongiorno* (good day) or *buonasera* (good evening) before launching into your question will go a long way around here.

What is the best way to meet locals and make friends?

My best advice is to slow down and take your time. Strolling is big in Orvieto—the Sunday *passeggiata* is legendary. To get the most authentic experience, eat where the locals eat and drink where the locals drink. Talk to people. Be interested. Be an Orvietano for a day.

Why should people make sure to visit Orvieto?

Besides the obvious (a magnificent *Duomo*, Etruscan wells, and charming cobblestone streets), Oriveto is a great place to visit because of its convenient location. Literally smack-dab in the center of Italy, it can be reached easily by car or train and is the perfect base from which to travel all over Italy.

Where can we go to take beautiful photos?

Head to the Medieval quarter of town, where panoramas of the lush, green Umbrian countryside can only be described as breathtaking.

Anything else you want us to know?

Umbria is the new Tuscany: less crowded, slower-paced, yet sophisticated and urbane. Art, music, culture, history, and grand traditions—Orvieto has it all and more.

Find Toni at: orvietoorbust.com.

PERUGIA & UMBRIA

Paciano

Welcome to the "green heart of Italy."

Alina Pinelli
Organic Farmer. Vacation Villa Owner. Sommelier. Chef. Blogger.

First, tell us about you.
I was born, grew up, and got my university degree in Rome and I moved to Paciano four years ago. My parents had bought *Fontanaro*, the property I am running now, the year I was born and I believe it was written in the stars that my life would take me here!

I am a professional wine sommelier and chef as a hobby. And now, since organic olive oil is the main product of my farm, I am also an oil sommelier. I love to collect wines in our wide wine cellar to share with friends and guests, as well as music.

And I love to travel as much as possible.

If someone is visiting Paciano for the first time, what do you recommend they see or do?
Paciano is a tiny Medieval village in the "green heart of Italy" (Umbria). Nature, art, and food are the focus here. From the Etruscans and the Romans to the Renaissance, this unpolluted country is full of history and culture. It is still possible to recognize in the paintings of Giotto, as well as Perugino or Raffaello, the sweet rolling hills and the lakes of the Umbrian landscape.

What neighborhoods or parts of town are best to stay in?
Well, I might say that nothing is better than Fontanaro...but Paciano village is so precious and typical within the Medieval walls that it is hard to decide. Personally, I cannot imagine living anywhere else in the countryside, with 360-degree views and our olive orchards, vineyard, and woodlands.

198

PERUGIA & UMBRIA

Let's talk about day trips...what nearby places should everyone make sure to visit?

Paciano is located on the border between Umbria and Tuscany, in a strategic position to explore both regions. By car, within an hour you can reach Orvieto, Todi, Spoleto, Assisi, Perugia, Gubbio, Cortona, Montepulciano, Pienza, Val d'Orcia, and Siena. From the nearby railway station, we are less than two hours from both Rome and Florence.

Tell us about the local dishes. What should people try?

Typical food for our village includes a very tasty pizza dressed with onion and sage (this is absolutely to die for). If you only eat one thing here, make it that pizza.

What are your top three favorite bars and restaurants?

I recommend Michele & Co, at *Via Novella 2* in Castiglione del Lago, for coffee, breakfast, aperitifs, brunch...It's unforgettable!

In Paciano, it is hard to choose between Oca Bruciata (at *Viale Roma 7)*, Loggetta (at *Via Guglielmo Marconi 10*), and Casale (at *Localita Cerreto 50*). Try them all if you can!

Is there anything tourists do that locals find rude or strange? What can we do to better fit in with the culture?

Don't eat dinner out too early in the evening. If you do, you're likely to only meet other foreigners. Italians eat late.

What is the best way to meet locals and make friends?

In Paciano, there are two bars. At the one just outside the walls, you can find more locals and get to know them. In the one in the municipality square, you will find mostly the English-speaking local community members that might tell you about the village.

Why should people make sure to visit Paciano?

Paciano is a typical village and its name recalls peace (the Peace of Janus, the God with two faces). David McTaggart, the founder of Greenpeace decided to settle here and was our neighbor. (I like to think that, since I am a member of Greenpeace, this is another sign that I had to come and live here.) The quality of life here is high, the people friendly, and the location perfect—close enough to my favorite city (Rome) and to the airport, from which I can keep traveling. I love to live in the true heart of Italy.

Where can we go to take beautiful photos?
The village itself is a perfect place for taking photos, while the landscape offers wonderful, unspoiled sites and rolling hills covered with olive groves, vineyards, and woodlands.

Anything else you want us to know?
Each village in central Italy is a wealth of culture, tradition, and history. Paciano, with less than 1,000 inhabitants, is loved and preserved by young and old alike.

Find Alina at: countryslowliving.com & umbriatuscanyreview.com.

LE MARCHE

Off-the-beaten-track and full of charm, Le Marche offers everything from beaches to hill towns to vineyards.

In this section: Ancona / Jesi / San Marcello

Ancona

Hugging the Adriatic Sea, this port town is a haven for seafood-lovers.

Alessandro Sternini
Linguist. Writer. Hiker. Guitarist. Native Italian.

First, tell us about you.

Hi, my name is Alessandro. I am Italian, 37-years-old, and a native (born and raised) of Ancona. Later in life, I lived abroad in Spain, Northern Ireland, and then Estonia.

I studied foreign languages (English and French) and I love writing, drawing, hiking in nature, and playing the guitar.

If someone is visiting Ancona for the first time, what do you recommend they see or do?

Walk from the port up to the old town, starting from *Teatro delle Muse*, walking along the *Via della Loggia*, where you can see the façade of the *Loggia dei Mercanti* and the beautiful Church of Santa Maria. From there, look for a narrow street called *Vicolo della Serpe*, which is a bit hidden off of *Via Saffi*, but, once you find it, takes you to the Church of San Francesco.

From there, the best choice is to go left along *Via Pizzecolli* to visit the local historical museum (The Archeological National

201

LE MARCHE

Museum...the most important museum in the region) and then reach the highest part of the old town, *Colle Guasco* (Guasco hill), where you can visit the Ancona Cathedral. Unfortunately, the Cathedral is only open until 12:30 p.m. and then opens again quite late, at about 4 p.m., so avoid lunchtime there.

After enjoying a panoramic view of the port, you can visit the old Roman amphitheater ruins (unfortunately very ruined) and decide: walk through Cardeto Park (a beautiful park with a spectacular view of the Adriatic Sea, particularly stunning in spring or autumn), whose entrance is near the old amphitheater (in *Via Birarelli*), or find a way down the hill, through the old town to *Piazza del Papa*.

If you choose the Cardeto Park route, make sure to see the old lighthouse, the Jewish cemetery, and Cardeto hill on the other side.

If you are ready for some nightlife, choose the *Piazza del Papa* route (which has nice nightlife, but isn't terribly crowded, even in summer).

Other places of interest: Passetto Beach (easy to reach from the *Monumento ai Caduti* at the end of *Viale della Vittoria* and famous for its fishermen's caves), south of the city center, and *Mole Vanvitelliana* (a massive pentagonal-shaped building by the port, not far from the train station, where lots of events take place in the summer, including concerts, cinema, exhibitions, etc.).

What neighborhoods or parts of town are best to stay in?
I recommend finding a place in the city center or the old town. I don't know hotels very well in town, but you can find a nice B&B in the old town on *Corso Garibaldi* (just one minute far from *Teatro delle Muse* on foot).

Let's talk about day trips...what nearby places should everyone make sure to visit?

LE MARCHE

I highly recommend coming to Marche in the summer. In August, there is Rosso Conero Wine Festival in Camerano, a village that has some beautiful and ancient labyrinthine caves where old sects (especially during the Napoleonic times) used to hide and gather in secret to plot against the church and state.

From Ancona, south and not far from Camerano, there is the beautiful natural reserve called *Parco del Conero*. The top of the Conero hill, which has views of the sea, offers some places to eat and is particularly nice in late spring.

I also recommend Portonovo, with its 18th-century tower and 11th-century Romanic church and a walk on the nearby free beach of Mezzavalle.

Due Sorelle Beach and its nearby villages of Sirolo and Numana are also beautiful places to visit.

If you love the outdoors, check out the Frasassi Caves, west of Ancona. In my opinion, these are some of the best natural caves you can visit in Italy. Not far from there, if you love to hike, you can visit the Sibillini Mountains and their natural park (which is about 1.5 hours from Ancona by car).

If you love sandy beaches and easy walks along the shore and especially if you like fifties rock 'n' roll music and style, check out Senigallia in August for its famous Summer Jamboree, one of the best 50s-dedicated events in Europe with big bands and festival-goers from every part of Italy.

Tell us about the local dishes. What should people try?

Typical food from Ancona is seafood, especially mussels (*moscioli*) served in any way, even as a pasta sauce.

Another popular dish is *brodetto*, a fish soup from a poor tradition but nowadays very appreciated. The most traditional dish in Ancona is *stocafisso all'Anconetana*, which is Norwegian stockfish cooked in a pan with potatoes and tomatoes. Fish is always good around here, particularly fried.

If you do not love fish, try *gnocchi con sugo di papera* (potato dumplings in duck-sauce) or *vincisgrassi* (a particular kind of lasagna).

What are your top three favorite bars and restaurants?

Gnao Gatti (at *Via della Beccheria 3*) in the old town is a good bar for every season. Ulderico (at *Via Terenzio Mamiani 9*) is a very good restaurant for fried fish (and don't worry about getting dressed up; it's a very working class atmosphere). Il Giardino (at *Via Fabio Filzi 2*) is a good restaurant for everything. And La Rocca di Offagna (at *Via della Arengo 71* in the village of Offagna) is very good for pizza.

Is there anything tourists do that locals find rude or strange? What can we do to better fit in with the culture?

Not really. Ancona is not really used to having tourists around, which is both bad and good. The bad news is that the city is not very prepared (like other Italian cities) to host and attract visitors and the monuments might be a bit more hidden or dirty. The good news is that you will always have a genuine and authentic experience here.

What is the best way to meet locals and make friends?

It's not very easy to meet new friends in Ancona. The best option would be using Couchsurfing.org or being introduced to the locals by a mutual friend.

Why should people make sure to visit Ancona?

Because it is one of the less stereotypical cities in central Italy and is still undiscovered and authentic. It has good food, a beautiful and sweet countryside (similar to Tuscany), small villages with cheap food, a lot of nature (*Parco del Conero* and the Sibillini Mountains, to start), and mild weather (compared to the hot south and humid north of the country).

Authentic Ancona is where you can find fishermen's caves by the sea, where you can experience the real local life in the summer by having a swim, canoeing, eating pasta with mussels with the locals, and staying in a cave by the sea at night (of course, first you have to know someone from there who can host you in a cave).

Where can we go to take beautiful photos?

I would take pictures in *Parco del Cardeto* and in the old town, especially near *Cattedrale di San Ciriaco*. For great shots by the sea, head to the caves, especially at dawn, when you can see the sun rising from the sea and projecting amazing light on the different-colored gates of the caves.

Anything else you want us to know?

Maybe Marche region, and especially Ancona, can look like a little bit poorer in touristic facilities compared to Romagna, Umbria, and Tuscany (our biggest competitors), but the point is: in Marche we are still authentic and there's so much to discover. Truly, our region is rich in art, nature, wine, and food. We would love for you to come and see.

Jesi

This Medieval town, located on the floodplain and surrounded by hills, is home to a fascinating old town and fish dishes.

Giuseppina Ambroggio
Creative Type. Traveler. Single Mother. Superhero.

First, tell us about you.

I was born in Jesi and have always had a strong connection with the city. I've worked and lived in many other places in Italy and in Germany, but for the past 24 years I've been back in my hometown. In my free time, I like to walk around the countryside of Jesi, to cook with friends, and to spend time with my daughter.

If someone is visiting Jesi for the first time, what do you recommend they see or do?

LE MARCHE

I recommend visiting the city center, because Jesi is a very nice Medieval town. I think that my city is full of interesting things to see like the *Pinacoteca* (picture gallery) of *Palazzo Pianetti*, the main street, and the Theater Square.

What neighborhoods or parts of town are best to stay in?
I live near the city center, but almost every part of town has something good. I like that Jesi is full of green spaces.

Let's talk about day trips...what nearby places should everyone make sure to visit?
Portonovo and Sirolo (both coastal villages).

Tell us about the local dishes. What should people try?
The Italian dishes are pretty much the same around Italy, but the specific dishes of my region are a lasagna called *vincisgrassi*, *olives all'ascolana* (stuffed olives), *crema fritta* (fried cream), and, near the sea, many fish dishes.

What are your top three favorite bars and restaurants?
La Grotta del Frate (at *Via Roma 10* in Staffolo) is very good.

What is the best way to meet locals and make friends?
Walk around the city center, especially during the weekend, and look for some good music played in the pubs in the center.

Why should people make sure to visit Jesi?
Because it is a small, precious city in the center of Italy, with arts, good food, and good wine. And because it's not one of the big tourist cities where you can't come in real contact with the culture of the place.

Where can we go to take beautiful photos?
Around the city, on the hills.

LE MARCHE

San Marcello

Tiny and authentic, San Marcello is a perfect place to meet some locals, practice your Italian, and slow down.

Mauro Piccotti
Software Engineer. World-Curious. Marche Native.

First, tell us about you.
I have always lived in my beloved San Marcello. I did some studies with my sister and we discovered that our ancestors lived here since 1830, always in San Marcello and often in the same street.

I like a lot of different activities. Some days I read and experiment with computer stuff because of my job. Sometimes I play poker with my friends. For some months, I took dance lessons. For a couple years, swimming lessons. I tried climbing...

When I can, I try to help my family with our vineyards and olive trees, but, unluckily, I'm lazy and I haven't enough time.

If someone is visiting San Marcello for the first time, what do you recommend they see or do?
If you are in the middle of Marche, the best thing you can do as tourist is hike Mount Conero Park; there are a lot of trails with wonderful views of the sea.

The second must-do is, in my opinion, the Frasassi caves. They are some of the best caves in the world, very well maintained, and, if you like adventure, you can visit some parts not open to the public with a speleologist.

What neighborhoods or parts of town are best to stay in?
Usually tourists come to le Marche in summer for our beaches, so perhaps the best option would be to stay along the sea. The *Portonovo* and *Sirolo* areas of Ancona are very nice, but also expensive.

LE MARCHE

You can also stay in the villages not too far from the sea, like Morro d'Alba or Camerano. Morro d'Alba is a nice village very close to mine; it's famous for the *Lacrima di Morro d'Alba* grape variety and wine, and it's close to beaches of Senigallia (less than 20 minutes by car). Camerano is very close to the Conero area, as well as the beaches of Portonovo, Sirolo, Numana, and Marcelli.

If you prefer the mountains, Serra San Quirico, Genga, and Cingoli are very good.

Let's talk about day trips...what nearby places should everyone make sure to visit?

Visit the Frasassi caves first, pass through the "Balcony of the Marches," Cingoli (so-called for its great views of the region), and then head to Camerano and visit the Conero area.

Tell us about the local dishes. What should people try?

In Marche, there aren't particular dishes that you should try, but it's very difficult not to find great wine or food.

Italy is full of little villages and usually people live in families like mine that produce wine, have a kitchen garden, and, very often, people breed and kill little animals for kitchen use. Usually people have lunch and dinner at home—and the quality of the food is very high—which is why restaurants that want to sell to the people of Italy must also keep their quality very high. We are too well-fed at home to put up with mediocre restaurant food.

The direct consequence of this is that even a cheap dish like a kebab is very good. In other words: anywhere and anything you eat will be very high quality here.

That said, here are some specific dishes: *olive ascolane* (fried olives filled with meat), *brodetto all'Anconetana* (fish soup), *vincisgrassi* (a kind of lasagna), and *coniglio in porchetta* (rabbit filled with pork rind and other things).

LE MARCHE

Be aware: if you are vegan, you cannot live in Marche; if you are vegetarian, you'll have a hard life.

What are your top three favorite bars and restaurants?
Bars in Italy are very different from foreign bars. My favorite bar is the one where I have gone since when I was a little child, where I go when I want to meet my friends without needing to call them, where I go to play cards with somebody I know or simply chat a little with the bartender, who is my friend. It's called Bar David and it's the only bar in my village. (Address: *Via Ring Road 28.*)

My favorite restaurants, in order, are: my house, where two of the best chefs in the world live (my mother and my aunt); Pulcinella (in Senigallia at *Lungomare Mameli 265*) for fish dishes; Le Piane (at *Via S. Giuseppe 31* in Camerata Picena) for fish dishes; Vintora (at *Via Circonvallazione 23* in San Marcello), which is a very nice restaurant where you can eat products from the hills; and Chioschino della Buona Piadina (at *Viale Don Minzoni 20* in Jesi), a *piadineria* where you can eat the best *piadina romagnola* in the world (this last restaurant is a small, one-room place where workers eat their lunch – very authentic).

Is there anything tourists do that locals find rude or strange? What can we do to better fit in with the culture?
Italian cities aren't so different from other cities in the world, but something weird happens when tourists come to little villages like mine, because a little village is like a family. When a foreigner comes into a bar here, everybody looks at them. My point is that a foreigner in a little, not-so-touristic village is something incredible and wonderful, so it's impossible to act like he isn't there. The best thing a tourist can do is try to chat with the locals, ask for info, even if it's difficult (because in villages there aren't a lot of English speakers and we mostly speak dialect rather than Italian).

What is the best way to meet locals and make friends?
Join a sport club. Take dance lessons. Go to a climbing gym.

LE MARCHE

If you are here more long-term, start going to the same bar; you'll start to see the same faces and get to know some locals. In an Italian bar, there are always people that are playing card games, darts, table tennis, or foosball, and playing against locals for a beer or a glass of wine could be great. You could also join a local "pro-loco," a local association of people that organizes celebrations and parties in the village.

Why should people make sure to visit San Marcello?
If you really want to understand Italy, you should speak with locals where there isn't tourism. Tourism in Italy is almost everywhere, but in Marche there aren't big and famous cities and, if we exclude our beaches, Frasassi caves, and Urbino, we don't have any famous tourist spots.

The point? We are authentic. Here you can meet people who cannot speak English, that never travel, people who live in their houses for their whole life. Passing your time with these Italian men and women could be the most amazing thing you do in Italy, and in this area there are a lot of these people.

Where can we go to take beautiful photos?
Our hills are breathtaking. And you will love the views from almost any hilltop village. One of the best places for taking pictures is at the end of *Passo del Lupo* in Conero Park.

Anything else you want us to know?
Marche is as pretty and hilly as Tuscany. Our wines are delicious. Everything is cheaper than in other regions like Tuscany, Lazio, or Emilia-Romagna because there isn't tourism.

Everybody knows cities like Roma, Venezia, and Firenze, and almost every tourist goes there. If you want something more challenging, authentic, and meaningful, Marche is your place.

ROME & LAZIO

Come for the Coliseum and the Vatican, stay for the sweet liquors, vibrant markets, and ruin-filled beaches.

In this section: Rome / Vetralla / Anzio

Rome

Bursting with history, culture, and the culinary arts, Rome has captivated millions.

Elizabeth Knight
Travel Writer. Blogger. Expat. Attorney. Baker

First, tell us about you.

I am originally from Nashville and have lived in Rome for six years. In my free time here, I like to eat Italian food, bake American sweets, and visit museums and monuments with friends who come and go through my apartment's revolving door. At least one weekend a month, I get out of town to absorb the rest of Italy—from the Alps to Sicily.

If someone is visiting Rome for the first time, what do you recommend they see or do?

Once you've seen all the usual suspects, I strongly suggest seeing the Basilica of San Clemente near the *Colosseum*. Underneath the Medieval *basilica*, there are shockingly intact remains of a fourth-century *basilica*. And below that is what's left of a 1st-century pagan temple and even residential dwellings.

I also strongly recommend a stroll through Trastevere, my favorite neighborhood in Rome. Winding alleys, only wide enough for a bicycle, and tightly packed ancient buildings hide funky shops and superb eateries. You'll miss out if you stick to the typical *Colosseum*-Spanish Steps-*Piazza Navona* triangle.

If you feel confident doing so, try a scooter tour of Rome. Several companies in town organize these. It is the fastest way to get around the city and you'll feel like Mr. or Ms. Cool with the wind in your hair. Be careful, but not scared; if I can drive one of these things, anyone can.

What neighborhoods or parts of town are best to stay in?

Anything in the historical center around *Piazza Navona* or the Spanish Steps is a dream, if you can afford it. You can walk everywhere. Apart from that, some of the best places to eat are in *Trastevere*, across the river in the Jewish Ghetto, and in the *Monti* neighborhood near the *Colosseum*. So, any of those would be fabulous as well.

Be careful of apartment rentals that are allegedly "fifteen minutes from downtown," as they're usually much farther. Get an address and map it online. And definitely avoid the area near the train station unless you are really on a student's budget.

Let's talk about day trips...what nearby places should everyone make sure to visit?

I firmly believe that Naples and Florence are not day trips from Rome. People try to do it, but it is just too far and there is too much to see there. Plus, there are loads of beauties near Rome that you can get to without spending half the day on the train. For example...

Calcata. About an hour north (by car) of Rome is a tiny village that seems to grow out of the top of a rocky hill like a mushroom. It sits practically unmodified since it was built in the Middle Ages. Head to Calcata with your camera for lunch at La Piazzetta, located at *Via S. Giovanni 47* (order anything; it's all delicious), and a welcome breath of fresh air.

Orvieto. An hour from Rome (by train) is Orvieto in Umbria. In the main *piazza* you'll see one of the most famous cathedrals in Italy, colorfully mosaicked and constructed in striped marble. Then, have an ice cream at Gelateria Pasqualetti right next door. You'll never forget either.

Assisi. Going to Assisi from Rome is a bit of a hike—two hours by train—but once you're there, everything to see is crowded together into an easily walkable radius. The 800-year-old Basilica of St. Francis is worth the trip alone, but the whole town is bursting with charm and views of sunflower fields around every turn.

Sperlonga. The beaches nearest to Rome tend to be crowded and, frankly, dirty. But just an hour away by train is Sperlonga, with clean, blue water, well-kept sand, and plenty of lounge chairs for rent. The town is also darling, with plenty of places to eat fresh seafood.

Tell us about the local dishes. What should people try?

There are a couple of kinds of pasta that are quintessentially Roman: *carbonara* (*al dente spaghetti* with egg, *pecorino* cheese, and *guanciale*, which is pork cheek) and *amatriciana* (tomato, *pecorino*, and *guanciale* sauce often served with long *bucatini* pasta, resembling mini-hoses).

Then there are *carciofi alla giudia*, flattened whole artichokes fried as crispy as potato chips, which are a Roman Jewish tradition. It's best to get these, obviously, in the Jewish Ghetto (I recommend the restaurant Nonna Betta, located at *Via del Portico d'Ottavia 16*). They are typically only available in late winter and spring.

Finally, Roman pizza. Unlike the famous pizza from Naples, Roman pizza has a paper-thin crust. Stay out of the way when arguments over which crust is better heat up.

What are your top three favorite bars and restaurants?

For pizza, my heart beats a little faster for Dar Poeta (at *Vicolo del Bologna 45* in *Trastevere*). You should try the mixed

213

bruschetta appetizer with everything from spreadable sausage to honey and gorgonzola on crusty bread, a plate of steaming, chewy pizza, and finally, a nutella calzone. There's always a long wait for a table.

Down the street, Zi' Umberto, located at *Piazza di San Giovanni della Malva 14*, is a small Roman restaurant with good outdoor seating, a decadent salami and cheese plate, and superb pastas—particularly the *gricia*.

Across the river from *Trastevere*, in the Jewish Ghetto, Nonna Betta (at *Via del Portico D'Ottavia 16*) is the place to try fried artichokes (*carciofi alla giudia*) and traditional kosher lamb and fish.

Bars: Near *Piazza Navona* (at *Piazza del Fico 26*), Bar del Fico is so small that the hoards of patrons have to spill out into the square with their glasses of wine and beer. This gives them the chance to look at each other, which is good, because everyone there is gorgeous. There are always a lot of locals.

Gusto (*www.gusto.it*), along the river, not far from *Piazza di Spagna*, has one of the best *aperitivi* in town. For 10 euros, you can get a fun cocktail (I get the Mediterranean Mojito with cherry tomatoes) and as many trips as you want to the very solid appetizer buffet.

The rooftop bar of the Hotel Eden (address: *Via Ludovisi 49*) is pricey, but you're paying for the best sunset view in Rome. If you're celebrating a special occasion, you can't beat it.

Is there anything tourists do that locals find rude or strange? What can we do to better fit in with the culture?

Italians are horrified when Americans get drunk (and some of them get so drunk) in public. Maybe because Italians have been drinking since childhood or maybe because they are always trying to look their best, they just do not think it's cute for groups of friends to act wildly drunk in a bar or in the street. And the worst thing ever for them is to see a drunken American girl walking home on the cobblestones barefoot, carrying her shoes. Don't ask me how I know this. So enjoy the wine, but stay sober.

This one is kind of funny: so many Italians ask me why tourists wear flip-flops around the city. They often remark with disgust that tourists' feet are always black with dirt. That may be true...Who among us hasn't rinsed off his or her feet in the hotel bidet?

Italians have a rule against cappuccino after dinner, while Americans love it. Ask an Italian the reason for this rule and he or she will tell you that it is quite unappetizing to consume hot dairy after a big dinner of pasta and meat. If they were consistent with this reasoning, I'd accept it. But when they, instead, order a big plate of creamy, eggy tiramisu or a giant ice cream cone with whipped cream or an assorted plate of cheese and honey, all with a scalding espresso on the side, the rule against cappuccino seems rather arbitrary to me. But if you want to do as the Romans, order a shot of espresso after your dinner and toss it back.

What is the best way to meet locals and make friends?

The first thing to remember is that Italians do not typically speak good (or any) English, unlike residents in northern European (or even northern Italian) cities. To get to know locals in Italy, it really helps to know some Italian, even a few words. But not to worry! Most Italians are happy to practice their English with you, whatever level it is.

For this reason and others, Rome isn't the easiest place to meet locals unless you're a young female tourist or student and want to meet only a certain kind of Roman man.

If you're a little older and/or you're interested in actual conversation, the best places are the many bars and squares in the *Trastevere* neighborhood, where the locals tend to congregate outside instead of huddling around tables indoors with their backs to you. Apart from that, any event that is outdoors and crowded will be better than sitting in a restaurant

215

or bar. Soccer games, concerts in *piazzas*, and the beach are all places that have worked for my expat friends and me.

Why should people make sure to visit Rome?

Rome has something for everyone. Ancient monuments and ruins, Renaissance art, churches, and food and wine for all. Plus, a small enough downtown area that you can walk to everything (this is fortunate, because the subway system is practically non-existent). Even the weather is agreeable. If you want to skip the monuments and just sit in sunny *piazzas* and sip things all day, that's okay, too. There are no rules. *Il dolce far nulla* (the sweetness of doing nothing) is an Italian motto and way of life.

Where can we go to take beautiful photos?

Cross the Bridge of Angels in front of the *Castel Sant'Angelo* at dusk and set your camera on the bridge's railing pointing towards the river and St. Peter's. The railing serves as a makeshift tripod, so your shot won't blur in the waning sunlight, and the giant dome against the navy blue sky makes an excellent photograph.

Rome is complicated. The things that make it wondrous—monuments, etc.—are precisely what make modern life difficult.

For panoramic shots of the city, climb up the Gianicolo hill near Trastevere. You can see all of the city's monuments gleaming white against a bright blue sky. Bring your wide-angle lens.

Photos of ruins are great, but predictable and usually filled with passing cars and people. So, for some atmospheric shots that look like you've stepped through a time machine, stroll around

Trastevere at night or very early in the morning. Narrow cobblestone paths, random fountains punctuating alleyways, and laundry hanging from windows combine with great, warm light to break up the monotony of white marble in your pictures.

Anything else you want us to know?

Rome is a complicated place. The things that make it so wondrous—the monuments, the fountains, and the crumbling marble everywhere—are precisely what make modern life difficult. Every time the city government tries to expand the pathetic (compared to other European cities) underground system or even widen a road, the builders run into a long-ago buried temple or amphitheater and construction is halted. This provides some context for why traffic is so bad, why parking is so elusive, and why there are only two metro lines. It can really feel like chaos.

I always try to remember that if I were speeding across town in a subway car, I'd miss out on the beauty that explodes everywhere in Rome. So just put on your comfortable shoes, walk, and look both ways before crossing.

Find Elizabeth at: romeifyouwantto.com.

Stephen Oddo
Co-Founder, Walks of Italy. American Expat. Travel-Savvy Explorer.

First, tell us about you.

I'm originally from California, but my heritage is Italian (via Sicily). I moved to Rome in March 2005 and was there until the end of 2011, when I headed north for the Alps and spent a winter season in Cervinia, Italy, before finally moving to New York in April 2012.

I still make frequent trips to Italy (about four to five times a year) and, when I'm in Rome, I spend a lot of my free time in the *Monti* district, where I lived previously. Taking walks, stopping for espresso, instagramming, zipping around on a *motorino* (scooter)—these are what I'm doing most days.

When I'm traveling outside Rome, I spend a lot of time exploring new places and researching sites, monuments, churches, etc. My favorite thing to do is take drives through the countryside and visit the more off-the-beaten-path regions like Molise, Le Marche, and Puglia.

If someone is visiting Rome for the first time, what do you recommend they see or do?

As cliché as it is, no first-time trip to Rome is complete without a visit to the major sights: The Vatican, Sistine Chapel & St. Peter's, the *Colosseum* & Roman Forum, the Pantheon, Trevi Fountain, *Piazza Navona*...these are, of course, very popular tourist sites, but for good reason. Rome has been a popular tourist destination for millennia, so if it's your first trip, definitely make sure to include these highlights in some form.

Now, my personal opinion is that the best way to visit these sites is with Walks of Italy. Visits are so much richer when you have exclusive access, a knowledgeable tour guide, and the ability to skip the lines.

I also recommend hands-on experiences with food, wine, and cooking classes.

What neighborhoods or parts of town are best to stay in?

Personally, I love the *Monti* neighborhood. I lived there for a number of years and, in recent years, it has become a hub of funky cafes, unique boutique and artisan shops, and local craft fair markets. It's also easy to walk to the city center (*Piazzas Venezia* and *Navona*), the *Colosseum*, and even *Termini* station (for day trips). The closest subway stop would be Cavour.

Let's talk about day trips...what nearby places should everyone make sure to visit?

ROME & LAZIO

Some great nearby day trips in Lazio include the *Castelli Romani* for wine tasting (try the *Frascati Superiore*, a common grape grown near Rome for centuries) and Lago Albano to see the Pope's summer residence (known as *Castel Gandolfo*).

I also love to visit the seaside port and beaches of Ostia and the nearby ruins at Ostia Antica, the ancient port of Rome. It's also worth a trip to Civita di Bagnoregio, to see the Medieval village seemingly floating in the sky — it's an amazing view!

Lastly, I'm a huge fan of Orvieto. While it's outside of the Lazio region, it's just over the border into another fantastic region: Umbria. There you can see the incredible paintings by Luca Signorelli in the *Duomo*, enjoy hearty Umbrian cuisine, see Etruscan remnants and tombs, and visit the city's underground caves and passageways used for millennia. Plus, the views from this Medieval hilltop city are spectacular.

Tell us about the local dishes. What should people try?
I particularly love the Roman artichokes. During artichoke season, it's popular to eat artichokes either in the Roman or Jewish style. I'm fond of the Roman style because they're soft and delicate and stuffed with breadcrumbs, mint, and garlic.

Another favorite dish is the *bucatini all'amatriciana*. This dish consists of simple, quality ingredients: *guanciale* (pork cheek, similar to bacon or *pancetta*), tomato sauce, and *pecorino* cheese.

What are your top three favorite bars and restaurants?
I'm a big fan of the historic restaurant La Campana (at *Vicolo della Campana 18* near the *Pantheon*). They do great seasonal dishes in a no-frills atmosphere and for reasonable prices. I've been going there for years.

As a thin-crust pizza fan, I also love La Montecarlo (at *Vicolo Savelli 13*). They also have great *fritti* (fried appetizers) and nice pasta dishes. Another great pizzeria is Giacomelli in *Prati*, located at *Via Faa di Bruno 25* near Vatican City.

ROME & LAZIO

There's a great, historic wine bar known as Il Goccetto, near the beautiful *Via Giulia* at *Via dei Banchi Vecchi 14*. Here you can try wines from all over Italy, along with meat and cheese appetizers.

Is there anything tourists do that locals find rude or strange? What can we do to better fit in with the culture?

Italians are quite particular about customs and traditions. For example, it's very rude in Italy to put your feet up on another seat, even if it's empty, even if it's the train. I've seen everyone from train conductors to McDonald's employees scold tourists for sticking their feet on an empty chair, so don't do it.

Also, when Italians eat out they often speak in a soft voice unless they are in a large group at, say, a pizzeria. In other cultures, it's more acceptable to be louder when eating out, but less so in Italy.

Lastly, it's never acceptable to order or drink a cappuccino after midday. Baristas and waiters will definitely scold anyone for this (though in Rome you'll get less scolding since there are so many tourists and some of the Italians have given up on us!).

What is the best way to meet locals and make friends?

Get out of the historic center. There are areas that are very popular with young Romans, like *Ponte Milvio*, *San Lorenzo*, or *Pigneto*. Visiting these areas, taking a *passeggiata* (stroll) through the squares, and trying the bars, cafes, and restaurants in these areas, you're sure to meet some real Roman locals. Also, one could always try visiting a *partita di calcio* (soccer match) and watching as Roma squashes their opponents. You're likely to meet some colorful Roman soccer fans at the same time. Just make sure to wear *giallorosso*—orange and red!

Why should people make sure to visit Rome?

Rome is the center of all things Italian. Sure, there have been other capitals and other important central places, but, really, everything begins and ends in Rome. There is truth to the phrase "All roads lead to Rome." You can get a snapshot of every great era leading back to pre-Roman days, some of the best examples of Roman, Renaissance, and Baroque construction, the center of the Catholic church, some of the world's top museums, fantastic food, the setting of countless Italian classic films...need I say more?

Where can we go to take beautiful photos?

You can't go wrong with overlooks: the Gianicolo hill has a wonderful overlook of the city, as do Monte Mario (where the observatory is) and the Aventine Hill at the *Giardino degli Aranci* (Garden of Oranges).

Of course, areas within the city are great for photography too: along the river near the Vatican and *Castel sant'Agelo*, in *Piazza Navona*, *Villa Borghese* (the largest public park in Rome), and *Pincio* (a hill northeast of the historic center).

Anything else you want us to know?

If you want to maximize your time, don't hesitate to take a tour. Tours are not like they used to be, especially in Italy. The classic bus tours of 50+ travelers herded around with a guide holding an umbrella and shouting on a megaphone are finally phasing out of style in favor of higher quality experiences. Now, tours allow you to see more, learn more, gain hands-on knowledge, or visit exclusive areas and skip lines.

Find Stephen at: www.walksofitaly.com.

Gillian McGuire
Serial Expat. Blogger. App Writer. Coffee Lover.

First, tell us about you.

I have lived in Rome since 2006. I grew up in eastern Tennessee and went to college in Washington, DC. After college and before Rome, I lived in west and southern Africa for over a decade.

ROME & LAZIO

I am an Instagram/iPhoneography addict. I love to explore the smaller streets and neighborhoods in Rome and capture (and share) images of hidden corners.

If someone is visiting Rome for the first time, what do you recommend they see or do?

A first-time visitor should absolutely hit the well-known highlights. See the ancient sites first. The *Colosseum*, Palatine Hill, the Roman and Trajan forums will give you some perspective on time and place. Next, book tickets ahead of time, skip the line, and spend a day inside the Vatican Museums, which hold a lifetime's worth of artwork. Once you see the big stuff, I love *Palazzo Valentini*, an interactive multimedia exhibit that brings to life a 2,000-year-old Roman villa. Then, go hunting for works by bad-boy artist Caravaggio in churches scattered all over town.

What neighborhoods or parts of town are best to stay in?

I am partial to the *Monti* neighborhood, where I live. Rome's first neighborhood was once a swampy, seedy place that was thick with brothels and rowdy gladiators. Now the cobblestone streets are lined with traditional trattorias, wine bars, and chic shops.

Let's talk about day trips...what nearby places should everyone make sure to visit?

In the summer, head to the beach. Less than an hour away by train, the seaside town of Ostia is easy to reach and you can escape the city heat for a mini Mediterranean vacation. There are beach clubs with sun loungers and restaurants that you can enter for a fee. Or look for one of the free beaches where you can plop down a towel and swim in the sea.

If it is not beach season, Orvieto is a picturesque Umbrian hill town only an hour away by train. The gilded gothic cathedral is filled with frescoes by Luca Signorelli. Shop for wild boar sausages and handcrafted ceramics in the local shops.

ROME & LAZIO

Tell us about the local dishes. What should people try?

My favorite Roman pasta dish is *amatriciana*. This hearty pasta sauce is made with crisp, salty guanciale, onions, tomatoes, and hot pepper.

With my pasta, I always order a side dish of *cicoria*. You will find this dark green, slightly bitter vegetable on just about every menu in Rome. (And if you don't see it, ask; they probably have it.) I love it *ripassata* in *padella* (boiled and then sautéed in a pan with lots of garlic, olive oil, and chili).

Roman pizza has a cracker-thin, crispy crust with almost burned edges.

Make sure to order a plate of delicious fried treats (vegetables, zucchini blossoms, olives) while you wait for your pie.

What are your top three favorite bars and restaurants?

Taverna Fori Imperiale: this is my neighborhood favorite. It is also the favorite of famous food critics and visiting movie stars, so make sure you make a reservation ahead of time. It is great for lunch after a day of touring the ancient sites or for an early dinner. Make sure you ask what the daily specials are. A standout is a twist on the Roman classic *cacio e pepe* scattered with shaved black truffles. Address: *Via della Madonna dei Monti 9*.

Pier Luigi: this is one of my go-to picks for a nice night (or long, lazy lunch) out. It is in a beautiful *piazza*, there are killer cocktails at a snazzy bar, and the fish-based menu has never disappointed. Address: *Piazza de Ricci 144*.

Bar Licata: this is my neighborhood bar. A friendly neighborhood place located close to the *Colosseum*, Bar Licata is a classic Roman bar. They have excellent pastries, salads at lunchtime, and an evening *aperitivo*. You can also buy bus tickets here. Open all day long, you can start your morning here with a cappuccino or end your day with a *cafe correto* (a shot of espresso with a shot of *grappa*). Address: *Via de Serpenti 165*.

Barnum Café: near the *Campo de Fori*, the mismatched chairs and an always-interesting soundtrack set this bar apart. Have a late morning cappuccino and catch up on your email with the free Wi-Fi. Or, for some of the best cocktails in Rome, stop by in the evening (Tuesday - Saturday). The bartenders here really know their stuff and your drink will often be accompanied by a cocktail history lesson. And a bar stocked with unusual spirits and bitters means even your most obscure request can probably be met. Address: *Via del Pellegrino 87*.

Is there anything tourists do that locals find rude or strange? What can we do to better fit in with the culture?

La bella figura means to make a good impression. How you present yourself is very important in Italy. The idea expresses itself in a multitude of ways. When you enter a store or bar, make sure you greet the owner with a smile and a *buongiorno*. Flip-flops and shorts are beach attire and not appropriate for touring the city.

What is the best way to meet locals and make friends?

Sign up for a language exchange or join one of the many expatriate clubs.

Why should people make sure to visit Rome?

Rome was once the center of the ancient world. Today it is a vibrant, chaotic, beautiful place filled with art, both ancient and contemporary, terrific food, and light that will take your breath away.

Find Gillian at: gillianslists.com, the Rome for Expats app, and instagram.com/gmcguireinrome.

Davide Corizzo
Student. Native Roman. Soccer Player.

ROME & LAZIO

First, tell us about you.
Hello everybody! I'm a student, age 26, who has always lived in Rome. In my spare time, I like to have walks throughout the center, go jogging in *Villa Borghese*, attend cultural events, and enjoy the nightlife.

If someone is visiting Rome for the first time, what do you recommend they see or do?
I would recommend places like the *Colosseum*, Trevi's Fountain, and the Spanish Steps, which are the symbols of the city.

What neighborhoods or parts of town are best to stay in?
The center, for sure, and *Trastevere*.

Let's talk about day trips...what nearby places should everyone make sure to visit?
Ostia (Rome's seaside), Cerveteri (famous as the biggest Etrurian necropolis), Castelgandolfo (with its beautiful lake and the Pope's summer residence), and Orvieto (a Medieval town in Umbria, just one hour away by train).

Tell us about the local dishes. What should people try?
The best option is always pasta: in Rome you could taste dishes like *carbonara* (eggs, bacon, and *pecorino*, which is typical of Rome and similar to *parmigiano*, but with a stronger flavor), *amatriciana* (tomato sauce, bacon, and *pecorino*), and *cacio e pepe* (*cacio*, which is another Roman cheese, and pepper).

For main courses, try *saltimbocca alla Romana* (meat dressed with ham, sage, and some white wine on top) and *carciofi alla giudia* (typical Roman-Jewish food; Rome had one of the largest European ghettos centuries ago).

What are your top three favorite bars and restaurants?
Pizzeria Panattoni (known as *L'Obitorio*, which, hilariously, means mortuary in Italian) is a favorite. The location is not great (address: *Viale Trastevere 53*), but the food is so excellent. Try the *suppli*.

225

ROME & LAZIO

Visit Caffè Sant'Eustachio (at *Piazza Sant'Eustachio 82*, near *Piazza del Pantheon* and *Piazza Navona*) and you will have the best coffee of your whole life!

Gelateria La Romana (at *Via Coriano 58*, close to *Porta Pia*) is a new *gelato* place with the best *gelato* in Rome.

What is the best way to meet locals and make friends?
Go to the center and *Trastevere*.

Why should people make sure to visit Rome?
Rome is the Eternal City. Walking through the center is like visiting an open-air museum. Its unique atmosphere enchants everyone.

Anything else you want us to know?
Check out sightseeing favorites *Terrazza del Pincio* (a beautiful terrace with one of the best city views), *Gianicolo* hill, and *Giardino degli Aranci* (the Orange Garden).

Giorgio Pastore
Lawyer. Cyclist. Native Roman.

First, tell us about you.
I was born in and have always lived in Rome. In my spare time, I love cycling, visiting museums, reading good books, going to cinema or theatre, and taking a walk in my favorite place in Rome: Music Bridge and the MAXXI Museum in the *Flaminio* zone.

If someone is visiting Rome for the first time, what do you recommend they see or do?
First of all, check out the views from Zodiaco Cafè (located at *Viale del Parco Mellini 88/90/92*), the Gianicolo hill, and *Pincio Terrazza*. Then take a walk in the small streets around *Trastevere* and *Campo de Fiori* downtown. And if you are not too tired, have a good coffee at the *terrazzo* above *Milite*

Ignoto, which has a breathtaking view of the *Colosseum, Via dei Fori Imperiali*, and *Piazza Venezia*.

What neighborhoods or parts of town are best to stay in?

In my opinion, the best place to stay is in *Prati* zone which is just a few meters from St. Peter, but is not as crowded or expensive as other places in Rome. It's well connected by metro and a tourist can easily reach every place in a few minutes.

Let's talk about day trips...what nearby places should everyone make sure to visit?

Don't forget to visit the beautiful small town of Calcata, located on a hill not far from Rome.

Tell us about the local dishes. What should people try?

Tonnarelli cacio e pepe (pasta with cheese and peppers), *pizza con i funghi porcini* (pizza with various mushrooms), *pasta carbonara* (pasta with bacon), and *fragole e crema vaniglia* (strawberries with vanilla cream).

What are your top three favorite bars and restaurants?

Caffè della Pace, located at *Via della Pace 3/7*, Caffè di S. Eustachio (at *Piazza Sant'Eustachio 82*), and, if you want to eat good fresh fish, Tempio di Iside (at *Via Labicana 50*).

Is there anything tourists do that locals find rude or strange? What can we do to better fit in with the culture?

Tourists usually mix all the flavors together at the table and sometimes, when you have cooked for two hours, it is very depressing watching foreign guests taste pasta and meat and...whatever...at the same time.

What is the best way to meet locals and make friends?

Going in the pubs around the *Monti* zone just a few meters from *Colosseum* or going out for some live music in a small club and talking about music, art, or culture with the people you meet.

Why should people make sure to visit Rome?

ROME & LAZIO

I really don't think Rome is the first city a tourist should visit in Italy. In my opinion, small cities in the northern part of Italy can be more interesting. That said, in Rome, a tourist can have a good experiences with Italian food, culture, etc.

Where can we go to take beautiful photos?
I think from the beautiful terrace on the roof of *Milite Ignoto*, *Gianicolo*, or inside the Pantheon.

Anything else you want us to know?
Be very careful in the metro stations because there are many pickpockets and gypsies.

Stefano Sandano
Italian Art Historian. Spanish Steps Expert. Author.

First, tell us about you.
I lived in Rome for 39 years—from the day when I was born a few inches away from the Spanish Steps, until I moved to the US in 2006 and married a US citizen.

In Rome, I worked as licensed art guide for American travelers coming to Rome (which is how I met my wife). In my free time, I like to write about the art produced in Rome and its monuments in order to facilitate an understanding of the Roman legacy.

If someone is visiting Rome for the first time, what do you recommend they see or do?
Start with a visit to the Colosseum and the Roman Forum, both of which are linked to the other interesting archaeological complex of Palatine Hill, which contains the remains of the first huts dating back to the period of Romulus and Remus (8th century B.C.) and which eventually developed into an integrated palatial residence where the Roman emperors lived.

228

ROME & LAZIO

After that, visit the Vatican museums and the Sistine Chapel, frescoed by Michelangelo. After the Sistine Chapel, enter Saint Peter's Basilica, which is the largest church in the world.

What neighborhoods or parts of town are best to stay in?

Stay near the Spanish Steps or Trevi Fountain or even at the Pantheon; from these monuments, it is easy to reach ancient Rome and the many churches that played a significant role during Renaissance and Baroque Rome on foot.

Let's talk about day trips...what nearby places should everyone make sure to visit?

Rome has an incredible legacy, even outside the perimeter of the city itself. As a day trip, I suggest that you visit the catacombs and the Appian Way, both located in the south of Rome, about three miles from the city center. The Appian Way is a testimony to the formidable nature of Roman engineering, as it was built by the Roman army to link Rome with the south of Italy and allowed the troops to travel straight to Greece. The catacombs are underground Christian cemeteries dug by the Christian community after the arrival of the apostles Peter and Paul in Rome to spread the gospels. The visual heritage of the catacombs, which consists of inscriptions and frescoes, is relevant to the comprehension of the rise of the new religion that, in only three centuries, superseded the pagan cult and helped to end the Roman Empire.

Tell us about the local dishes. What should people try?

Try Piperno Restaurant, (at *Monte dé Cenci 9*, opposite Tiber Island). While you're there, try *bruschetta*, a popular antipasto or appetizer in central Italy, which comes from the Romanesco word for "bread," *supplì* (fried rice croquettes stuffed with beef ragout and mozzarella), *bucatini alla matriciana* (pasta with tomato sauce, *guanciale* vegetables, and grated *pecorino romano* cheese), and *spaghetti alla carbonara* (pasta with meat sauce).

And, for those who really want to try local, the Roman tripe (edible offal from animal stomachs) is a very good and rich dish.

ROME & LAZIO

What are your personal top three favorite bars and restaurants in the area?

My preferred restaurants in Rome are Ristorante Piperno (at *Monte dé Cenci* 9), which features the popular *carciofi alla giudia* (Jewish-style artichokes), and La Buca di Ripetta (at *Via Ripetta* 36), located near *Piazza del Popolo* and famous for its Tiramisu.

The only bar I love is one with a good espresso near the Pantheon, Caffe' Sant' Eustachio (at *Piazza Sant'Eustachio 82*).

What is the best way to meet locals and make friends?

Before you come, watch some Italian movies like *Roma Citta' Aperta* and *La Dolce Vita of Fellini* and you'll have a better grasp of the Roman culture. Please also remember that famous actors such as Anna Magnani and Alberto Sordi were from Rome and embody the Roman culture and its contradictions.

Meeting friends in Rome is not complicated; today Italians use social media, such as Facebook and Twitter, extensively.

Why should people make sure to visit Rome?

Visiting Italy without Rome is like carving a statue and then leaving it incomplete. There is so much culture that other towns borrowed from Rome. One example from Florence: we all love *Piazza della Signoria*, the *Uffizi*, and the Medici family, but few people know that under *Piazza della Signoria* there are the vestiges of a Roman theater and the remains of a Roman military outpost devoted to exchange of goods between Rome and the north of the Italian peninsula. Need more? If you go to Sicily, the Roman Civilization spread there, as well, after having taken Sicily and its granaries from Hannibal at the end of the second Punic war. By visiting the beautiful town of Agrigento, travelers will marvel at the Greek temple adjacent to a Roman theater or forum.

Where's the best place to take photos?

230

The best places to take photos of Rome are, in my opinion, two: the top of the dome of Saint Peter's Basilica and the Janiculum Hill, which is very close to the Vatican. Both places highlight the main monuments of Rome and the domes of popular churches.

Anything else people should know about Rome?

Rome deserves more than three days to be visited and understood in its entirety. However, travelers do not have to miss the bigger picture; the Lazio region, which includes Rome, is full of Etruscan tombs. The Etruscans were absorbed into the Roman civilization, but Romans owe a lot of their culture to the Etruscans: the arch, the augural bird watching religious practice, and the technique of wine making. A day trip outside Rome should include a visit to the towns of Tarquinia and Cerveteri.

Find Stefano on: Amazon.com (search: Stefano Sandano).

Vetralla

Crossed by the original Roman roads, Vetralla is just a hop, skip, and a jump from many historic gardens and castles.

Mary Jane Cryan
Author. Blogger. Cultural Holiday Leader.

First, tell us about you.

Born in the Boston area, I studied in Buffalo, NY and Dublin, Ireland. Then, in 1965, I flew to Rome, where a position in an international school was waiting for me. Over the years, I've been a teacher and school administrator and earned an Italian university degree.

I also have published many guides and books on Italian history and culture, been a guide in St. Peter's Basilica and director and lecturer for Elderhostel, and created start-ups for universities, schools, and artists' workshops.

For the past eight years, I have traveled the Mediterranean, the Black Sea, and the Baltic as an enrichment lecturer aboard luxury cruise ships.

If someone is visiting Vetralla for the first time, what do you recommend they see or do?

After living in Rome for 35 years, I now live one hour north, with easy access by train into the Eternal City. This area is known as Etruria or Tuscia and borders on Tuscany and Umbria. It has always been a special, yet mysterious, area and a great favorite of travelers, artists, and archeologists.

The area is crossed by the original Roman roads (*vias Cassia, Aurelia*, and *Flaminia*) and the ancient pilgrims' route, *Via Franchigena,* which connects northern Europe with Rome. When spring comes, we have numerous modern pilgrims trekking or biking on these trails.

Let's talk about day trips...what nearby places should everyone make sure to visit?

The best day trips in the area include the many historic gardens and castles (Ruspoli Castle, *Palazzo Farnese*, *Villa Lante*, and *Sacro Bosco*). The area abounds in Etruscan and Roman archaeological sites such as Tarquinia, Vulci, and the newly discovered Etruscan pyramid. There is a huge variety of things to do and places to visit and the food and wine are magnificent, too. The only thing lacking are hordes of tourists.

What are your top three favorite bars and restaurants?

There are three great family-run restaurants in Vetralla: Da Benedetta (located at *Via della Pietà 76*), La Lanterna (located at *Via Roma 26* and specializing in fish dishes), and Il Pigno (located at *Via Don Benedetto Baldi*).

The bars, pastry shops, and pizzeria I recommend are Di Carlo in Cura di Vetralla (located on *Via Cassia*), Il Bersagliere

ROME & LAZIO

(located at *Via Roma 1*), and Fiordalisi (at *Via Cassia Sutrina 3*) in Vetralla.

What is the best way to meet locals and make friends?

I constantly run into visitors at the supermarket, swimming at the local hot baths (such as *Terme dei Papi*), or relaxing at one of the sidewalk cafes. In spring and summer, there are concerts, festivals, and happenings every weekend. During the winter, people meet at conferences, opera, and music evenings or the local library.

Why should people make sure to visit Vetralla?

Vetralla and surrounding towns in the Roman countryside are where city-dwelling Romans come for the weekend. Many foreigners have bought and fixed up houses here that they share with friends. You can rent a villa or a beach or lake house to enjoy a laid back vacation. Vetralla is one of 60 different hill towns, each with its own personality and interesting history.

Where can we go to take beautiful photos?

There are numerous great photo opportunities, especially during the festivals when local people dress in the costume of days gone by. I have a small camera always with me.

Anything else you want us to know?

Spring festivals such as San Pellegrino in Fiore (May 1 - 4) bring many visitors to the main city of Viterbo, 14 kilometers north of Vetralla. Most visitors come because they have done research and know what they want. After having seen the big three (Rome, Florence, Venice) real lovers of Italy want to see the unspoiled areas off the beaten track. The only site that is quite famous is Civita di Bagnoregio, since it is mentioned in a well-known guidebook.

Find Mary-Jane at: www.elegantetruria.com and 50yearsinitaly.blogspot.it.

Anzio

This harbor town is also the home of some fascinating WWII history, Roman ruins, and important art.

Moyan Brenn
Photographer. Traveler. Hiker. Native Italian.

First, tell us about you.
I am a photographer and a traveler. I am also a security consultant and have lived in Anzio since I was born, 30 years ago. My mother's family is from Lazio and my father's is half Sicilian and half Lazian. My passions are music, hiking, photography, traveling, documentaries, cartoons, and gourmet chocolate.

If someone is visiting Anzio for the first time, what do you recommend they see or do?
Start with the *grotte di Nerone* (the caves of Nero) and Ostia, a nearby region known for its old ruin-filled beach, formerly owned by the Roman emperors. There, you can still see the basements of the rich villas and the rest of the Roman harbor.

You should also visit the very famous Nettuno American International Cemetery in Nettuno.

Finally, in Anzio itself, there's the little commercial harbor, which is full of lovely restaurants, and the WWII museum, which is full of clothes and photos.

What neighborhoods or parts of town are best to stay in?
We have very few hotels and B&Bs and, as always, the best thing to do for accommodation is to rely on reviews of users on websites like Booking.com. There's no better choice than this, based on my own traveling experience.

Let's talk about day trips...what nearby places should everyone make sure to visit?

Well, my opinion differs greatly from most tourist organizations. Whether you're visiting my town or basing yourself in Rome, I'd recommend:

The Garden of Ninfa, a beautiful, well-known garden with a little stream and a miniature waterfall. They are astonishing. I have visited them six times and still want to take more pictures.

The hill town of Sermoneta: the best and the most typical Medieval Italian town in the Ciociaria mountain region. Visiting here is like going back in time. And, on your way home, stop by the Abbey of Valvisciolo, which is beautiful, Medieval, and free.

For those who like WWII history, the Piana delle Orme Museum, located at *Strada Migliara 43 e Mezzo 29* in Borgo Faiti, is an incredible museum full of old vehicles and a large-scale reconstruction of the famous Auschwitz station of Poland. It's simply unbelievable.

For those who like beaches, I suggest the Island of Ponza, whose ships depart from the harbor of Anzio (and which was recently visited by Nicolas Cage). The sea is beautiful there. That said, be careful because it's a risky zone for tourists. Before choosing a hotel, B&B, or restaurant, be sure to check Booking.com or Tripadvisor.com, and don't trust the boat men who want to take you to beaches with their boats once you arrive. Be sure to go only to beaches recommended on your favorite guide or possibly try to rent a little vehicle so that you can be self-guided.

Finally, for the history buffs, I suggest the famous Cassino Abbey, well known for the American aviation bombing during WWII.

Tell us about the local dishes. What should people try?

Fish! Anzio is very famous for its fish dishes and even people from Rome come to Anzio to try them. We don't really have

ROME & LAZIO

tourist traps, junk food, or high prices, so wherever you decide to go along the main harbor, you'll be safe and have great food.

What are your top three favorite bars and restaurants?

The most famous recommended restaurants are Romolo al Porto, located at *Via Porto Innocenziano 19*, and Alceste, located at *Piazza Sant'Antonio 6*. Both are situated along the harbor.

For a more romantic view, Il Turcotto, located at *Riviera 44 Mallozzi*, faces the Caves of Nero.

Pastry bars: Graziosi (at *1/3 Corso Del Popolo*), Stampeggioni (at *Via Nettunense 219*), and Marotta (at *Via Filibeck 17*). All three are close to the main square and they are the best places in town for breakfast or cakes.

Is there anything tourists do that locals find rude or strange? What can we do to better fit in with the culture?

Italian people don't like people who easily get drunk.

What is the best way to meet locals and make friends?

Here's a simple trick to make friends in Anzio: just ask people to tell you about their favorite football (soccer) team (the exact phrase is *di che squadra sei?*). The most common answers are Roma and Lazio. Once you know the person's favorite, just say *Forza Roma!* or *Forza Lazio!* (whichever team they prefer), which means "I love Roma!" or "I love Lazio!" I guarantee you that it will be like having a VIP pass on your hand. You will be impressed by how friendly they will suddenly become.

Why should people make sure to visit Anzio?

Anzio is the old sea heart of Italy. It was one of the first Italian harbors in the Roman Empire and visiting the Caves of Nero, especially at sunset, will make you feel like you are in a time machine.

ROME & LAZIO

Where can we go to take beautiful photos?
The Caves of Nero at sunset and the main harbor in the early morning (before 9 a.m.).

Anything else you want us to know?
Anzio is famous for two reasons: 1) its popularity during the Roman Empire, along with Ostia, and 2) its role in the conquering of Rome by American soldiers during WWII. That is why we have a little war museum, a wide American international cemetery, and the Piana delle Orme Museum.

Find Moyan at: earthincolors.wordpress.com.

NAPLES & CAMPANIA

Where the birthplace of pizza
meets the candy-colored cliffside
towns of the Amalfi Coast.

In this section: Naples / Portici /
Pompei / Sorrento / Amalfi /
Positano

Photo by: Jimmy Harris (jimmyharris) on
Flickr.

Naples

*This gritty Italian city is the home of real pizza and breathtaking
human drama.*

Renato Bova
Native Neapolitan. Soccer Player. Explorer.

First, tell us about you.

I was born in Napoli, but I live in Acerra, a town just 10
kilometers from the city, which is really a suburb of Naples. The
town where I grew up (Pulcinella) is famous for a mask that
everybody believes came from Napoli. I have lived here for 35
years (my whole life).

I grew up playing soccer in the street (like 99% of the men
here). In my free time, I prefer to walk with friends in the center
of Napoli, especially near the old university (*Spaccanapoli, Via
Tribunali*, and around), which is a really young area of the city.

I also love to discover new places in the city; I think that Napoli
is unique in this aspect. At 35 years old, I continue to discover
squares, bars, *trattorias*, churches, and buildings every year. My
Napoli is rich in everything.

238

NAPLES & CAMPANIA

If someone is visiting Naples for the first time, what do you recommend they see or do?

I recommend taking a walk among the people. Napoli is like an open theater, full of life (in a good and a bad way). In order to touch the "real" city, seek out the popular markets (the city is full of all kinds of them). The fish market near *Porta Nolana* is the best (and really loud).

For pizza, I send everybody to Michele (at *Via Cesare Sersale 1/3*) restaurant; it's great!

Then, of course, I recommend going to the aristocratic places too: *Piazza Plebiscito, Posillipo* (the best views are from this hill), and the *Santa Lucia* area, next to the sea. There's so much to see here, but, of course, it depends how much time you have. Personally, I think Napoli deserves a week or more.

What neighborhoods or parts of town are best to stay in?

I recommend the big hotels in *Santa Lucia*, just in front of the sea. They are very expensive, but the views are beautiful. In the old city center, I recommend staying on *Via Tribunali, Spaccanapoli,* or *Via Toledo*. Then you really could say to your friends "I was in Napoli," because this is the heart of the city.

Make sure to avoid hotels near the central train station.

Let's talk about day trips...what nearby places should everyone make sure to visit?

With the Vesuviana train, you can easily move from Pompei to the Herculaneum ruins, from Stabia to the Oplonti ruins, and from the Vesuvio crater to Sorrento. Many people visit these places in one day.

Another interesting option is *Campi Flegrei*, an old Greek volcanic area in the west.

If is your first visit, I suggest you visit at least one island—Capri, Ischia, or Procida—especially if there's good weather.

Finally, a less well-known and more off-the-beaten-track spot that I love is *Reggia di Caserta*, a huge royal palace surrounded by a big Versailles-style park. (Also, an amazing place to play soccer.)

Tell us about the local dishes. What should people try?

Mmm...Start with *sfogliatella* (very sweet pastry with ricotta cheese), *babà* (another sweet, soft pastry with rum), and *pastiera* (a cake made with grain cereal).

Pizza is actually just from Napoli...even 10 kilometers away it tastes different.
Photo by: Sebastian Mary on Flickr.

Pizza! (Do I even have to say this?) Many people abroad think that pizza is good all over Italy. This is not true! Pizza is actually just from Napoli (even in my town, just 10 kilometers away, pizza tastes different). So make sure to have a pizza here—and not just pizza, but also a *fried pizza*.

Also: pasta with beans and mussels, *menesta maritata* (vegetable and meat soup), *zuppa di cozze* (normally they serve you an enormous dish, so make sure to come hungry if you order this one), and *spaghetti a vongole* (clam spaghetti).

If you come during Easter, try *casatiello* (a cake full of cheese, salami, and black pepper). For Christmas, order *struffoli* (fried little bread balls with honey).

What are your top three favorite bars and restaurants?

Restaurants: Michele (at *Via Cesare Sersale 1/3*), Zi'Teresa (under Castel Dell'Ovo at *Via Borgo Marinari 1*), and Luise (located at *Via Toledo 266* and good for little fried things).

Bars: Attanasio (best *sfogliatella* pastries near the station at *Vico Ferrovia 1/2/3/4*), Bar Mexico (at *Piazza Giuseppe Garibaldi 72*, for the coffee), and drink bars in *Piazza Bellini* (for a nice atmosphere with tables in the square).

Is there anything tourists do that locals find rude or strange? What can we do to better fit in with the culture?

Strange: Old people with socks (normally white) and sandals, asking for a tea at lunch with a pizza, and the fact that foreigners don't use the bidet.

Rude: when people assume that southern Italians are mafia.

For me, it is also offensive when a tourist says that they came here just to visit Pompei and I tell them they are missing out on such a unique city (Naples) and they tell me my city is too dangerous.

I also wish women didn't think that all southern Italian men were the stereotypical *machismo*.

What is the best way to meet locals and make friends?

I think you just have to avoid stereotypes about mafia (*camorra*), garbage, or other bad things when you speak. Then it is very easy in every context to meet people— especially if you eat with them. (But don't be surprised if every time they try to offer you the bill.)

Why should people make sure to visit Naples?

Because Napoli is older than Roma. Because Napoli is a constant, stimulating contradiction of good and evil. Because Napoli is the home of 2,500 years of art and architecture. Because Napoli was one of the great capitols of Europe. Because you didn't know that Napoli was so beautiful. Because, just in one day, you can learn something (Napoli is really a theater of humanity).

Where can we go to take beautiful photos?

NAPLES & CAMPANIA

From *Parco Virgiliano* in Posillipo there is an incredible view of the city. Moreover, there's the contrast between the green of the park, the blue of the sea, and the red of Vesuvius.

I would also suggest the view from *Castel Sant'Elmo* and from *Castel dell'Ovo* (near the sea).

Anything else you want us to know?

If there's a soccer match on Sunday, that's a good excuse to see the famous passionate soul of the Neapolitan. The stadium is very big (70,000 people) and many times full. It's also nice to see all the life around the stadium, with its mix of supporters and merchants selling everything you can imagine.

Teatro San Carlo is the oldest opera theater in Europe and it's just amazing.

Personally, I love Positano (Amalfi coast) by night and the path of the gods, a walking path along the mountains of Amalfi coast.

Every time I see a tourist, I hope he will meet some citizens, because it is really the best way to see the city, to drink, to eat, and to see the people from another perspective.

As tourists, we hear that Naples is dangerous and has a lot of pickpockets. Is this true? How can we be safe?

Yes, there's a magic aura about our thieves! They are famous for their speed and cleverness.

To stay safe, avoid a few dangerous areas (I'd say, *Sanità*, *Forcella*, and *Quartieri Spagnoli*, but you can ask other locals for their opinions too), though I do walk in those areas at night myself. Pay attention when you are on buses or if you are on a deserted street and hear a motorcycle coming up behind you. If you can blend in a little, not seem like a typical tourist, that's the best thing.

NAPLES & CAMPANIA

Antonio Ag

Doctor. Soccer Enthusiast. Native Neapolitan.

First, tell us about you.

I was born in Naples and have always lived here (except for two years in Paris in my late twenties). In my free time, I like to see friends, go out for a drink, take walks, eat, enjoy good music and good conversations, go to the cinema, see a soccer match (a decidedly Neapolitan pastime at the stadium called *San Paolo*). I am also a sports enthusiast (especially for soccer). Sometimes I like to stay alone just reading a good book or listening to music.

If someone is visiting Naples for the first time, what do you recommend they see or do?

Take a walk in the historical center from *Piazza Plebiscito* to *Piazza del Gesù* and then *Spaccanapoli*, *Via dei Tribunali*, *Piazza Bellini*, and *Piazza Dante*. You'll find yourself deep in the true atmosphere of Naples.

What neighborhoods or parts of town are best to stay in?

I like the historical center; in particular, the area between *Piazza Dante*, *Piazza Bellini*, and *Piazza del Gesù,* and the *Riviere di Chiaia* (though that last neighborhood can get a little expensive).

Let's talk about day trips...what nearby places should everyone make sure to visit?

I strongly suggest a visit to *Campi Flegrei*, a vast area at west of Naples around the seaside town of Pozzuoli. There you'll find a lot of Roman ruins, spas, and small, picturesque harbors.

Tell us about the local dishes. What should people try?

Pizza, of course, is something to try in Naples. It's unlike anything you can find in any other part of the world. The best places to eat pizza are in *Via dei Tribunali*, *Via Pignasecca*, *Via Paladino*, and *Via Benedetto Croce* in the historical center.

NAPLES & CAMPANIA

Other local dishes to try include *pasta col ragù* (pasta with meat sauce), *gattò di patate* (a traditional dish made with potatoes, eggs, herbs, cheese, and ham), *sartù di riso* (rice balls filled with meat and vegetables), *pasta al forno* (oven-baked pasta), *crocché di patate* (potato fritters), *pasta provola e patate* (potato and provolone pasta), and *pasta alla Genovese* (pesto pasta).

For fish lovers, try *spaghetti con le vongole* (spaghetti with clams), *impepata di cozze* (peppered mussels), *pasta cozze e fagioli* (pasta with mussels and beans), and *orata all'acqua pazza* (fish in a garlic and tomato sauce).

For desserts, try *baba al rum* (rum cake), *bignè alla crema* (cream puffs), *sfogliatelle ricce e frolle* (flaky, cream-filled pastry), and *pastiera* (an Italian cake made with ricotta cheese).

And, of course, you should have some *caprese* (tomato and mozzarella with olive oil and spices).

What are your top three favorite bars and restaurants?
Restaurants: La Stanza del Gusto (located at *Via Santa Maria di Costantinopoli 100*), Palazzo Petrucci (at *Piazza San Domenico Maggiore 4*), and La Scialuppa (on *Borgo Marinari*).

Bar: Archivio Storico (on *Via Morghen*), Nea Art Gallery (in *Piazza Bellini*), and Babar (at *Via Bisignano*).

Is there anything tourists do that locals find rude or strange? What can we do to better fit in with the culture?
Italian people dress quite well on average. If you dress sloppy, you'll stand out as a tourist immediately.

What is the best way to meet locals and make friends?
The best way is to have a Neapolitan friend introduce you, but Couchsurfing.org is also a good option.

Why should people make sure to visit Naples?

244

NAPLES & CAMPANIA

Naples is one of the few really authentic places left, not only in Italy, but in Europe. Many places are structured for tourists, but in this way they lose their true identity. Naples is always itself; it is not for sale, ever.

Where can we go to take beautiful photos?
One of the best places is surely *Via Petrarca a Posillipo*. Another is the Castle Sant'Elmo a San Martino.

Anything else you want us to know?
The more you know the local people, the more you can know the true Naples.

Yeny Yohana
Spanish Teacher. Expat. Film Buff. Yogi.

First, tell us about you.
I'm Peruvian, from Lima. I've been living in Naples for 10 years. I came to study and now I teach Spanish at the university and I am pursuing a PhD.

In my free time, I like going to the cinema, because there are so many options here and it is cheap. I also like going for walks on the weekend with my friends and visiting sights around the city, because there are always many different activities to take part in. Recently I have taken up yoga, which is very relaxing for me, and sometimes I go to the library to read.

If someone is visiting Naples for the first time, what do you recommend they see or do?
On the first day, walk around the city to take in the atmosphere—because Naples is very lively. Also, walk along the coast and the historic center and eat a pizza in a traditional Italian restaurant, where locals go. I would also suggest visiting the palace, the castles, the monasteries, and the churches, including the *Duomo, Santa Maria La Nova*, and *San Domenico*. You could also sit outside and have a coffee in one of the many bars.

NAPLES & CAMPANIA

What neighborhoods or parts of town are best to stay in?

There are many hotels in *Chiaia* and along the coast. However, they are very expensive. The best place is the historic center because the prices are more reasonable and it is interesting to stay there.

Let's talk about day trips...what nearby places should everyone make sure to visit?

Many people visit Pompei, Sorrento, the Almalfi Coast, and Mount Vesuvius. Also, you can't miss the islands of Ischia, Capri, Vietri sul Mare, and Procida. Recently, I was in *Palazzo Suriano*; it's one of the most prestigious buildings in Vietri sul Mare (near Costiera Amalfitana). I loved it.

Tell us about the local dishes. What should people try?

In Naples, you can eat well without spending a lot. Try a typical green vegetable called *friarelli* with sausage, as well as *ragu* (meat sauce) pasta, sausage and French fry pizza, and fried fish. You can buy slices of pizza and various fried foods in a cone on the street. And don't forget gelato and other sweet delights such as *babà*, which is a cake soaked in rum.

What are your top three favorite bars and restaurants?

Pizzerie DiMatteo (located at *Via Tribunali 94*), Starita (at *Via Materdei 27*), Da Michele (at *Via Cesare Sersale 1/3*), Sorbillo (at *Via dei Tribunali 32*), Da Pellone (at *Via Nazionale 93*), and Brandi (at *Salita Sant'Anna di Palazzo 1-2*).

The street food is very famous here: *fritture* (fries), *pizzette* (mini pizzas), and *rustici* (puff pastry filled with veggies or meat). In the university area, try the street food at Luise (located at *Piazza dei Martiri 68*).

My favorite restaurant is Gigino (located at *Via degli Archi 15*). I love it for the home cooking and friendly atmosphere.

Is there anything tourists do that locals find rude or strange? What can we do to better fit in with the culture?

246

Don't drink cappuccino at night or in the evening or eat dinner at six in the evening or leftover pasta the next day. Italians always eat pasta freshly made.

What is the best way to meet locals and make friends?
The best way is to meet people on the street or at San Pasquale (a place where there are many small bars) or the university zone. Obviously, if you work here, then it's easier.

Why should people make sure to visit Naples?
People should visit Naples because it is different than other Italian cities, especially compared to the north of Italy. It is a city full of contradictions and people on the street are friendly and welcoming.

Where can we go to take beautiful photos?
You can take pictures of people living their day-to-day lives on the streets. You can also take pictures in the historical center, where there are many historical buildings, or along the coast, where there are good views of Mount Vesuvius.

Portici (Naples)

At the foot of Mount Vesuvius, along the Bay of Naples, Portici is known for its expansive former Royal palace.

Diego Piermatteo
Genealogical Researcher. Traveler. Culinary Hobbyist.

First, tell us about you.
My name is Diego. I'm 36 and live in the perfect center of the Gulf of Naples, in Portici, a little town very close to Naples. Portici was the suburban district of ancient Ercolaneum (1st century) and the ancient summer residence of Borboni Naples Kings (XVII – XIX century).

NAPLES & CAMPANIA

My family is all from Naples, at least from XVIII century; the grandfather of my grandfather (dad's side) moved to Naples from the Abruzzo mountains when the first factories were built in the Kingdom of Two Sicilies. And the grandfather of my grandmother (mom's side) arrived in Naples after the Union of North Kingdom with South Kingdom (1861) during the *piemontesizzazione* process (when the northern people were sent to the south).

If you're wondering, I know the full history of my family's story because my first hobby is genealogical research.

I lived in Naples from birth to 25, when I spent six years in the extreme north (Varese) and the extreme south of Calabria, passing through Genova, Modena, Parma, Roma, Brindisi, and, now, returning in Naples.

My favorite hobbies are historical research (as you know), reading, traveling through every Italian region, cooking and drinking, and staying with foreign people.

If someone is visiting Portici and Naples for the first time, what do you recommend they see or do?
My first work, when I was a student, was as a tourist guide and I created some tours in order to show people as much as possible in little time. My tours are focused on old stories, legends, myths, and ancient gossip—things that interest tourists of every age and culture—all of which Naples has a lot of. My goal is to show you a particular Naples...Naples that is only known by Neapolitans.

Naples is a very strange and particular town, where poverty is mixed with richness, where ancient lives in close proximity with new, where folklore is the everyday. Only by walking around can you truly appreciate and fall in love of it.

Obviously, every tour must start from the historical center (a UNESCO World Heritage Site), with all its dark alleys and darker bassi (with a literal meaning of "low," these homes on ground floor consist of only one room and house whole families).

While you're walking around, stroll down Spaccanapoli, a long alley that cuts old Naples into two parts. This is one of most ancient streets—from the 25th century—and along it you can see workshops for many different things.

Another street—San Gregorio Armeno—is the most special street in the world. This little street is where all the presepi craftsman make and display their tiny nativity scenes.

In a small corner, you'll find Santa Patrizia Church, which is probably the most artistic Baroque church complex and convent, in which nuns, Neapolitans orphans, and abandoned children live their lives.

San Lorenzo Church and its museum are a very, very interesting place, where you can walk through three different historical periods by walking on three different roads superimposed on each other. One is an ancient Greek market road, another a Medieval market road, and the third a Middle-Age street. You'll discover that nothing has really changed in 20 centuries!

The ancient Monte di Pieta (pawnshop) is a wonderful palace, rich in different, incredible, unusual, sad, and funny stories.

There's also the Santa Chiara Church, Neapolitan Pantheon, and San Gregorio Armeno—the oldest Naples church, where the Borboni Kings of Naples are buried.

San Severo and Cristo Velato are considered the most beautiful sculptures in the world and are shrouded in mystery because their author was a magician.

San Gennaro Church, dedicated to the patron of the city, is seen by Neapolitans as a living person, with all its legends. This is not to be missed.

249

NAPLES & CAMPANIA

If you still have time after seeing all that, go to the Royal Palace, located on the sea, with its Plebiscito Plaza (one of the largest in Italy), San Carlo Theatre (built in only eight months), King Umberto I Gallery (a very wonderful place), *Maschio Angioino* (a Medieval castle with five towers, each with its own name and heroic story), the Botanic Gardens, Fuga Palace (which King Borbone built to host the city's poor and which, later, become a prison for children during the Nazi occupation), and the San Gennaro Door (which opens to another world...the popular *Sanità District*).

Also, check out Toledo Street, with all its shops and local markets and old wonderful palaces (on the left, along its entire length, is the *Quartieri Spagnoli*—Spanish district—one of most popular and dangerous districts). Go through Dante Plaza (and look to the right for the ancient door of *portalba*, which gives access to the ancient district of booksellers and Bellini Plaza, where you'll find the oldest remains of ancient Greek Naples). Then go to Cavour Plaza and visit the Archaeological Museum, which preserves everything found in Ercolaneum and Pompei.

On the sea, there is the *Caracciolo Street*; for Neapolitans (and not only us), this is the most beautiful walk and view in the world. You can see the gulf, Vesuvio (the volcano), Capri, and the Ischia and Procida islands. On the walk, you'll see *Castel dell'Ovo* (a white castle whose name means egg), which is wrapped in thousand legends of wizards, alchemists, and ghosts, and is joined to the mainland by a rock bridge. You'll also pass the wonderful *Villa Comunale*, which houses a lot of statues and the oldest Italian aquarium (all built on an artificial embankment of remains of wars on the sea), the little, but very rich touristic harbor of *Mergellina* (which means silver sea), Sannazzaro Plaza (where you'll see the statue of the mythological siren, Partenope, the symbol of Naples), and the *Posillipo* district (the richest district, made up of only old palaces and villas on the sea).

Finally, *Napoli sotterranea* (Naples underground) and tunnel *borbonico*—an entire city 40 meters underground, born of

250

aqueducts and tanks for the ancient city, which was used as a refuge from bombing during Second World War and is now an authentic museum—are worth seeing, as is Seiano Tunnel and the *Posillipo* district, an authentic paradise of hills, parks, and Roman history, where ancient kings took their holidays.

What neighborhoods or parts of town are best to stay in?

Stay in the center, avoiding popular and far-away districts, in order to fully experience the city and stay safe. The serious problems of Naples are petty crime and inefficient public transport.

If you're staying in the center, I recommend the Central Station area (avoiding the station's immediate surroundings), *Corso Umberto I/Rettifilo* and its squares, the university area, *Via Duomo*, the *San Ferdinado* district, or, if you'd like to be a bit farther out, the *Vomero* district.

For simple living people, there is a good hostel on Salvator Rosa Street.

If you'd rather stay outside the city and if you have a car, consider nearby towns like Ercolano, the wonderful Pozzuoli, San Giorgio, and my own Portici.

Let's talk about day trips...what nearby places should everyone make sure to visit?

It is mandatory to go to Sorrento and the Amalfi Coast. If you're going by car, take freeway A3, exit in Vietri (where the Amalfi Coast starts), and drive the coast, stopping in the towns along the way—Vietri (with its ceramics), Cetara (known for anchovies), Maiori, Minori, Amalfi (with its cathedral), Praiano, Positano (with all its endless stairs)—and returning through the Sorrento Coast (Sorrento, Piano, Meta, Vico).

When you stop in Amalfi, park your car along the harbor and visit the wonderful cathedral (where Saint Andrew is buried) and the small village. Entering the Cathedral Square from the small streets of the harbor, the view will leave you breathless.

NAPLES & CAMPANIA

In Positano, after you climb the giant staircase to the beach, turn toward the mountain behind you and contemplate a unique view in the world.

In Sorrento, the most beautiful view is from the balcony of Saint Francis Convent.

Of course, you'll also want to visit the Ercolaneum and Pompei, remains of two ancient, rich Roman cities. In Pompei, you can see elements of Roman urban architecture.

I also recommend the little-known *Oplontis Villa* in Torre Annunziata very close to Pompei; it is a wonderful imperial villa, perfectly intact. Also, if you want, the Amphitheater of Santa Maria Capua Vetere, near Caserta, the second biggest Roman amphitheater after Rome's Colosseum.

To stay in theme, I think it's necessary to go up Mount Vesuvius; the climb starts in Ercolano or Torre del Greco and continues for 10 kilometers (you can go by car) through National Vesuvio Park and a green park (with every type of Mediterranean plant and flower growing on the lava!) and stops in a parking lot. From there, you can go on foot for a kilometer to the mouth of the volcano!

Another very singular experience is visiting *Piscina Mirabilis* (the "wonderful pool") in Pozzuoli; this is the largest tank for drinking water ever built by Romans, made as a water reservoir for Roman ships. In Pozzuoli, you can also admire Serapide Temple in the middle of the main square, a very singular Greek temple (indeed, an ancient market) where the ground rises and falls (in a phenomenon called *bradisismo*) over time.

After all that, go north to visit Caserta and its Royal Palace and gardens, which are the most beautiful in the world (or so say the greatest experts and historians). Also north are the ancient Medieval villages called Caserta Vecchia, Old Caserta, and San Leucio.

To the south, try Paestum (with its three ancient temples, including the Athens Necropolis) and all villages of the Cilento Coast. That said, I think it is better to spend more days on these, because all of them are very beautiful Medieval sea villages—and you should definitely visit the sea.

Finally, farther away (two hours by car), but absolutely worth a visit, I recommend Matera: an entire city carved out in the rock, with thousands of caves used like homes (this is now a UNESCO World Heritage Site and where Mel Gibson made The Passion of the Christ).

Tell us about the local dishes. What should people try? What are your top three favorite bars and restaurants?

Obviously, Naples is known for its pizza. In Naples, we have codes about how pizza must be prepared—even for the type of wood to use in the oven! (Keep in mind that home delivery is an American idea, not an Italian one.)

Neapolitans invented fast food centuries ago. Pizza is, of course, the queen of all these; some succulent variations are *pizza salsicce e friarjelli* (two pizzas layered with stuffing of sausage and particular bitter herbs that grow only on volcanic lands), *pizza di scarole* (two pizzas layered with a stuffing of fried salad with anchovies and olives), *ripieno fritto* (fried dough stuffed with ricotta, pepper, lard, and ham), and *frittata di maccheroni* (pasta omelet).

You should also try *montanara* (a little, fried pizza *margherita*), *zeppole* and *zeppole d'alghe* (simple fried dough with or without seaweed), *panzarotti* (breaded cylinders of potato, mozzarella, and ham), *scagnuozzi* (fried cornmeal), *arancini/palle di riso* (breaded balls of boiled rice with or without tomato sauce, meat, and peas), *panuozzi* (a big crusty bread, emptied and stuffed with meat, sometimes mozzarella, and bitter herbs), *cuozzo* (crusty bread stuffed with bean salad and onions), *brodo di polpo* (octopus broth), *o pere e 'o musso* (raw pork with salt and lemon), veggies fried in batter, and fried fish, in batter or not. All these you can find in every pizza shop or stand. The best are in the historical center.

253

The locals are also fond of *cozze crude* (mussels), but, for safety reasons, I don't recommend them.

Another very particular dish that you can only get in Naples is *taralli*—a little twisted donut made from salt dough with pepper and almonds. Legend says that a poor old lady invented them by gathering scraps of bread from the seawater to sell. In fact, tradition dictates that *tarallo* must be eaten sponged in seawater.

Moving on from street food, let's talk about sweets: the queen of Neapolitan sweets is *pastiera*—a very old invention of a Sorrento nun, this wonderful cake is made from wheat and ricotta and is typical around Easter. Its variant from the mountains is called *migliaccio* and is made with semolina flour. The best place to buy one is Scaturchio in San Domenico Square.

Other dishes Naples is known for include *sfogliatelle ricce* and *sfogliatelle frolle* (shortbread stuffed with cream, ricotta, dried and candied fruit, and lemon liquor and eaten hot—the best place to eat it is Attansio near Central Station), *babà* (soft dough soaked in rum), *delizia* (soft dough covered with lemon cream—the best place to try it is the bar in front of Amalfi Cathedral), and *struffoli* (hard fried dough balls dipped in honey and candied).

Finally, Naples is a coffee town, so you must have a coffee in Bar Gambrinus in Plebiscito square, for historical and traditional reasons, or a coffee shaken in Bar Cimmino in the *Posillipo* district.

Why should people make sure to visit Portici and Naples?
The greatest authorities in the world consider Naples the most beautiful city in the world; J.W. Ghoete wrote "see Naples and then you can die."

Where can we go to take beautiful photos?

NAPLES & CAMPANIA

To take unforgettable photos, I recommend panoramic places, like the street on the sea (*Lungomare Caracciolo*), especially near Mergellina harbor, near castles, in the short streets the historic center, Plebiscito Square, Santa Lucia beach, Municipio Square, Maschio Angioino Castle, behind the Royal Palace.

Outside Naples, I recommend photos of Vesuvio and on the street to Sorrento (though you'll have to take that quick and from the passenger seat, as there's no place to stop).

Finally, a place known only to Neapolitans (and not all), where you can see the most beautiful and complete view of Naples (including Mount Vesuvius and the Sorrento Coast) is a little terrace in Nevio Street, in Posillipo district, where you can take the best photos!

Anything else you want us to know?
Going to Ercolano from Naples, you must pass through Portici and you can stop to see the Borboni Summer Royal Palace (a very singular Royal Palace with a great hunting park on one side and the sea on the other), the ancient military harbor of Granatello (one of the most beautiful views of all Naples), and Pietrarsa Rail Museum (where you can find some of the oldest locomotives in Europe).

Pompei

After you've walked the ancient ruins in the sunshine, try a nighttime tour as well.

Saverio Danubio
Art & Nature Enthusiast.

First, tell us about you.
My name is Saverio Danubio. I was born and still live in a little village near Pompei. I am a friendly and sunny guy and like

meeting new people and discovering new things. My passions go toward art, nature, sustainability, sports, design, and technologies.

If someone is visiting Pompei for the first time, what do you recommend they see or do?

First of all, spend at least one day visiting the ruins of old city. In Pompei, there is a rare (perhaps even singular) opportunity to see how exactly a Roman village was 20 centuries ago.

The entrance gates, in Porta Marina Inferiore Square and next to Immacolata Square, are closer to the center of the new city and the train stations. Inside the ruins, the roads of old Pompei are made of ancient square stones and lead to the temple of Apollo, the theater, the baths, and many other public and private structures.

In some houses, there are visible plaster casts of citizens and the animals that died covered by the ashes. The mosaics and fresco paintings clearly show the habits of wealthy Romans. And everything is fixed at year 79 A.D., when the old city was completely covered by the Vesuvius volcano eruption. Sometimes you can visit the ruins by night on guided tours; do not miss this awesome experience.

Sometimes you can visit the Pompei ruins at night on a guided tour. This is a must-see.
Photo: Carlo Mirante on Flickr.

Pompei also offers another kind of tourism. The new city is an important religious destination, visited several times by various popes. Even if you aren't coming to Pompei to pray, the awesome sanctuary of blessed Virgin of the Rosary and its

NAPLES & CAMPANIA

tower bell are worth admiring. Inside the structure, there is the tomb of Blessed Bartolo Longo, the founder of the shrine.

The touristic area with many restaurants and bars is around the Bartolo Longo Square garden and the adjacent Roma street, which has souvenir stores, where the tourists pass hours buying fancy things, postcards, and fake pieces of ruins.

What neighborhoods or parts of town are best to stay in?

I suggest remaining in the city center, where there are a lot of accommodation options suitable for any budget. There are luxury Hotels like the Palma and Forum, both next to the sanctuary. And, located in Plinio Street, near the gate to the ruins, there are numerous camping options and bungalows.

Let's talk about day trips...what nearby places should everyone make sure to visit?

If you're interested in archeology, there are lots of interesting sites in Campania that merit a visit. In less than half an hour by the local train (the *Circumvesuviana*), you can visit the ruins of Antiquarium, Ercolano, Oplonti, Stabia, and Longola. The latter is a really promising prehistoric installation in Poggiomarino that just recently came to the light and is not yet open.

If you want to escape from the monuments and enjoy some relaxation, you can go to the termae located on the beautiful Island of Ischia or in Castellamare di Stabia, where I advise you, also, to taste a really good Italian *gelato* and wander along the waterfront.

For those interested in the religious monuments, Amalfi cathedral, Montevergine, and Sant'Anastasia sanctuaries are all within an hour. Each Easter Monday in Sant'Anastasia, there is a traditional procession in honor of the *Madonna dell'Arco*, which draws more than 10,000 visitors.

Other nearby places to see include the islands of the gulf of Naples: Capri, Ischia, and Procida. All three are accessible by ferries from Beverello marina.

NAPLES & CAMPANIA

Capri is a little and charming island with two tall, iconic rock spurs called *faraglioni*. It is the island of very important people and, actually, in the summertime, it is not rare see Hollywood stars lounging there. There are a lot of important hotels and villas on Capri that have been the locations of movies and TV fictions.

Ischia is the bigger island. It is a thermal location, also appreciated for its beautiful summer places. Tourists seem to stay in Ischia much longer than the other islands—usually more than just a weekend. When people think of Ischia, they often picture the mushroom-shaped rock in front of the beach of Lacco Ameno.

Procida is the smallest of these three islands. It is a pretty, quiet fishing island. The port where little boats are moored and its colorful houses are picture perfect.

Finally, there is one place where you can see all of the places I've mentioned at one time. This is the top of the Vesuvius volcano. By car, it is about one hour from Pompei, but part of the trip to the top is on foot (for 15 minutes).

The mouth of volcano has a diameter of hundreds of meters, as does its inner cavity. Today, the soil there is dark and porous. And while the volcano is still active, it does not smoke at all.

Tell us about the local dishes. What should people try?
As far as I know, Pompei does not have a typical dish. The meals here are obviously influenced by the Mediterranean and Neapolitan culinary traditions.

In the touristic area next to Roma Street, many restaurants serve good, characteristic meals. My ideal menu, which you will easily find in the restaurants, starts with a rich *antipasto* made of fried tiny fishes, algae batter, potato croquettes, grilled vegetables in oil, and buffalo mozzarella, ricotta, Neapolitan salami, and other local cold cuts.

Next, I'd have *pasta di Gragnano* with seaweed, fish, or octopus. Another typical first dish is the *gnocchi alla Sorrentina* (dumplings in tomato sauce with mozzarella). Pair this with good and cheap homemade wines from the local farmers or famous wines like *Lacryma Christi* (a really tasty wine with ancient origins, made from the grapes grown on the slopes of Vesuvius).

As second dish, I'd choose grilled or roasted fish.

Then, for dessert, try *caprese*, wheat tarts, *babà* (a small cake doused in rum), and *sfogliatelle* (shell-shaped filled pastries). Depending on the time of year, you can also try the *struffoli* (deep fried dough balls available during Carnival) and the delicious *zeppole* (more deep fried dough balls) of Saint Joseph, prepared on the days around March 19th. Each meal should be closed with the famous lemon drink of Sorrento, *Limoncello*, and Neapolitan coffee.

Finally, some foods I didn't mention, but are typical in this region: *pomodorini di piennolo* (Vesuvian tomatoes), Neapolitan bagels with black pepper and almonds, *casatiello* (stuffed Easter bread), *panuozzo* (traditional thin-bread sandwiches) made in Gragnano, hazelnuts, and the Annurca apple.

And important wines of the region: *Falerno*, *Fiano*, *Greco di Tufo*, *Aglianico*, and *Taurasi*.

Of course, there's also the food that made Naples and Italy famous in every corner of world: the pizza. The pizza of Naples is absolutely the best and there is no way to copy it.

What are your top three favorite bars and restaurants?

Zi Caterina (located at *Via Roma 20*): inside this old restaurant, there is a traditional and warm atmosphere and the waiters are very friendly and efficient. They offer cheap touristic menus with a wide selection of Neapolitan dishes. The *spigoletta panatenea* (a local fish dish) is very good.

NAPLES & CAMPANIA

Il Principe Restaurant, located at *Piazza Bartolo Longo 8*, has a refined and elegant style and the waiting service is perfect. Try the old Roman meals there, especially the *oplontis cassata* (their signature cake).

Kobe, located at *Via Carlo Alberto 76/80*, is a grill, pizzeria, and more. It's just five minutes from the main square. This is not exactly a restaurant, but a fashionable and famous place to enjoy the nightlife in Pompei and eat something.

For bars, I recommend: the De Vivo pastry shop (located at *Via Roma 38\42*). It is a very famous, historic bar and pastry shop. There is always a long line of people for its ice creams.

Next: Gabbiano Dulcis (located at *Via Lepando 153*), which is just a five-minute walk from the sanctuary. It is a modern and elegant bar with a first-level Neapolitan pastry shop. Its sweets are delicious and there are also some cakes made from old Pompeian recipes.

Finally: hcca24 (located at *Viale Giuseppe Mazzini 48*). It is a full bar and offers a wide selection of sweet and salty foods. This bar is the ideal place for happy hours and meeting new people at night.

Is there anything tourists do that locals find rude or strange? What can we do to better fit in with the culture?

Italians, in general, do not like to see half-bare people walking around the city (or inside the churches). Don't drink cappuccino or colored sparkling water with vitamins next to a delicious dish of pasta. It is not properly in harmony with our tastes. And if you are not sure what you should order and would like eat as Italians do, feel free to ask somebody next to you. It will be a nice way to make acquaintances as well.

What is the best way to meet locals and make friends?

People here are basically friendly and it is a welcoming culture. It is very easy make new friends here. The locals who have some free time usually go walking in the city center or sit in bars drinking coffee or aperitifs at happy hour. They will be glad to talk with a polite and smiley new friend. (And they will love to give you recommendations regarding the stay in Pompei).

If you see a table of scopone (a card game) players, try to join them. Your partner will try to tip you off about his hand with colorful facial expressions and it will be very funny. If you want to see a preview about the typical southern Italians, watch the movie Welcome to the South.

Why should people make sure to visit Pompei?

The city is well connected by many trains and buses, which will take you to Naples, Sorrento, or Rome within an hour. Pompei, with its ruins and the sanctuary, is a nice, interesting destination and a good base for day trips to the other wonders of south Italy.

Where can we go to take beautiful photos?

The ruins will offer many inspirations, behind columns or inside the amphitheater. You can also stand next to the souvenirs shops in Via Roma, outside the shrine, or in the Bartolo Longo Square garden. Also, do not miss the top of the bell tower.

Anything else you want us to know?

A few last recommendations: visit the lovely cities of the coasts (these should be more than a day trip, even though they're close enough to visit in a day). Sorrento and Amalfi are the most representative cities, but all the little cities are worthwhile. These places are full of narrow streets facing the sea, and the mountains of both coasts fall directly into the sea, creating beautiful and sometimes hidden beaches that only locals know. Their lemons are sweet and fragrant. And the view of Amalfi Coast from Villa Cimbrone in Ravello will leave you breathless.

You should also visit the city of Naples. Even though it's only 30 minutes away, it's another place that merits more than a day. The city was the capital of south Italy for many centuries and its monuments are strongly influenced by its many dominations. When I go to Naples, I like to see some of the following places:

NAPLES & CAMPANIA

The king's palace, Plebiscito Square, *Maschio Angioino* (a castle also known as *Castel Nuovo*), *Castel dell'Ovo*, and the area around the Saint Gregorio Armeno, with its figurine handicraftsmen. Also, do not miss *Via Tribunali*, where every pizzeria is amazing.

Finally, go to the royal palace of Caserta. It is a complex of three buildings and has been the summer residence of Spanish kings in the city of Caserta—only about one hour from Pompei. The abundance of marble, paintings, crystal chandeliers, tapestries, etc. clearly show how they lived in richness. Behind the palace, there is a huge green area with meadows, the botanic garden, and a sequence of numerous poles adorned with ancient figures. The Royal Palace of Caserta is essentially the Italian version of the French Versailles.

Sorrento

Enjoy views of Naples, Vesuvius, and the Isle of Capri, perfectly prepared limoncello, and a mild Mediterranean climate

Flavio Caccaviello
Beach-Lover. Surveyor. Local.

First, tell us about you.
I live in a small town near Massa Lubrense and Sorrento. I'm 22 years old and I am a surveyor. In my spare time, I enjoy going to the beach, staying with friends, and going to the gym.

If someone is visiting Sorrento for the first time, what do you recommend they see or do?
To get to Sorrento, take the panoramic road that connects us to Naples; there is a particular point—called Scutari—where you can see all the beauties of the Sorrento peninsula and where there is also a street vendor who makes a delicious

NAPLES & CAMPANIA

lemon *granita*. This is the best welcome and introduction to the region you can get.

What neighborhoods or parts of town are best to stay in?
Surely, the hotels that overlook the Gulf of Naples are the prettiest. For budget travelers, though, hotels in *Sant'Agnello* are only a five-minute walk from Sorrento and are cheaper.

Let's talk about day trips...what nearby places should everyone make sure to visit?
Surely, Capri, Positano, and Amalfi. For those who love nature, the beautiful marine *crapolla* (a fjord nearby) and *jeranto* (the Bay of Sirens) are accessible on foot if you're up for a long walk.

Tell us about the local dishes. What should people try?
Everything is good in Sorrento—from starters to desserts and from coffee to *limoncello*. Definitely do not miss the *paccheri Sorrento* (a tomato and onion pasta), pizza, *Provolone del Monaco*, *spaghetti* with clams, and *penne* with zucchini.

What are your top three favorite bars and restaurants?
For a sunset drink, try Marinella Sant'Agnello (located at *Piazzetta Marinella*).

What is the best way to meet locals and make friends?
Certainly, in the bars, waiters and owners are ready to joke with tourists in a very natural way with Italian-style hospitality.

Why should people make sure to visit Sorrento?
Even though Sorrento is very small compared to Rome and Florence, it's the 5th most visited Italian city. It has certainly charmed a lot of people and there's a reason for that.

Where can we go to take beautiful photos?
Villa Comunale or the bar, La Marinella Sant'Agnello.

NAPLES & CAMPANIA

Nino Miniero
Sorrento Tourism Expert. Soccer Enthusiast.

First, tell us about you.
I am from Sorrento and have lived here from my birth, 63 years ago. In my spare time, I like meeting friends, playing soccer with friends, and watching sports or movies on TV. I work in tourism.

If someone is visiting Sorrento for the first time, what do you recommend they see or do?
See the old town center, the fishing village of Marina Grande, and, of course, a view of the Gulf of Naples from any terrace.

What neighborhoods or parts of town are best to stay in?
In town, it is best to stay in the old center. The *Massa Lubrense* and *Sant'Agata sue due Golfi* neighborhoods are also nice, quiet places to stay, only a 20-minute drive from the center.

Let's talk about day trips...what nearby places should everyone make sure to visit?
Capri, the Amalfi Coast, and Pompei/Herculaneum are the highlights. Then Naples, the islands of Ischia and Procida, Paestum, and Oplontis if you still have time.

Tell us about the local dishes. What should people try?
Gnocchi alla Sorrentina (gnocchi Sorrento style) is one of the most well-known local dishes and is made with potato dumplings, tomatoes, basil, and mozzarella cheese.

Of course, you should also try pasta with seafood or *parmigiana di Melanzane* (fried eggplant with tomato sauce, mozzarella cheese, and basil), and, of course, local fresh fish.

What are your top three favorite bars and restaurants?
Fauno (located at *Piazza Tasso 13 -15*), Ercolano (located at *Via Santa Lucia 15*), and Syrenuse (in *Piazza Tasso*) are good bars in the town center.

NAPLES & CAMPANIA

Da Emilia (at *Via Marina Grande 62* in the fishing village of Marina Grande), Il Buco (a Michelin starred restaurant at *Rampa Marina Piccola 5*), and L'Antica Trattoria (at *Via Padre Reginaldo Giuliani 33*) are my top three restaurant picks. Furthermore, Pizzeria Aurora (at *Piazza Tasso 10/11*) offers 50 different kinds of pizza and is well worth a visit.

Is there anything tourists do that locals find rude or strange? What can we do to better fit in with the culture?
To fit in with the culture, always accept an invitation for a drink, a coffee, or a party, because any invitation comes from the heart.

What is the best way to meet locals and make friends?
Restaurants, bars, and even walking are good places to meet local people and also at the Foreigner's Club (a bar/restaurant in the town center with a sea view, address: *Via Luigi de Maio 35*) where everybody is welcome.

Why should people make sure to visit Sorrento?
Sorrento is the best home base to visit the whole region.

Where can we go to take beautiful photos?
Sorrento is high above the sea—about 90 meters—so any viewpoint is a good place to take photographs. Also, the town center (with its old archways, gates, and shops) and the fishing village are top spots for taking photographs.

Anything else you want us to know?
There are many places in the world where the food is very good, other places where the climate is very mild, other places where it is really beautiful, still other places rich in culture, archaeology, history, etc....But Sorrento has it all, plus the art of hospitality and friendliness handed down from generation to generation. All who come here as a tourist will return as a friend.

Find Nino at: www.sorrentotourism.com.

The Amalfi Coast (Erchie)

This famed coast offers a series of UNESCO World Heritage Sites, as well as the world's best limoncello.

Senem Sonmez
Expat. Trekker.

First, tell us about you.
I was born and raised in The Netherlands, but originally I am from the border between Syria and Turkey. I left the Netherlands for a indefinite world trip on foot, but when i arrived in Italy, I fell in love with a beautiful man and the country and decided to continue my walking in Italy.

On my birthday last year, we decided to do one of the hiking paths between Cetara and Maoiori and we enjoyed it so much that we bought all the maps of the more than 100 paths and started visiting the coast as much as possible. Then, in June last year, we decided to come and live here permanently.

The Amalfi Coast is famous for its coastline, which is beautiful, with houses clinging to the rocks and a clear, blue sea. For me, the best thing about the coast is the combination of the sea and the mountains.

I enjoy fishing with our fisherman friends, rowing with a boat or canoe, being able to swim (even in winter), being able to go on a mountain trek so close to home, picking wild herbs and fruits in the mountains, and meeting old farmers, shepherds, and goats which live freely and eat the best grass possible.

If someone is visiting the Amalfi Coast for the first time, what do you recommend they see or do?
Erchie is a small town—with just 83 inhabitants in winter—which is great. I love the quiet and the beauty of the beach and the

people in winter. In summer, the tourists arrive and the peace goes away (in all of the coastline). In summer, I prefer to be in the mountains, where it is fresh and quiet.

As for the towns along the coast, I like Cetara a lot; it is a fishing town, but very lively. Also, Vietri sul Mare is one of my favorites, because of the ceramics they make and the streets, which look like an open ceramic museum. Minori is where the most generous and sympathetic people of the coast live.

Amalfi is very touristic, but it is definitely worth seeing, especially the white tunnel-arch streets between the houses. About 1,000 meters away from the busy town is one of the most beautiful hiking paths (*valle dei mulini*); it passes through many rivers and waterfalls, which are just magic. In the middle of the river, there are some huge, abandoned paper mills, which are just lovely.

Other towns worth a visit include Ravello (a town of music and extraordinary beauty) and Positano (very characteristic of the region, but also very on-the-beaten-track). One of the most famous paths ends up there in Positano: the path of the gods. (The village of Bomerano is the starting point for the walk, which takes about 4 to 5 hours normally.)

Tell us about the local dishes. What should people try?
Fish! You can buy fish directly off the fishermen's boats. Cetara is famous for having the biggest fleet in Europe for fishing tuna and anchovies...but there are also many other fish here.

Lemons: Amalfi is famous for the *sfusati* lemons. Here they use lemon in everything! *Pasta al limone, dolce al limone,* and even coffee with lemon skin inside...

What are your top three favorite bars and restaurants?
For restaurants I only have two favorites: Ristorante il Convento (located at *Piazza San Francesco 16* in Cetara), which uses many local products and is just delicious. My second favorite, in Minori, is called A Ricetta, (located on *Corso Vittorio Emmanuelle*).

NAPLES & CAMPANIA

Is there anything tourists do that locals find rude or strange? What can we do to better fit in with the culture?

Just have respect for everyone around. Don't leave your plastic bottles on the beaches. Note that in the smaller towns like Cetara it is strange to be topless; save that for the big beaches.

Also, if you rent a wave runner, please go as far away as possible from the beach. It is dangerous for swimmers and petrol in the sea is just a shame. I hear many locals complain about that.

What is the best way to meet locals and make friends?

Just go on the beach and watch the people; they are extraordinarily friendly and like to talk with travelers, so if they see you interested in whatever they are doing (repairing nets for fishing, for example), they will come talk to you.

When you walk around in the mostly abandoned mountains, just smile at the farmers you meet and they'll tell you all about their life.

Why should people make sure to visit the Amalfi Coast?

The Amalfi Coast is just wonderful. It's beautiful with the old houses on the rocks and the many, many lemon terraces that make you feel like you're in a fairytale. The combination of sea and mountains so close to each other is hard to find in Italy and the rest of the world. The whole coastline is full of very strong colors...I really could continue forever...

What is the best place to go take beautiful photos?

The different hiking paths have panoramas like you have never seen before. Every time I go up into the mountains, I regret that we do not have a good camera to take pictures. Also, the beaches are full of characteristic boats and people and it is beautiful.

Positano

This colorful port town is a popular tourist destination and part of the Amalfi Coast—a UNESCO World Heritage Site.

Giuseppe Cuccaro
Tourism Expert. B&B Owner.

First, tell us about you.
My name is Giuseppe Cuccaro and I was born in Positano. I worked with tourists for several years in the wonderful and famous Hotel Il San Pietro di Positano, one of the most beautiful in the world. And now I dedicate myself to running my own B&B, Casa Cuccaro.

If someone is visiting Positano for the first time, what do you recommend they see or do?
Positano is the pearl of the Amalfi Coast and is beautiful from the sea to the top of the mountains. You can discover the city by strolling through the hidden alleys. And you should also see the church with the beautiful Black Madonna and the remains of the crypt and the ruins of the Roman villa.

What neighborhoods or parts of town are best to stay in?
I suggest staying in Nocelle; we are far from the bustle of downtown and the view is wonderful.

Let's talk about day trips...what nearby places should everyone make sure to visit?
You can make several day trips to Capri, Pompei, Amalfi, and Ravello. Also, take a walk along the path of the gods (which is especially nice for trekking lovers).

Tell us about the local dishes. What should people try?
Buffalo mozzarella with fresh tomatoes, spaghetti with seafood, and delicious eggplant *parmigiana*—don't miss any of these while you're here!

NAPLES & CAMPANIA

What are your top three favorite bars and restaurants?
To enjoy a delicious breakfast with a cappuccino and a sea view, try the Caffe Positano (at *Via Pasitea 168/170*) and the Buca di Bacco (at *Via del Brigantino 35/37*).

The restaurants that I prefer and recommend are Il Ritrovo (at *Via Montepertuso 77*), La Tagliata (at *Via Tagliata n32b*), and Le Tre Sorelle (at *Via del Brigantino 27/29*) on the beach.

Is there anything tourists do that locals find rude or strange? What can we do to better fit in with the culture?
Often, our guests complain about the stairs, but Positano is like that—in the mountains and on the sea. Just come prepared for some climbing.

What is the best way to meet locals and make friends?
All young people meet and make new friends at the *rotonda* on the beach. Sometimes even love is born!

Why should people make sure to visit Positano?
It is a magical, romantic place that brings all the colors and scents of the world together.

Where can we go to take beautiful photos?
Every corner of Positano has wonderful views for memorable photos—from the first viewpoints as you enter town, from the beach, and from our terrace of Casa Cuccaro Nocelle, where you can see everything up to the cliffs of Capri!

Anything else you want us to know?
In the summer, there are hourly ferries from 10 a.m. until 1 p.m. to take tourists to the other beaches in the area: Laurito, Arienzo, and Fornillo. It's really nice to dive in a different place each day.

Find Giuseppe at: casacuccaro.it.

NAPLES & CAMPANIA

De Martino
B&B Owner. Gardener. Long-Time Local.

First, tell us about you.
I have always lived in Positano. My business is a B&B. And I like to garden in my free time.

If someone is visiting Positano for the first time, what do you recommend they see or do?
Visit the *Chiesa Madre*, the Medieval crypt, and other beautiful, smaller churches. Go to the beach called Fornillo. Admire the wonderful views from the top of the town. Go shopping in the fashion and ceramic boutiques. Go sailing along the coast.

What neighborhoods or parts of town are best to stay in?
Stay at mid-height in the city, where you can enjoy unobstructed views of the sea and the landscape, there is more peace, and the
prices are cheaper.

Let's talk about day trips...what nearby places should everyone make sure to visit?
The most typical places to visit are: Capri, Sorrento, Pompei, Amalfi, and Ravello.

Tell us about the local dishes. What should people try?
Local dishes to try: *pasta ai frutti di mare* (seafood pasta), *pesce locale* (local fish), *mozzarella* and other fresh cheeses, raw and roasted veggies, and pizza.

Sweets: *gelati e granita di limone* (two different types of lemon ice cream), *sfogliatella* (shell-shaped filled pastries), *babà* (rum cake), *delizia al limone* (lemon cupcakes), and *crostata di frutta fresca* (fresh fruit tart).

Wines: *D.O.C. Costa d'Amalfi and D.O.C. Vesuvio.*

Liquors: *Limoncello* (lemon liquor) and *Mirto* (liquor made from the myrtle plant).

What are your top three favorite bars and restaurants?

Bars: Internazionale (located at *Via Guglielmo Marconi 306*), La Zagara (at *Via dei Mulini 8/10*), and Li Galli (at *Via del Saracino 4*).

Restaurants: Pupetto (located at *Via Fornillo 37*), Vincenzo (at *Viale Pasitea 172*), and La Taverna del Leone (at *Via Laurito 43*).

Is there anything tourists do that locals find rude or strange? What can we do to better fit in with the culture?

Stay in Positano for several days in order to admire the landscape in different light conditions, day or night. Learn about the ancient history of Positano, the characters who have chosen to live here, and the artists who have found inspiration here.

What is the best way to meet locals and make friends?

Spend your time in *La Piazzetta dei Mulini*, on the beaches, in the church that holds mass in English, and on the steps of the rotunda with the lions—and simply talk to people.

Why should people make sure to visit Positano?

People who come to Positano always return. There's something special about this place.

Where can we go to take beautiful photos?

There are so many places to take beautiful photos: the Belvedere, *Punta Reginella*, from the beach looking back up toward the houses, and the many stairs between the houses, which have amazing panoramic views down to the sea.

Anything else you want us to know?

NAPLES & CAMPANIA

You should also visit the hillside villages of Positano, Montepertuso, and Nocelle and walk some of our famous paths, like the way of the gods.

Find De Martino at: www.casasoriano.it.

PUGLIA, MOLISE, & CALABRIA

These lesser-known regions have a few tricks up their sleeves—including hilltop castles, world-famous truffle mushrooms, and colorful port towns.

In this section: Campobasso / Terlizzi / Brindisi / Catanzaro / Lecce

Photo by: Fedewild on Flickr.

Campobasso

Authentic, off-the-beaten-track Italy featuring a hilltop castle and a region famous for truffle mushrooms.

Peter Farina
American Expat. Entrepreneur. Founder, italyMONDO!

First, tell us about you.
I have been in Italy on-and-off for over eight years and have been in Campobasso for the past year.

I'm originally from upstate New York and, though the concept of free time is fairly foreign with an ever-growing business, lately I've been finding the time to rediscover my passion of for fishing.

If someone is visiting Campobasso for the first time, what do you recommend they see or do?
Campobasso has a wonderful historic center, complete with cobblestone alleyways, Medieval gates, and a castle overlooking the entire city. The shopping is great and, since it's not a traditional tourist destination, the prices are reasonable. The food is absolutely mind-blowing. It also makes a perfect

base camp for exploring the entire region of Molise, of which it's the regional capital.

What neighborhoods or parts of town are best to stay in?

There are plenty of B&Bs popping up in the historic center of town and, although there are a few three- and four-star hotels in the city, what makes Campobasso and the entire region of Molise wonderful is the warmth of the people, which is better experienced via B&B.

Let's talk about day trips...what nearby places should everyone make sure to visit?

You can't go to Campobasso without visiting the Medieval city of Termoli. What Termoli lacks in Campobasso's green hills and nearby snowcapped mountains, it adds with sandy beaches and the blue, clear waters of the Adriatic.

In addition, there are the villages of Oratino and Sepino—both registered as one of the *Borghi Piu' Belli d'Italia* (most beautiful villages in Italy). Sepino also offers one of the best-preserved Roman cities in Italy: the ruins in Saepinum (also known as Altilia).

For fishermen, skiers, hikers, and other nature-lovers, nearby Guardiaregia—another picturesque Medieval village sitting over 2,000 feet above sea level—serves as the region's gateway to the Matese Mountains. The World Wildlife Foundation protected area above town is also the second largest wildlife preserve in Italy.

From there, you can then head into the highlands of Alto Molise in the province of Isernia (the other province of the region of Molise). Here, every village is like a postcard.

If I had to pick one place in Isernia, the area known as Alto Volturno, where the Volturno River begins to flow, is a perfect day trip with something for everyone: fantastic restaurants, beautiful walled Medieval villages, charming, perfectly preserved castles, snow-capped mountains, and crystal-clear

PUGLIA, MOLISE, & CALABRIA

streams boasting some of the best fly fishing in southern Italy. This area is always a client favorite.

And no trip to Campobasso and the region of Molise is complete without a cheese tasting in Capracotta (the *Pallotta Caseficio* dairy at *Via Nicola Falconi* is a particular favorite), a visit to the Marinelli Bell Foundry and the rest of the historic center of Agnone, and a stop at the Samnite/Roman ruins in Pietrabbondante.

The region also has countless traditions and festivals that are mostly undiscovered and, thus, authentic, so the to-do list varies by time of year, too. The above are year-round staples, though, and are a must for anyone planning a visit.

Tell us about the local dishes. What should people try?
Where do I begin? The ideas of organic and farm-to-table are a way of life in Campobasso and Molise and, as a result, you'll only be eating food that is fresh and in-season. Dishes can change as fast as week-to-week.

It's hard to beat freshly discovered truffles from the province of Isernia (Molise is the truffle capital of Italy, unbeknownst to most!) or *porcini* mushrooms picked the in the Matese Mountains by the restaurant owner's uncle that very morning.

This is still a reality in Molise…and the moment you sip some olive oil, taste a fresh, wild asparagus, or bite into a tender piece of lamb that just came off an open fire, you'll be in love.

What are your top three favorite bars and restaurants?
How can I choose just three? Anyone visiting Campobasso has to eat at La Grotta, also known as Da Concetta, located at *Via Larino 7*. It's the quintessential farm-to-table, family-run trattoria (and you may even find 85-year-old Zia Concetta still working the kitchen!). The beans and greens are absolutely divine and my fiancé can't go there without getting the lentil soup. Tell Fabio and Lucia I sent you.

PUGLIA, MOLISE, & CALABRIA

Monticelli is also a personal favorite. Located in the heart of the historic center at *Via Monticelli 6*, the chef and co-owner, Simona, (along with her brother Stefano) offer a seasonal menu focusing on old traditional recipes and ingredients. It's particularly charming in the summer, when you can eat outside with the Medieval alleyways lit up around you.

Finally, I'm partial to Miseria e Nobilta, located at *Via Sant'Antonio Abate 16*, which offers a style of cooking called *rivisitata*, which revisits traditional recipes and flavors, kicking them up a notch to turn them into fine cuisine. This is always a client (and personal) favorite, and owner/sommelier/head waiter, Pasquale—a sincere, genuine, and friendly guy— embodies Molisana hospitality, while the restaurant itself boasts an impeccable, classy ambiance. If you go there, be sure to have a glass of *Tintilia*, a regional wine that's rarely exported (and is a secret treasure of the locals, as a result).

Is there anything tourists do that locals find rude or strange? What can we do to better fit in with the culture?

Italians—particularly southern Italians—are warm, naturally social creatures, very generous, and very proud (sometimes to a fault) of their local culture, traditions, and towns. As a result, visitors should attempt to socialize as well as to try local dishes and traditions.

Not a lot of people speak English and the area is not touristy, so don't expect English-speaking waiters, trinkets to buy, and stores that always accept credit cards.

That's all part of the local charm, though. It's easy to find yourself making local friends and eating at people's houses here. There's a quote from a recent movie that encapsulates the mentality well. In it, a southern Italian wanted to invite a northern Italian to dinner and he replied: "We don't even know each other." The southerner's response? "Well, we'll get to know each other!"

So, just try to speak what Italian you can (and always do so with a smile), make it a point to socialize, and enjoy the locals, the culture, and the area in general.

Why should people make sure to visit Campobasso?

Just an hour and a half from Naples and two and a half hours from Rome, Campobasso is an easy destination with all the conveniences of any other major city in Italy, but in an area seldom seen by tourists. If someone is looking for something truly authentic, they simply can't go wrong with Campobasso and the entire region of Molise.

Where can we go to take beautiful photos?

It really depends on what you're looking for. As an amateur photographer myself, I LOVE food photography, while some photographer clients of mine couldn't tear themselves away from the locals (both in Campobasso and the surrounding villages). In the city itself, though, you have to be sure to get shots of *Castello Monforte* from below and then of the entire city as seen from the castle. The Medieval alleyways in the evening are a perfect setting for photos as well.

Anything else you want us to know?

Leave Tuscany and Umbria behind and escape the crowds in Rome. Give the real Italy a chance. You'll thank me later.

Find Peter at: www.italymondo.com.

Terlizzi

Discover la dolce vita in the southern countryside.

Paul Cappelli
Walker. Chef. Co-Owner, Villa Cappelli.

PUGLIA, MOLISE, & CALABRIA

First, tell us about you.

I have lived here for two years full-time now, but we have been back and forth for about half the year for 10 years before that. I was born in Pisa, moved to Boston when I was seven, and lived in New York City for over 25 years before moving back to Italy. Our place, Villa Cappelli, sits on the ancient Appian Way, and we now hosts guests from all over the world and love introducing them to the life and culture here.

In my free time, I love to take long walks in the neighboring fields looking for ancient artifacts. Newly plowed fields can hold all sorts of wonders around here, from ancient pottery to loom weights that are hundreds, if not thousands, of years old. I also enjoy cooking and entertaining when I'm not working.

If someone is visiting Terlizzi for the first time, what do you recommend they see or do?

Terlizzi has wonderful restaurants that serve excellent food at VERY reasonable prices. It is an ancient town with a Norman and Swabian past. The clock tower dates to the 12th century and the church of *Santa Maria di Cesano* was built in 1055 A.D. We've been told it is the largest backlit clock in Europe, after Big Ben.

Outside Terlizzi, make sure to visit our beautiful coasts and coastal towns, the *Mugria* area (a beautiful national park with charming ancient towns) and some of the simple, local farming towns, each with their own charm and personality.

What neighborhoods or parts of town are best to stay in?

Terlizzi and the surrounding towns really are central to a ton of sites in the area, so you won't be in a car your entire trip, but actually out experiencing and enjoying Italy.

If you prefer something on the coast, we'd recommend Giovinazzo. It's a small fishing village with an amazing hotel and wonderful B&B. The town itself is beyond charming.

Terlizzi is a small town that will literally let you experience the true Italian lifestyle, so it is perfect for travelers looking for something off the typical tourist path.

Let's talk about day trips...what nearby places should everyone make sure to visit?

Castel Del Monte: built by Frederick II, the Swabian king and Holy Roman Emperor, it is a mystical edifice with a 360-degree view of northern Puglia—from the Murge all the way to the Gargano peninsula.

The town of Polignano a Mare is a sight to behold, atop a rocky promontory that juts into the sea. On your way, you can stop by Bari, the capital of Puglia, which boasts the remains of St. Nicholas (yes, Santa Claus) among many other gems. Take a ride through *La Murgia*, with its beautiful fields of grain and trulli covering the countryside, to visit Gravina, which features a large ravine with some spectacular views and an ancient Roman bridge that is right out of a postcard.

Just 12 kilometers away, on the Adriatic, Giovinazzo is a jewel of a town. It features the most romantic tiny fishing port and some spectacular Medieval architecture.

Walk the winding ancient streets of Matera, so well-preserved that it has been used as a movie set for films like Passion of the Christ. Matera features homes, restaurants, and hotels built out from caves in the soft *tufa* rock. Many of the cave homes were inhabited until the 1950s.

Mount Garagnone: these ruins of a feudal castle are nothing short of majestic, sitting atop a hill overlooking some amazing views. You might need very specific directions or a guide to help you find it (it is very off the beaten path) and there is a steep hike to the top, but it's totally worth it.

Trani's beautiful cathedral sits right on the water in this quaint costal town. Wander through the port and enjoy the views. Be a little wary of all the restaurants right on the water, as they

PUGLIA, MOLISE, & CALABRIA

tend to overcharge for a meal. You might find something a little more authentic, less touristy, and cheaper a few blocks in from the port.

The Battle of Cannae is a major battle of the Second Punic War and its site is well worth a visit. It took place on August 2, 216 B.C. in Pulia. The army of Carthage under Hannibal decisively defeated a larger army of the Roman Republic. It is regarded as the worst defeat in Roman history.

And that's just the beginning. Many visitors come to find the towns where their ancestors came from, take culinary tours, or go on a bicycling tour or adventure tour (from hiking and hot air balloon rides to spelunking and boating).

Tell us about the local dishes. What should people try?

Try *orecchiette alle cime di rapa* (homemade pasta with garlic broccoli sauce), *puree di fave e cicoria* (fava bean puree with wilted wild greens), *focaccia* (a flat, oven-baked bread that is usually topped with tomatoes, onions, herbs, and the like), *riso, patate, e cozze* (rice, potatoes, and mussels), fresh seafood (since it is so fresh in the coastal towns, a lot of it can be and is eaten raw...even mussels, sea urchins, and sardines), grilled meat (Terlizzi is actually known for its butchers), fresh *mozzarella, stracciatella,* and *burrata* cheeses, and *caprese* salad (mozzarella, tomatoes, basil, and olive oil with fresh cheese and super sweet Puglia tomatoes—this is to die for).

What are your top three favorite bars and restaurants?

I Tigli, located at *Corso Giuseppe Garibaldi 21*, is a great place to sit outside and enjoy watching all the locals pass by. All the food is good. Ask for a sampling and they will bring you small plates of lots of local dishes, including lots of seafood, for the whole table to try. If you are still hungry after that, their pizza is also very good.

La Lupa, located at *Largo La Ginestra 12*, is in an old olive mill in Terlizzi, You can't go too wrong with the grilled meats here and the atmosphere is beautiful.

PUGLIA, MOLISE, & CALABRIA

Da Marchino, located at *Parma Via Riccio 43*, is, by far, our favorite pizza place in Terlizzi. It's a bit of a local dive, but every thing on the menu is great. Ask for a few sample *antipasto* plates, especially the grilled octopus, before diving into their delicious pizza.

Adriatica, located right on the water between Giovinazzo and Molfeta, serves excellent seafood. Plus, the view is great.

Is there anything tourists do that locals find rude or strange? What can we do to better fit in with the culture?

Do not ask for extra virgin olive oil and balsamic to dip your bread in. That is a very American thing. No Italian does that.

Do not ask for any kind of salad dressing besides oil and vinegar or American Italian meals like spaghetti with meatballs, chicken parmesan, or *fettuccine alfredo*. They really don't even exist.

Try and speak at least a little Italian. Very few people in the area speak another language and even less speak English. Be prepared to use some sign language, be patient, and have fun with it. Everyone will be more than willing to help you and/or try to understand, as they are always excited to have visitors from another area.

Do not drink cappuccino in the afternoons or after a big meal. Italians feel the heavy milk is not good for digestion after eating. And do not order a coffee and expect an American-style cup of coffee. You will get a small espresso. Also, there is no to-go food in Italy. You drink your coffee at the bar and you never see anyone walking around with coke or water bottle.

If driving, use the left lane only to pass. Italians drive *very* fast in Italy. If you stay in the right lane and only use the left for passing, you will be fine.

What is the best way to meet locals and make friends?

Take the *passeggiare* (stroll) at night with the locals. They close the old part of town to traffic from 7 to 10 p.m. every night so locals can stroll freely through the street and visit with friends and neighbors.

Why should people make sure to visit Terlizzi?

This is authentic Italy. While you might see a few other tourists at some of the major sites, you could easily go all day without seeing a single other foreigner. Here, you get to experience what it is truly like to live *la dolce vita*. Relax. Soak up the great life.

Where can we go to take beautiful photos?

A better question would be where is there *not* a good place? We love *Castel Del Monte* for a 360-degree view of the countryside, pretty much anywhere in *Terlizzi* for quaint Italian village scenes, Polignano a Mare for amazing views of the sea and cliffs, Gravina for its ravine, caves, and ancient Roman bridge, Giovinazzo for fishing shots, Matera for ancient scenery, and *Mount Garagnone* for a top-of-the-world experience.

Anything else you want us to know?

Terlizzi and Puglia are undiscovered parts of Italy. You will not fight crowds for a seat in a restaurant or stand in line for hours to see any site. You will have to rent a car to get around and not a lot of the locals speak English—but that is the joy and adventure of it all. This is where you can truly understand what it means to live like an Italian. This is where you come to live *la dolce vita*.

Find Paul at: st8567.wix.com/vcvilla.

Brindisi

This trade port is also a former Greek settlement.

PUGLIA, MOLISE, & CALABRIA

Gianluca
Puglia Tour Guide.

First, tell us about you.
I am from Brindisi. I am a tour guide. And when I have free time, I travel the world.

If someone is visiting Brindisi for the first time, what do you recommend they see or do?
Stroll through the historical center, take a boat to the *Casale* area, visit the temple of St. John at Sepolcro, and eat seafood and good *gelato*.

What neighborhoods or parts of town are best to stay in?
Downtown is the best.

Let's talk about day trips...what nearby places should everyone make sure to visit?
Lecce, Ostuni, Alberobello, and Natural Reserve of Torre Guaceto are my personal favorites.

Tell us about the local dishes. What should people try?
Orecchiette (homemade local pasta), *turcinieddi* (lamb intestines), and watermelon in the summertime.

Is there anything tourists do that locals find rude or strange? What can we do to better fit in with the culture?
The area is still low-key for tourism, so the locals love anything weird and different.

What is the best way to meet locals and make friends?
Hang out in the evenings near by the Verdi Theater or spend an afternoon on one of the local beaches.

Why should people make sure to visit Brindisi?
It is the gateway to the east; it has been this way since Roman times. It is easy to reach (airport, train station, and port are all

within few kilometers). The food is genuine. Everything is reachable on foot. You'll get an authentic experience as a local, unlike the usual tourist spot.

Where can we go to take beautiful photos?
On top of the sailor monument in *Casale* district.

Anything else you want us to know?
It is the gateway to Salento, the new off-the-beaten-path of Italy. You must stop here before discovering the rest of the region.

Find Gianluca at: www.toursofpuglia.com.

Catanzaro

This "city of two seas" is also the capital of Calabria.

Cherrye Moore
Expat. Blogger-Turned-Business-Owner.

First, tell us about you.
I grew up in southeast Texas, in a little town just outside of Beaumont. (Go Kountze Lions!) After college, I spent time at Walt Disney World in Orlando, which led to a temporary position at Disneyland Paris. There was a tall, dark, handsome southern Italian working around the corner and, after an extended long-distance relationship, I married him. Hence, I now live in Calabria.

I've been here since 2006 and love it. In early 2007, we opened a small bed and breakfast and, soon after that, started organizing ancestry tours to southern Italy through my blog-turned-travel business, My Bella Vita Travel. Today, we specialize in ancestry tours and custom vacations throughout southern Italy.

PUGLIA, MOLISE, & CALABRIA

If someone is visiting Calabria and Catanzaro for the first time, what do you recommend they see or do?

Calabria is deceivingly big and, even though we don't get a lot of press, there is a lot to see, do, and discover here. I'd recommend first-time visitors plan enough time to see two to three different areas or villages. Many of the Tyrhennian seaside towns are nice, including Praia, Diamante, Pizzo, and Tropea, as well as the Ionian towns of Cariati or Gerace. I like for travelers to plan a stop in a seaside town, as well as an inland mountain village. Many people like to include great, local foodie experiences, wine tours, tastings, or cooking classes.

What neighborhoods or towns are best to stay in?

Since many of the travelers I work with have ancestral roots in Calabria, we usually choose their base location accordingly. For travelers who just want to see and experience the best of Calabria, the Catanzaro area is nice because it is centrally located and makes a good base for day trips. As I mentioned above, many of the seaside towns are also stunning!

Let's talk about day trips...what nearby places should everyone make sure to visit?

From the province of Cosenza, I'm in love with Civita. It is a precious Albanian village that dates to the 1400s and is home to Europe's deepest gorge. It is history and nature all in one! From Catanzaro, I like the ruins of Scolacium, ancient Greek and Roman ruins with a forum, theater, and necropolis all set in a beautiful olive plantation.

From Crotone, my all-time favorite place to take my family is Le Castella.

Tell us about the local dishes. What should people try?

Calabria is known throughout Italy for having amazing, local, rustic food like grandma would make. Spicy red pepper can be added to anything. (Seriously, anything! I asked my father-in-law once what he wouldn't put red pepper on and he was

PUGLIA, MOLISE, & CALABRIA

stuck for an answer!) Besides that, there is a fabulous baked pasta with meatballs, stuffed eggplant, spicy, spreadable sausage called 'nduja, and sausage from the mountains.

What are your top three favorite bars and restaurants?
La Cascina (located at *Via Corace 50* in Catanzaro Lido) is my current favorite wine bar/restaurant. The owner, a local sommelier, knows everything about Calabrian wine and helps you with your selection without being stuffy or pretentious.

In La Sila, I love Villa Marinella, a family-owned mountain restaurant with homemade everything (located at *Villaggio Racise*).

When I want a nice seafood lunch, I go to San Domenico (located on *Via Colapesce* in Pizzo). It has an amazing setting, fresh, creative cuisine, and a young, friendly staff and chef.

Is there anything tourists do that locals find rude or strange? What can we do to better fit in with the culture?
They think it's funny that we drink wine all day (they only have it with meals), but they just smile and pass the bottle. They love having people visit the area.

What is the best way to meet locals and make friends?
I think it would be very hard for tourists to make real friends with Calabrians because, for the most part, they are friends with the same people they've been friends with since childhood. They are, however, really caring, generous, and friendly people. The best place to meet locals is going to be at a local cafe or in the town's main *piazza*.

Why should people make sure to visit Calabria?
Calabria is still under the radar, which means we enjoy Italy's beauty, food, and culture without having to share it with a load of tourists. Now is the time to visit!

What is the best place to go take beautiful photos of the area?

PUGLIA, MOLISE, & CALABRIA

Since Calabria is so mountainous, many great photo opportunities can be found by walking through the historical part of a town and taking pictures from one of the lookouts. There are typically a lot of nice mountain, hill, valley, and sea views, many with little Italian housetops and clotheslines thrown in for fun.

Find Cherrye at: mybellavita.com.

Lecce

They call it Baroque's city for a reason. Architecture buffs, welcome.

Roberto Frisino
Guitarist. Basketball Player. Language & Literature Student.

First, tell us about you.
I am originally from a little town near Taranto. Two years ago, I moved to Lecce to study in the university and now I'm enjoying my life here. Lecce isn't a very big city, but you can find everything you need here.

In my spare time, I like to play basketball, play the guitar, and go out with my friends. The nights are always full of events.

If someone is visiting Lecce for the first time, what do you recommend they see or do?
First of all, Lecce is known as Baroque's City because there are Baroque monuments spread all over the city. *Piazza Sant'Oronzo* is a must-see, with its Roman amphitheater and the column holding the statue of Saint Oronzo. Then there is *Piazza del Duomo*, with its amazing cathedral. There are a lot of things to see, but I recommend taking a tour of the monuments both in the morning and at night (at night, everything has a different look).

PUGLIA, MOLISE, & CALABRIA

What neighborhoods or parts of town are best to stay in?

I think that the historic center is the best place to stay as a tourist, but if you want to live in Lecce and you're young, there's the neighborhood near *Porta Rudiae* that's full of students and the shops here are very cheap, though the houses are a little bit old. And if you like a modern house and a quiet life, the neighborhood near *Piazza Mazzini* is what you need.

Let's talk about day trips...what nearby places should everyone make sure to visit?

Lecce is surrounded by beautiful places, especially in the summer. Puglia is famous for the amazing beaches and you can see this in cities like Gallipoli, Otranto, Santa Maria di Leuca, and Santa Cesaria. Here there are huge beaches with crystal-clear water and you can reach them easily by train or bus from Lecce.

Tell us about the local dishes. What should people try?

Try the *friselle*, a hard bread that is dipped in water, drizzled with olive oil, and topped with chopped tomatoes. Then, try the *sagne ncannulate sciattariciati*, long, twirled, ribbon-like pasta with fried eggplant strips, Leccese olives, and tomatoes.

If you want some meat, you can try the *turcineddhri*: heart, liver, lungs, and spleen seasoned with salt, pepper, and parsley, then wrapped with intestines and grilled.

If you want to eat something quickly, I advise you to take the *puccia*, a sort of sandwich usually filed with meat, pepperoni, onions, tomatoes, and salad.

The dessert of Salento is the *pasticiotto*, a shortbread crust (typically made with lard instead of butter) with pastry cream. Sometimes cherries are added to the cream.

What are your top three favorite bars and restaurants?

My favorite pizzeria is La Bufala (at *Via Dei Mocenigo 15*), which is really nice and right in the center (so you can eat and take in the views of Lecce).

PUGLIA, MOLISE, & CALABRIA

Another place that I like is the Trattoria of Nonna Tetti, located at *Piazzetta Queen Mary 17* in the historic center. It's a little bit hard to find, but it's worth it. An inviting restaurant, popular with all ages and budgets, this *trattoria* serves a wide choice of traditional dishes, is not expensive, and really makes people feel at home.

One of the bars that I like the most is the Caffé Letterario (at *G. Paladini 46* in the center). They make very good cocktails and have good wines. If you like art and music, it's a great place to go.

Is there anything tourists do that locals find rude or strange? What can we do to better fit in with the culture?
It's actually pretty difficult to annoy the Italians, but do try to have some respect and not dirty the monuments with papers, chewing gum, and cigarettes. Lecce is full of trash cans, so if you have some trash, please walk a little bit and you'll find one for sure.

What is the best way to meet locals and make friends?
The best way to make friends in Lecce is to go out to a nice pub in the evenings. The local people are very open, so it's easy to start a conversation and you will enjoy the night. One thing that I like about Lecce is that it's a little city, but there's always something to do and you can meet people from all over the world.

Why should people make sure to visit Lecce?
Lecce is a city with a beautiful history, full of art and emotions. Above all, if you come in summer, everything is full of colors and you can enjoy the best that this region can give. If you like music, the Salento is the father of the *pizzica*, a genre of music accompanied by an amazing dance.

Where can we go to take beautiful photos?
I think that the best place to take photos is in *Piazza del Duomo*: for lovers it's very romantic and for thinkers it's very inspirational.

PUGLIA, MOLISE, & CALABRIA

Piazza Sant'Oronozo and *Porta Napoli* are also good places for taking a postcard photo of Lecce.

Anything else you want us to know?

Puglia is full of beautiful places like Taranto, which has a bad reputation because of its industry, but has an ancient history. It was one of the principal ports of *Magna Grecia* and is it full of Greek and Roman monuments. I'd advise a visit.

SICILY

Sicilians believe so firmly that theirs is the best food in Italy that Sicilian mommas actually pack food for sons when they head to the mainland. If that doesn't make you want to try the food, I don't know what will.

In this section: Siracusa / Vittoria / Palermo / Agrigento / Messina / Santo Stefano Medio

Photo by: gnuckx on Flickr.

Siracusa

Enjoy seafood, authenticity, and laid-back culture in this big Sicilian city.

Davide Mauro
Reader. Writer. Thinker. Native Siracusan.

First, tell us about you.
I was born in Siracusa and I have spent all my life here. Generally, I like to read books or write article or novels in my spare time. When the weather is good, I enjoy joining my friends to walk around town in search of old monuments.

If someone is visiting Siracusa for the first time, what do you recommend they see or do?
I recommend visiting Ortigia. You'll need a car to really explore the area. There are many historical places like Pantalica, where you can touch Sicilian history, but you need a good guide or a local.

What neighborhoods or parts of town are best to stay in?

SICILY

Feel the atmosphere of the country in Ferla or swim in the natural reserve of *Vendicari*. If you have time, you can go to Isola delle Correnti, the southern point of Sicily.

Let's talk about day trips...what nearby places should everyone make sure to visit?
Don't miss Ragusa, Modica, and Scicli, or the other baroque towns of Noto and Palazzolo Acreide.

Tell us about the local dishes. What should people try?
In Siracusa, you can eat good fish everywhere. It's also interesting to taste *pizzolo*, a kind of closed pizza from Sortino, near Siracusa.

What are your top three favorite bars and restaurants?
Try Bar Cassarino-Midolo, located at *Corso Umberto I 86*, for *arancini* (traditional fried rice balls), Bar Artale, located at *Via Landolina 32*, for sweet *cannoli*, and Pecora Nera, located at *Via Malta 34/36*, for a nice pizza.

Is there anything tourists do that locals find rude or strange? What can we do to better fit in with the culture?
Generally tourists are more polite than the Sicilian people; perhaps we should ask what tourists find strange about us!

What is the best way to meet locals and make friends?
The best way is to find someone on Couchsurfing.org, but it's pretty easy to make friends in general here, because people are really friendly, especially with foreigners.

Why should people make sure to visit Siracusa?
Because Siracusa is the town where the genius, Archimedes, was born, because the first impressive influence of Greek style to the Roman Empire came with the conquest of Siracusa in 212 B.C., and because the first Christian church in Europe was built here after St. Peter's passage.

Where can we go to take beautiful photos?

SICILY

Pillirina: a place in front of Siracusa where it is possible to take pictures of the harbor of Siracusa and there is a nice landscape near the sea.

Anything else you want us to know?
"To have seen Italy without having seen Sicily is to not have seen Italy at all, for Sicily is the clue to everything." - Goethe

 Sebastian Leggio
Hiker. Star-Gazer. Photographer. Austro-Sicilian. Tour Guide.

First, tell us about you.
I'm 37 years old and I was born and have always lived in Siracusa. My mother comes from Austria, so I also know the Austrian culture and I consider myself a sort of Austro-Sicilian.

During my free time, I like walking and hiking around Sicily and looking for minor archaeological sites, taking photos, and watching the stars with my telescope.

If someone is visiting Siracusa for the first time, what do you recommend they see or do?
The Neapolis Archaeological Park with its Greek and Roman ruins is an absolute must. I also recommend the old town, the island of Ortygia, which is utterly charming with its tiny streets, the fish markets, the little restaurants, the sea, and the impressive main square with the cathedral. A boat trip around Ortygia can be very nice.

What neighborhoods or parts of town are best to stay in?
The old town center (which is the Island Ortygia) is the best place to stay. There are monuments, but also pubs, bars, and restaurants. It's the focal point of the nightlife in Siracusa. Public transport is very bad in my town, so try to stay within walking distance of the center.

SICILY

Let's talk about day trips...what nearby places should everyone make sure to visit?

North of Siracusa, visit the volcano, Etna, and the town of Taormina, also known as the pearl of Sicily for its wonderful panorama.

South of Siracusa, check out Noto, a little town on the UNESCO World Heritage list for it's impressive Baroque churches, and the province of Ragusa, which offers a look at genuine Sicily with typical country views, dry stone walls, olive trees, and great sandy beaches.

Tell us about the local dishes. What should people try?

Siracusa is on the sea, so I always suggest fish. Typical here is pasta with black octopus sauce or sea urchin sauce. Mussels and crawfish are fantastic. Great desserts are the typical Sicilian *cannoli* with fresh *ricotta* cheese and, during the summer months, the Sicilian *granita* ice cream with lemon or almond.

What are your top three favorite bars and restaurants?

Bars: Leonardi (located at *Viale Theocritus 123*, near the archaeological park), Del Duomo (at *Piazza Duomo 18/19*, with great view of the cathedral), and Gelati Bianca (which has three or four shops in the city, with the most popular in the main square, *Piazza Duomo*, in front of the church of *S. Lucia alla Badia*). These bars are great, especially during the day, for desserts, street food, coffee, ice cream, and so on. To have a drink at night in Sicily, usually we go to a pub. There are a lot of them in the little streets of Ortygia.

Restaurants: for fish, try Porta Marina, located at *Via dei Candelai 35*, and La Rambla, located at *Via Dei Mille 8*. For meat dishes, try Da Mariano, located at *Vicolo Zuccolà 9*.

Is there anything tourists do that locals find rude or strange? What can we do to better fit in with the culture?

Sicilians are very easy-going people and they like tourists (though, of course, they do think tourists are strange). Eating spaghetti with the help of a spoon is strange. Having dinner before 8 p.m. is also strange. Eating a round pizza at lunch is strange. Wearing sandals with socks is German. But Sicilians like strange people!

What is the best way to meet locals and make friends?

Going out for the nightlife in Ortygia or going on local free beaches is a good way. Sicilians are friendly, but also a bit shy. Being introduced by a local is a good idea. Couchsurfing.org is great for that.

Why should people make sure to visit Siracusa?

Siracusa is one of the most ancient towns in Italy (Siracusa was a great metropolis when Rome was just a little village). In Siracusa, you can find great monuments from every age—from prehistory to Baroque.

The surroundings are beautiful and you can enjoy everything from sandy beaches and blue sea to trekking in the Sicilian canyons in the nearby Hyblean Mountains.

Where can we go to take beautiful photos?

Ortygia offers great views for every type of photo: monuments, little roads, local culture, and sea panoramas.

Anything else you want us to know?

Sicily is, sadly, very badly organized for tourism. There isn't great public transportation and it's always difficult to have updated information. Plan your trip carefully and ahead of time.

Find Sebastian at: www.hermes-sicily.com.

Vittoria

This young city is famous for its wine and remains relatively undiscovered by the tourism industry.

SICILY

Beatrice Cinnirella
Lawyer. Thinker. People Person. Native Sicilian.

First, tell us about you.

I am Beatrice Cinnirella. I am 33 years old and I have a degree in law. I have lived in Vittoria my whole life, with the exception of my five years away at university.

During my free time, I like to meet new people, especially foreigners. I love to learn about different cultures and to exchange ideas, thoughts, and points of view, especially with people who have vastly different backgrounds. This is like oxygen to me. Living in a Sicilian town, it is easy to fall into routine, so to have a coffee or a tour with someone from another part of Italy or the world is a moment to discover yourself and another person.

I also like to go to some exhibitions (photographic or other), shows, and cultural events.

If someone is visiting Vittoria for the first time, what do you recommend they see or do?

I would recommend a visit to the historic center (it is the heart and soul of town), *Piazza del Popolo* (which is wonderful for concerts, comedies, social events, etc.), the church of *Santa Maria delle Grazie* (near *Piazza del Popolo*), and the small, recently restored monastery near *Santa Marie delle Grazie*, where you can find some cultural events and a library full of cultural books.

You should also visit *Basilica di San Giovanni Battista* (San Giovanni is the saint of the city), the small artistic shops in the city center, and the former prison (Henriquez Castle), which is now a wine association headquarters. Vittoria is internationally famous for its *Cerasuolo di Vittoria* wine.

Il Calvario is a little square and monument that becomes popular during Easter, when they put on a version of the Passion of the Christ.

What neighborhoods or parts of town are best to stay in?
The historic center, where there are some nice B&Bs.

Let's talk about day trips...what nearby places should everyone make sure to visit?
Donnafugata Castle; Ragusa Ibla and Scicli for Baroque architecture; Modica for chocolate (home of the oldest chocolate factory in Sicily, *www.bonajuto.it*); Scoglitti (a fishing village and UNESCO World Heritage Site); the archeological ruins of Kamarina (near Scoglitti); Pozzallo, whose port connects to Malta Island; and the seaside villages of Marina di Ragusa, Punta Secca, and Punta Braccetto.

Tell us about the local dishes. What should people try?
Focacce bread (called *scacce* in Sicilian dialect), *arancini* (fried rice balls), *cannoli,* sweets in general, and, of course, local wine!

What are your top three favorite bars and restaurants?
There are so many good ones! Some of my favorites are Acqua e Vino, located at *Via Principe Umberto 98* in Vittoria, Al Castello di Beatrice in nearby Comiso (address: *Via S. Biagio 38*), Pasticceria Di Pasquale at *Corso Vittorio Veneto 104* in Ragusa, and Pizzeria La Perla at *Via Giardina 4* in Modica.

Is there anything tourists do that locals find rude or strange? What can we do to better fit in with the culture?
I think tourists are just more open-minded than Sicilians. In Sicily, it is still seen as strange and rather dangerous for a woman to travel alone. That said, even if they aren't the most open-minded people in the world, Sicilians are very hospitable and if you need help, they are ready to help you however they can.

What is the best way to meet locals and make friends?

Go to a pub, bar, or restaurant and you can meet someone to chat with.

Why should people make sure to visit Vittoria?

Vittoria is a young city in the southeast area of Sicily. Most tourists only know the principal Sicilian cities of Palermo, Catania, Trapani, Messina, and Siracusa. Which means Vittoria and the Ragusa province in general is a more genuine area with good sea, good food, lots of history, and so many traditions to discover and live. Here, you can choose so many different experiences: cultural, sea, gastronomic, etc.

Where can we go to take beautiful photos?

Villa Comunale—the central, green, natural park. It's the nicest park in the Ragusa province. I would also recommend the old electrical center near the wine association, which is a modern space for shows and events, *Piazza del Popolo*, and the historic center of town.

Palermo

History, culture, architecture, food...this capitol city has it all.

Luisa Cerniglia
Master's Student in Russian Literature. Native Sicilian. World-Traveler.

First, tell us about you.

I was born and grew up in Palermo. I started exploring the city on my own when I was in my teens and I fell in love with Palermo's colors. For three years, I was forced to leave for my studies and I learned to appreciate its beauty from a distance.

I'm a culture freak, so in my free time I like to visit new exhibitions and go to the theater or cinema. I also love to eat, so I'll never skip sharing a meal with my friends.

SICILY

If someone is visiting Palermo for the first time, what do you recommend they see or do?

Palermo is an architectural city. You have to pay attention to its buildings in order to grasp its history. So, I would recommend visitors explore its churches and palaces because they are unique.

Certainly the highlights are the Norman Palace, the cathedral, the Church of St. John of the Hermits, the Church of La Martorana, *Casa Professa* (another church), Serpotta's Oratories, *Palazzo Steri*, and *Palazzo Mirto*.

As for the museums, I wouldn't miss the chance to visit *Palazzo Abatellis* (where you can find Antonello da Messina's finest paintings) and GAM—the Museum of Modern Art.

If you're interested in contemporary art, you can go to RISO or try to get a glimpse of the Sicilian art world today by visiting some of its art galleries. Far from the canonical touristic paths, there's also *Via Dante*, with its stunning Modern-style villas.

If you wish to understand Palermo's soul, get lost in its noisy markets. Buying fresh fruits and vegetables at *Capo* or tasting street food in *Ballaro`* might be an interesting anthropological experience!

What neighborhoods or parts of town are best to stay in?

As a tourist, I think it's better to stay in the city center, especially if you're young and you want to experience Palermo's nightlife. In fact, most of the hotels, B&Bs, and hostels are concentrated in this area. That said, during the summertime, it would be nice to stay in *Mondello* or in *Sferracavallo*, Palermo's seaside suburbs, to enjoy their relaxed atmosphere and beautiful landscapes.

Let's talk about day trips...what nearby places should everyone make sure to visit?

Palermo is a very nice place. You might get tired of its chaotic traffic, though!

So, if you love small, nice, Medieval sea towns, you can get on a train and go to Cefalù. If you're into archeology and you're eager to see one of the UNESCO World Heritage Sites in Sicily, Agrigento is the place to be. Closer to Palermo, there's also another Greek colony: Segesta, with its perfectly preserved theatre.

If you're bored with sea and beaches, you can go to Ficuzza, a very small village 50 kilometers from the town, and hike in the woods down Rocca Busambra, the highest peak of Monti Sicani.

Tell us about the local dishes. What should people try?

This is a tricky question! I think that people shouldn't miss Palermo street food, which is becoming more and more glamorous lately. In fact, Palermo will host its first Street Food Festival in May 2014.

So, what's so special about Palermo's street food? It's tasty *and* cheap! Have a bite of *pane and panelle* (a sandwich filled with chickpea flour fritters) or *arancine* (crispy-fried rice balls stuffed with Italian *ragù* or *besciamella* and ham or spinach or fried eggplant) and you'll soon become addicted to Sicilian food. I must also mention *sfincione* (a traditional thick pizza with tomato sauce, onions, anchovies, and *caciocavallo*–a Sicilian traditional spicy cheese) and *pani ca' meusa* (veal spleen served in a soft bun).

As Palermo is a coastal city, fish is one of the main ingredients of its traditional cuisine. Perhaps *pasta con le sarde* (pasta with anchovies and fennel) and *sarde a beccafico* (sardine rolls stuffed with breadcrumbs, raisins, and pine nuts) are two of the most celebrated Sicilian dishes.

In my opinion, though, the best part of visiting Palermo is enjoying its sweets! From *cannoli* to *gelato* and from *cassata* to *granita*, exploring in a patisserie could be a mystical experience.

What are your top three favorite bars and restaurants?

SICILY

Despite my love for street food, my favorite restaurant in Palermo is Freschette (at *Piazzetta Monteleone 5*). They serve fresh, organic food, reinventing traditional Italian dishes. They also have vegan options menus and a good choice of organic wine and beers.

My favorite café in Palermo is Ristoro del Massimo, a very small bar in the city center (located at *Via Maqueda 364*). There you can have the best espresso in Palermo (and you might also try some of their ricotta buns).

Finally, my favorite bar is called Malox (located at *Piazzetta della Canna 8-9* in a small mall in the city center. They often organize nice gigs and free film screenings. Plus, Peppino—the most famous barman in town—is part of their crew. He never fails to prepare the perfect cocktail, according to your mood and taste.

Is there anything tourists do that locals find rude or strange? What can we do to better fit in with the culture?

People in Palermo might be sensitive to talk about the mafia. Showing disregard or ignorance towards this issue might upset people. Associations against mafias in Palermo are doing an amazing job. Getting informed about their role and their campaigns could give you a new perspective on Italian society.

What is the best way to meet locals and make friends?

I think the best way to meet locals and make friends in Palermo is to go out in *Vucciria* or in one of the hundreds of bars in town, share an *aperitivo*, and start talking. Young people are quite easy going.

Why should people make sure to visit Palermo?

Because it's an interesting, unusual, multicultural, Roman, Arab, Norman, Medieval, French, Spanish town. It's chaotic, crowded, and incomprehensible, at times. Nevertheless you might fall in love with its eclectic architecture and spectacular views. It's not flawless, but it's fascinating.

Where can we go to take beautiful photos?

The *Magione* area or *Vucciria*, one of Palermo's oldest markets. Its charms reside in the almost destroyed buildings, now redecorated by street artists. I also recommend photographing *Monte Pellegrino*, a promontory celebrated in Goethe's Italian Journey.

Anything else you want us to know?

If you have time, I recommend visiting the Sicilian archipelagos, especially in April/May, when the temperatures are already warm and you can enjoy their landscapes quietly. Moreover, travel the southern/oriental coast of Sicily.

Agrigento

A rich archaeological and Greek civilization history draw thousands each year.

Alberto Sardo
Basketball Player. Traveler.

First, tell us about you.

Truthfully, I live in a small village about 15 minutes from Agrigento. However, I'm always in Agrigento because I love it and my mother's side of the family lives there. In my spare time, I love to play basketball, socialize, and travel.

If someone is visiting Agrigento for the first time, what do you recommend they see or do?

Having hosted people from all over the world, I've discovered the best things to see are the theaters, churches, and rustic side streets of the city. I would also recommend really living in the culture by eating local food and spending time with someone from here.

What neighborhoods or parts of town are best to stay in?

SICILY

In my opinion, *San Leone* is the best because it is situated on the Mediterranean coast and has constant access to vibrant bars and nightlife.

Let's talk about day trips...what nearby places should everyone make sure to visit?

Naturally, I would recommend my own village, Racalmuto, where you will find two ancient castles, a theater, and a cathedral. Then there is a white mountain, called *La Scala dei Turchi*, and *Castello a Mare*, a castle in the sea linked to the land by a simple man-made road. Finally, check out the *Maccalube*—mini volcanoes on the land, forming a sort of hot lake of clay.

Tell us about the local dishes. What should people try?

Arancine (fried rice balls), *mpignolate* (filo pastry pies with onion, meat, and olives), *cannoli* (pastries with ricotta cream filling), and *ricotta* cream cheese cake.

What are your top three favorite bars and restaurants?

I'd recommend Agorà (located at *Viale Sciascia 27*) which has a cheap, exquisite buffet and great *pasticceria*, Capotavola (located at *Via Paolo Paternostro 40*) for refined dining in the center, and Il Capriccio (located at *Piazza Luigi Storzo*), which is a relaxing restaurant opposite the sea.

For bars, I like Mojo (located at *Via San Francesco D'Assisi 15*, where you can get a cocktail in a historic *piazza* in the center), Oceanomare and Magaria (for cocktails on the beach, both at *Viale Delle Dune*), and Folli Follie (a chic wine bar on *Viale della Vittoria*).

What is the best way to meet locals and make friends?

In my opinion, the best place to make friends and meet locals is in the wide selection of bars in Agrigento, where the local people of all ages congregate to drink their ritual morning and afternoon coffees. There you can chat with and get to know people.

Making friends in Sicily is not a problem. Once you know one person, you know everybody!

Why should people make sure to visit Agrigento?
It genuinely is a hidden gem. Mostly because of it's ancient Greek, Spanish, Norman, and Arabic history, art and architecture, culture, and a buzzing nightlife.

Where can we go to take beautiful photos?
There are too many! Like *Via Atenea*, *Teatro Pirandello*, the *Viale*, and the Greek amphitheater. That said, the obvious choice would be the famous valley of the temples where, depending on which side you take the photo from, you either get the amazing backdrop of Agrigento or the wonderful display of the Mediterranean Sea.

Anything else you want us to know?
If you ever visit Agrigento, you can't limit yourself to the city itself. Instead, venture to the surrounding locations in the region, also full of awesome stuff. Racalmuto, Realmonte, Naro, Canicattì, Sciacca, and many more.

Messina

Come for the land shrouded in myth and legend; stay for the granita.

Gianluca Molino
Rock Climber. Hiker. Native Messinan.

First, tell us about you.
I'm a 35-year-old man born and raised here in Messina. In my free time, I like to meet friends and go rock climbing, trekking, swimming, etc. I'm all about nature.

If someone is visiting Messina for the first time, what do you recommend they see or do?

SICILY

Take in the sea and the mountains. Go for a swim or a walk along the shore. See the city center and the view of the city from the mountains.

Capo Peloro and the two lakes, the cathedral with the mechanized clock tower, and other monuments/churches in the city center of Messina are all worth seeing.

What neighborhoods or parts of town are best to stay in?

The place where I live—*Capo Peloro*, the northeast cape of Sicily—is very nice. It's a place full of myths and legends (Scylla and Charybdis). The place will soon be a UNESCO World Heritage Site.

Tell us about the local dishes. What should people try?

The list is very long! In the summer, you can't miss *granita*, our typical semi-frozen, sweet breakfast, which comes in many flavors, including coffee, soft cream, lemon, almond, pistachio, strawberry, fig, and prickly pear.

Then, of course, you can't miss *parmigiana* (made with eggplant), *pasta 'ncaciata* (an eggplant pasta specially made to celebrate the Assumption on the 15th of August), *pasta alla norma* (pasta with tomatoes, ricotta, and fried eggplant), and *caponata (cooked vegetable salad)*.

Also, you should try some of the typical Messinan food that you can't find anywhere else in Sicily, including *braciole alla Messinese* (meat rolls with cheese and bread crumbs), *focaccia alla Messinese* (a kind of pizza, but thicker, with cheese, tomatoes, endives, and, traditionally, anchovies), and *pitoni* or *pidoni* (essentially fried focaccia, often eaten on New Year's Eve).

What are your top three favorite bars and restaurants?

The best bar where you can have a very good *gelato* is Bar De Luca, located at *Via Nazionale 208*. I think they do the best ice cream in all of Sicily, which means the best ice cream in the world. The place is far away from the city center, in the south

SICILY

part of Messina, but it's always crowded—and with good reason.

In the summer (but closed in the winter), a very good café/bar to visit is Eden, located at *Via Palazzo III 2*. I often go there with my guests to have *granita*; they have tons of flavors.

As for restaurants, there are two places run by the Mancuso brothers, where you can eat delicious fish and pasta. They are next to each other and just in front of Ganzirri Lake. The first is called Trattoria le Sirene (address: *Via Lagogrande 96*) and the other is attached.

Another good restaurant in the city center is Il Padrino, located at *Via Santa Cecilia 54-56*.

In Messina, we also have lots of *rosticcerie*, where we go to buy the *rustici* (*pitoni, arancini, mozzarella* in *carrozza*) and *focaccia*. The most famous one is Famulari, at *Via Cesare Battisti 143* in the city center; they make 35+ kinds of *arancini* and some of them are very, very tasty.

Is there anything tourists do that locals find rude or strange? What can we do to better fit in with the culture?
People might get offended if you refuse when they offer food, so accept graciously.

What is the best way to meet locals and make friends?
Couchsurfing.org, maybe.

Why should people make sure to visit Messina?
Because it is the door of Sicily. Because we have a great story. Because we have very nice natural places. Because the region is amazing—Taormina, Eolian islands, Etna, Milazzo. And because it is a place of myth and legend.

Where can we go to take beautiful photos?
The are a lot of viewpoints on the mountains where you can see both the Ionian and Tirrenian seas and Eolian islands. From the shore you can also take nice photos.

Anything else you want us to know?

In June, a miracle happened in this city. We have a new mayor. He is an activist and very far from the old/very bad traditional political figure. We are all very hopeful that the city will be reborn under his leadership.

Santo Stefano Medio

Just south of Messina, you'll find castles, churches, and fried rice balls to die for.

Salvatore Bate
Engineer. Party Planner. Tourist Website Curator. Native.

First, tell us about you.

I am a 34-year-old civil engineer. I studied at Messina's University and have always lived in Santo Stefano Medio. My family arrived in this village in 1926 and my great grandfather bought a big plot of land from a noble family, De Gregorio Alliata.

When my friends and I have free time, we organize events in the village. We have an association that researches information on the history and tradition of the village and I manage a little website. We organize part of the Saint Anthony party on 17 January.

If someone is visiting Santo Stefano Medio for the first time, what do you recommend they see or do?

Visit the church, where there are some beautiful paintings. The most important is a painting by Girolamo Alibrandi, a local painter and one of the most important students of Antonello da Messina. The painting was created between 1514 and 1516 and there is a beautiful picture frame (though that is not original, but from the 17th century).

SICILY

I also recommend a visit to the castle, which has only three towers. It was built in the 8th century and is now a ruin.

In a village near Santo Stefano Medio, Santo Stefano Briga, there is a Byzantine church, where it is possible see original paintings, though it is a ruin, too.

In other villages, such as Mili San Pietro, it is possible see a monastery built sometime around 1100. In Scaletta Zanclea, you can visit a castle with a museum of arms.

What neighborhoods or parts of town are best to stay in?

It's best to stay in the center of Messina if you are young or in winter when things are quieter. In the summer, though, you can choose to stay nearer to the sea. There are some hotels in the north of the city near Ganzirri, Torre Faro, and Paradiso.

Let's talk about day trips...what nearby places should everyone make sure to visit?

I think that you must visit Taormina (which is called the pearl of Messina because of its beautiful views), the volcano Etna, Tindari, Castelmola, Montalbano Elicona, Savoca, and Forza d'Agrò. If you have more time you must visit Siracusa, Noto, Catania, and the Temple Valley in Agrigento.

Tell us about the local dishes. What should people try?

In Santo Stefano Medio, you can eat the best *arancino* (fried rice balls). They are particularly good at Pizzeria Tony, located at *Via Comunale 163*, which also offers *focaccia, pasta sapori dell'Etna* with bacon and pistachio of Bronte, *pasta alla norma* with tomato and eggplant, and *funghi e salsiccia* with mushroom and sausage.

Another favorite place is Bar De Stefano, located in *Piazza S. Giovanni*, which is in Santo Stefano di Briga and has very good nougat ice cream. Then there's Pasticceria Crupi, which is located at *Via C. Battisti 374* in Messina and has the best *cannolo Siciliano* (Sicilian cannoli) in the city.

One other typical dish is *pisci stoppu a ghiotta* (stockfish with potatoes and capers) and the best place to eat it is in Trattoria Don Nino, at *Viale Europa 39*, or in Trattoria Al Padrino, at *Via Santa Cecilia 54* (both in Messina).

Is there anything tourists do that locals find rude or strange? What can we do to better fit in with the culture?

Arrive with a smile on your face, have the desire to speak with the people, have patience if you wait for a bus or a train, and don't worry about dieting.

What is the best way to meet locals and make friends?

You can find always people in the bars or in the village square.

Where can we go to take beautiful photos?

You can take photos from the Saint Gaetano Church and square.

Anything else you want us to know?

If you come in Messina, you must taste the *granita*—a typical breakfast in Messina with many different flavors. Also, in my village and the neighboring village, there is a local DOC wine called *Faro,* which you should try.

Find Salvatore at: www.santostefanomedio.com.

SARDINIA (SARDEGNA)

History and seafood abound on this less-touristed island.

In this section: Cagliari / Sassari / Iglesias

Photo by Cristian Santinon on Flickr.

Cagliari

The capitol of Sardinia is all about seafood, ocean views, and history.

Paolo Piras
Walker. Swimmer. Music Buff. Local.

First, tell us about you.

I've been living in Quartu S. Elena, in the countryside of Cagliari since 2002. Before that, I lived in Castello, the old town inside the walls of Cagliari proper.

I love animals, walking along the beach, swimming, eating *al fresco* with friends, music, and many other things.

If someone is visiting Cagliari for the first time, what do you recommend they see or do?

In the morning, you can head to Poetto, a 10-kilometer beach, where you can have a walk and stop in one or more of the 40 cafes located along the beach (we call them *baretti*) to have a drink or lunch with sea views.

In good weather conditions, sunbathing and diving are popular. And, in the summertime, all the bars along the beach offer live music, DJ sets, and entertainment for every taste.

SARDINIA

In the evening, have a walk in Castello, the old town, enjoy the sunset, and visit the historical churches, expositions, sights, tiny, typical streets, old houses, cafes, and restaurants.

What neighborhoods or parts of town are best to stay in?
The best place to stay is downtown Cagliari, which is divided into three neighborhoods: *Stampace*, *Marina*, and *Castello*. You can find B&Bs and hotels there and can walk around the city from any of them.

The three districts are close to the port, train, and bus station, shopping area, restaurants, fancy bars, and all the facilities you may need.

Let's talk about day trips...what nearby places should everyone make sure to visit?
My number one choice is Chia, one of the best beaches in Sardinia. It is about 50 kilometers by car to the west of the city. My second choice would be Villasimius, another of the best beaches in Sardinia, about 40 kilometers east by car. My third choice is *Barumini*, a very important archeological site north of Cagliari (about 50 kilometers).

Tell us about the local dishes. What should people try?
Seafood. This is my perfect menu: mussel soup (*zuppa di cozze*), spaghetti with clams and *bottarga* (salted, cured fish roe), and mixed fried fish with white wine.

What are your top three favorite bars and restaurants?
Libarium: a well-known and fancy bar in Castello (located on *Via Santa Croce*). Paillotte: a bar, restaurant, beach, and disco pub in an amazing location right next to the sea (on *Viale Calamosca sul Mare*). And Royale, located at *Viale Diaz 52/A*, which is my favorite restaurant, which serves Tuscan cuisine and has a friendly atmosphere—all at the right price.

Is there anything tourists do that locals find rude or strange? What can we do to better fit in with the culture?

SARDINIA

Sardinians are easy-going and kind people; they share what they have with a smile; and they like people who are also easy-going.

What is the best way to meet locals and make friends?
Just hanging around downtown Cagliari or in some Poetto cafes you will meet friendly people.

Why should people make sure to visit Cagliari?
It's an ancient land, almost untouched. You can find genuine food, good wine, and true people.

Where can we go to take beautiful photos?
Everywhere. Just don't forget your camera anytime you leave the house.

Anything else you want us to know?
You can't go wrong in Sardinia. It's not the usual Italian destination.

The best time to visit is April to October, when you can enjoy sunny and warm days, eating *al fresco*, lots of friendly people, and wonderful *aperitivo*.

Sassari

The second largest city in Sardinia is also home to the oldest university on the island.

Luigi Romagnino
Artist. Gardener. World-Traveler.

First, tell us about you.
Originally from Iglesias, I have lived in Sassari for 48 years. In my free time, I do tai chi, study massage, draw, paint, and work in my vegetable garden.

SARDINIA

If someone is visiting Sassari for the first time, what do you recommend they see or do?

First, walk-around the city center, the old walls, and the old entrance gates to the city. Then, visit the National Museum G.A. Sanna, Pinacoteca of Canopoleno (another good museum), the *Fontana del Rosello* in the *Monte Rosello* quarter, *Cathedral di San Nicola*, and the Church of Sant'Antonio Abate.

What neighborhoods or parts of town are best to stay in?

There are many B&Bs in the city center and the surrounding countryside.

Let's talk about day trips...what nearby places should everyone make sure to visit?

Platamone, Castelsardo, Stintino, and Alghero.

Tell us about the local dishes. What should people try?

Lamb's feet in garlic and white or red sauce, snails with sauce, and lamb entrails roasted or sautéed with peas.

What are your top three favorite bars and restaurants?

Bar Trattoria Zia Forica, located at *39 Corso Di Savoia Margherita*, Cassaforte Ristorante Pizzeria, located at *6/A Corso Angioy Giovanni Maria*, and Trattoria L'Assassino, located at *Via Pettenadu 19*.

Is there anything tourists do that locals find rude or strange? What can we do to better fit in with the culture?

Don't pick your nose or eat with your mouth open.

What is the best way to meet locals and make friends?

Use the Internet: Facebook or Skype. Schedule a tour and you can make some acquaintances that way.

Why should people make sure to visit Sassari?

Sassari is cheaper than other places, is well located to other great places to visit, and is a nice place to be.

SARDINIA

Where can we go to take beautiful photos?
It depends on the time of day and the season, but some good options are the old walls, the main square, the front of the churches, and the old city, including *Pozzo di Villa*, the first nucleus of the original city.

Anything else you want us to know?
Near Sassari, you can visit some ancient ruins of the Nuragic civilization.

Marco Corposanto
Windsurfer. Photography Buff. Musician.

First, tell us about you.
I have lived in Sassari for 29 years. I like to windsurf, take long Sunday walks in nature, go out with friends, take photos and videos, travel, write poems and songs, and watch films.

If someone is visiting Sassari for the first time, what do you recommend they see or do?
Sassari has a wonderful *Duomo* in the center (and the rest of the center is also very nice). I'd start exploring Sassari from there.

After you've seen the center, I recommend going out for tea, coffee, or an *aperitivo*, visiting the beautiful beaches near town, walking around *Piazza d'Italia* and *Via Roma*, having a *pizzetta* at a local pizzeria called Gavina (located near Piazza d'Italia at *Via Florinas* 6), eating pasta from Sandrino (a restaurant located at *Via Torre Tonda* 26), visit the archeological site near the town, taking in one of Dinamo's basketball games, and visiting nearby Alghero, Stintino, Castelsardo, Isola Rossa, Bosa, and Marina.

What neighborhoods or parts of town are best to stay in?
I prefer *Cappuccini - Monserrato* (there is a very nice park there) or the historic center.

SARDINIA

Let's talk about day trips...what nearby places should everyone make sure to visit?
Alghero, Stintino, Castelsardo, Isola Rossa, Bosa, and Marina.

Tell us about the local dishes. What should people try?
In Sassari, you *must* try *il panino dallo zozzone* (a traditional sandwich), *lo zimino* (a traditional dish made with lamb or beef offal), *il panino da renato* (local sandwiches), *pizzetta* (from Gavina Pizzeria, located near *Piazza d'Italia* at *Via Florinas 6*), and pasta from Da Sandrino (a restaurant located at *Via Torre Tonda 26*).

What are your top three favorite bars and restaurants?
Sandrino's Spaghetteria (located at *Via Torre Tonda 26*), Ristorante Masia (located at *Via Macomer 27*), and Ristorante Lina (located at *Via Lepanto 30* in Stintino).

Is there anything tourists do that locals find rude or strange? What can we do to better fit in with the culture?
In Sardinia, you will find that people are accepting and educated.

What is the best way to meet locals and make friends?
Stop by the Style Cafè (at *Via Napoli 28*), Refral Restaurant (at *Via Roma 118*), and Vineria Tola (at *Piazza Tola Pasquale 39*).

Why should people make sure to visit Sassari?
In short, Sardinia is paradise. There are so many great places to see. And the people are friendly and comical.

Where can we go to take beautiful photos?
Duomo di Sassari, Fontana di Rosello, Monte d'Accoddi (a nearby archealogical site), *Platamona* (the nearby coast), and the cute coastal towns of Stintino, Castelsardo, Alghero, and Santa Teresa.

Find Marco at:
www.youtube.com/channel/UCjee5bG6sKgv5xwElMpjauQ.

SARDINIA

Iglesias

This city of many churches is heaven for dessert lovers.

Giuliano Langiu
Skating Instructor. Entrepreneur. Third-Generation Iglasian.

First, tell us about you.

I was born in Iglesias, left to study in Cagliari at age 19, and have spent a few years working and having other adventures between Cagliari and Iglesias. The origins of my family are in the village of Oschiri and we have been in Iglesias now for three generations.

In my free time, I am a skating instructor. For several years, I have coached at a high level, with my students competing nationally and internationally and achieving a lot. Now I have a company of my own—Roller Skating Team Sardinia Academy—where the goal is the world title in 10 years.

In addition, I recently opened a shop called Quarryville Gourmet, close to Cagliari, which means I travel every day. So my day starts at 6 a.m. and ends at 10 p.m. when I get home.

If someone is visiting Iglesias for the first time, what do you recommend they see or do?

Visit the churches! Iglesias means "many churches" in Italian. (So, if you thought it was a city dedicated to Julio Iglesias, sorry.) Many of the churches have beautiful frescoes that should be admired.

After the churches, tour the historic walls of the castle and the remains of the city gates.

If you can, come to the city when there is a Medieval procession (I have not personally been, but I hear they are absolutely beautiful), which always includes throwing events

317

and crossbows. You should also see the processions during the holy week (the week before Easter).

Also, you must go to the beach (one of the most beautiful in the world). If you come to our area and do not visit the sea, we like to joke that we'll send you to prison.

We also have beautiful mountains and pristine hills. This is also an old mining area and some old mines are open to visitors.

What neighborhoods or parts of town are best to stay in?
You can either stay in Iglesias or in the neighboring counties. Carbonia may be best because it is a little farther from Cagliari, but is the perfect link in between mountains and sea.

Let's talk about day trips...what nearby places should everyone make sure to visit?
First, head to the mountains, up to the ancient Temple of Antas. Then head to the sea for lunch. Doing both in one day is such a beautiful experience and the photography opportunities are amazing.

Tell us about the local dishes. What should people try?
Here, as in all of Sardinia, we love to eat the famous roast pork, but also lamb and roast *caprettino* (goat). (Though the pig is the best.)

Iglesias is also a great place for Sardinian desserts. Try any of the traditional bakeries. You won't be disappointed.

Is there anything tourists do that locals find rude or strange? What can we do to better fit in with the culture?
Recently, the local population has become quite open minded. But one thing we cannot ever forgive is white socks with sandals or flip-flops. Ha!

In general, Sardinians do not like people who are too snobby. Also, when you go into a house, it is good practice to accept everything that is offered to eat and (especially) drink. In the villages of central Sardinia, saying no to food or drink is considered an insult.

What is the best way to meet locals and make friends?

Go to *Via Nuova* and *Piazza Sella*. The center of much of the social life here is bowling.

Why should people make sure to visit Iglesias?

If you love the sea or have a passion for mining history (in which case, visit our mining museum), you'll love Iglesias. It is also close to many nice places to visit, including Carbonia, the Island of Sant'Antioco, and the village of Portoscuso, famous for factories and fishing traps.

Anything else you want us to know?

Sardinians speak parallel languages (not to be confused with dialects, as our root languages are different). In practice, we have four different types of Sardinian—a different one for each of the old provinces (Cagliari, Oristano, Nuoro, Sassari). Nuoro, which has less tourism, has the purest language. You will also find that Carloforte (Genoese dialect) is still spoken, as the island's inhabitants are the descendants of the Genoese, former prisoners on the island. Finally, you'll also find Alghero Priato, an ancient dialect of Catalan.

Find Giuliano by searching Roller Team Sardegna-Accademia di Pattinaggio on Facebook.

ABOUT THE AUTHOR

Gigi Griffis is a world-traveling entrepreneur and writer with a special love for inspiring stories, new places, and living in the moment. In May 2012, she sold her stuff and took to the road with a growing business and a pint-sized pooch.

These days, she's living in the Swiss Alps, planning epic European adventures, and working on her next couple books (watch for 100 Locals: Paris, Geneva, and Prague – coming soon!).

Love what you read here? Find more at *www.gigigriffis.com*.

ACKNOWLEDGEMENTS

First, a MASSIVE thank-you to everyone who contributed an interview. Obviously, without you there would be no book.

Other massive thank-yous go to:

My lovely editors, friends, and the brilliant people who let me bounce marketing ideas off them: Emily, Lisa, Lucia, Carlos David, Ali, Dani, Anita, and Anna. The entire staff at Airtime Café in Lauterbrunnen, Switzerland, where I edited most of this book. And my designers, Karen Kimball and Björn Musyal.

Special thanks to Ali of *www.aliadventures.com* for the back cover photo on the print version of this book and to all the other photographers featured throughout (whose names you can find credited near their photos), who made their photos available for public use through the Creative Commons license.

And, finally, thank you to all my lovely blog readers—those of you who write to me, those who read, and those who have quietly shown your support by buying this book, recommending it to your friends, promoting it on social media, and leaving it reviews. You guys make all the research, writing, and long editing hours worth it.

Love, Gigi

FLY INTO ROME

ROME TO SALERNO FAST TRAIN 70MIN
SALERNO TO CETARA BUS/TAXI 13MIN
PARKING IN CETARA
AMALFI COAST FERRIES APRIL 1-OCT 31.

CETARA TO SALERNO BUS/TAXI
SALERNO TO PARSTUM TRAIN 32MIN.

SALERNO RENTAL CAR TO POMPA 40MIN
HOTEL
POMPEI TO AIRPORT 2:30 DRIVE.
OVER NIGHT PARKING IN CETARA?